T0317048

Peoples Temple and Black Religion in America

Peoples Temple and Black Religion in America

EDITED BY
Rebecca Moore, Anthony B. Pinn,
& Mary R. Sawyer

Indiana University Press

BLOOMINGTON AND INDIANAPOLIS

Publication of this book is made possible in part with the assistance of a Challenge Grant from the National Endowment for the Humanities, a federal agency that supports research, education, and public programming in the humanities.

This book is a publication of

Indiana University Press
601 North Morton Street
Bloomington, IN 47404-3797 USA

http://iupress.indiana.edu

Telephone orders   800-842-6796
Fax orders   812-855-7931
Orders by e-mail   iuporder@indiana.edu

The paper used in this publication meets the minimum requirements of American National Standard for Information Sciences—Permanence of Paper for Printed Library Materials, ANSI Z39.48-1984.

MANUFACTURED IN THE UNITED STATES OF AMERICA

Library of Congress Cataloging-in-Publication Data

Peoples Temple and Black religion in America / edited by Rebecca Moore, Anthony B. Pinn, and Mary R. Sawyer.
         p.   cm.
Includes bibliographical references and index.
    ISBN 0-253-34371-2 (cloth : alk. paper)—ISBN 0-253-21655-9 (pbk. : alk. paper)
    1. Peoples Temple. 2. Jones, Jim, 1931–1978.
3. African Americans—Religion. 4. African American churches—History. I. Moore, Rebecca, date II. Pinn, Anthony B. III. Sawyer, Mary R.
    BP605.P46P44 2004
    289.9—dc22

                                                            2003017152

1 2 3 4 5 09 08 07 06 05 04

In memory of all who sought hope
in the promise of Jonestown

C O N T E N T S

ACKNOWLEDGMENTS

Many people helped in the preparation and production of this book: friends, families, colleagues, and associates. We would like to name just a few.

Fielding M. McGehee III served yeoman duty as transcriber, copyeditor, indexer, and advisor on a number of issues. Thank you, Mac!

Rebecca Moore thanks the Department of Religious Studies at San Diego State University, and the department chair, Dr. Linda Holler, for arranging release time for two semesters in a row to complete the manuscript. She also appreciates the help of the Reverend Richard Lawrence, and John and Barbara Moore for their comments and support along the way.

Anthony B. Pinn would like to thank his wife, Cheryl Johnson, for her understanding, patience, and good humor. In addition, he is grateful for the assistance offered by his mother, the Reverend Anne H. Pinn, with the preparation of his essay. And good friends—Ramon Rentas, Robbie Seals, Benjamin Valentin, and Eli Valentin—helped keep this writing in perspective. Thanks.

Mary Sawyer expresses her appreciation for the timely affirmations provided by Beverly Reddick and for the collaborative spirit of her co-editors, which made working on this difficult topic a positive experience.

The editors are grateful to Archie Smith Jr. and the *Bulletin of the Pacific School of Religion* for their permission to reprint his essay, "An Interpretation of the Peoples Temple and Jonestown: Implications for the Black Church," which appears in this book. We also thank *The Other Side* for permission to republish the article "America Was Not Hard To Find" by the late Muhammed Isaiah Kenyatta. Finally, we would like to express our appreciation to *Religion In Life* and to Lawrence Mamiya—acting on behalf of himself and his late co-author C. Eric Lincoln—for permission to publish "Daddy Jones and Father Divine: The Cult as Political Religion." We have made a few minor typographical changes in these articles so that they will conform in style to the rest of the book.

We all thank the helpful staff at Indiana University Press, and especially Robert J. Sloan, Kendra Boileau Stokes, Jane Lyle, Dawn Ollila, and Drew Bryan for their patience and encouragement.

INTRODUCTION

Peoples Temple began as a racially mixed, independent congregation in Indianapolis, Indiana, in the early 1950s. Initially called "Community Unity," in 1955 the congregation took the name "Peoples Temple Full Gospel Church." In 1959, the congregation affiliated with the Christian Church (Disciples of Christ). In 1965, some 70 members of the congregation, including both white and black families, relocated to Redwood Valley, California, where they were known as the Peoples Temple Christian Church. In 1966, the total membership was 86 and by 1968 it had grown to 136. Throughout the late 1960s, a number of young white people—who had either "dropped out" from society and become part of the counterculture scene, or who had been influenced by the Civil Rights and anti–Vietnam War movements—were drawn to the movement. Some of them came from religious backgrounds; more of them were committed to secular ideologies of racial integration and economic democracy.[1]

In 1968, the Temple began establishing relations with black churches in San Francisco by attending special events at those churches, winning the trust of the local black ministers, and inviting their congregations to visit Peoples Temple in Redwood Valley in an exchange of fellowship. In 1970, a large building was purchased in San Francisco, which enabled Peoples Temple to hold services in the city. Within a short time the membership had grown to three thousand, with the numbers of visitors swelling to thousands more. During these years, Peoples Temple members also went on bus tours to other large cities on the West Coast (a branch church was purchased in Los Angeles) and throughout the country, where they held evangelistic-style services and recruited hundreds more to the movement. In 1976, the headquarters of the Peoples Temple of the Disciples of Christ were relocated to San Francisco.[2]

Some of the individuals who became part of Peoples Temple in its San Francisco years were black youth and young adults who were taken in off the streets to be placed in drug rehabilitation, employment, and educational programs. Some had been placed in the custody of state agencies or were under the supervision of probation or parole officers. But many African Americans who joined the Temple came from San Francisco's black churches. Quite commonly, two- and even three-generation families would join as a unit, although a significant number of those who came from churches were retired or elderly, and many of these were women.

In the Bay Area of the 1970s, black churches were expressive of two different strands of the black Christian tradition. One minister who was active at that time, speaking of the majority of black churches in San Francisco, recalls that "we were just gospel-preaching, fundamental churches" which were not given to an activist role.[3] San Francisco itself was less affected by the Civil Rights movement than by the secular "New Left" political movement; most black churches were influenced by neither. Their focus remained evangelization, individual salvation, and life in the hereafter. Many of them emphasized the gifts of the Spirit—including healing—as did Peoples Temple.

But other models of black religiosity were present at that time, including the social action ministry of Glide Memorial United Methodist Church in San Francisco and the ecumenical body in Oakland known as Alamo Black Clergy. Alamo Black Clergy was one of numerous ecumenical groups that came into being across the nation in the 1970s in response to the development of black liberation theology. But its members represented the very small, prophetic remnant of Bay Area black clergy.[4]

There was, too, a highly visible, non-Christian expression of black religion—the Nation of Islam—that had been made popular in the early 1960s by Minister Malcolm X. Added to the theological and ideological mix of the times was a communist perspective held by individuals such as scholar/activist Angela Davis and by numerous socialist organizations.

It seems decidedly a stretch of credibility to think that African American members of Peoples Temple were uninfluenced by these religious-political currents, both in their decision to join the Temple—which was itself engaged in a variety of social protest and social service activities—and in the subsequent decision of many of them to leave the United States.

In 1974, the leadership of Peoples Temple negotiated an agreement with the government of Guyana—a cooperative socialist republic whose citizens were predominantly people of color—to build an agricultural settlement on land located in the midst of a Guyanese jungle. Over the next several years, members relocated—or were relocated—to this settlement and many became permanent residents. Here, for a few brief years, members of Peoples Temple pursued their utopian vision of a racially integrated and economically equitable community. The Peoples Temple Agricultural Project, which came to be known as Jonestown, built homes and developed gardens, provided sophisticated medical care to local residents and ran a school for the community's children.

But allegations of misdeeds leveled by former members and subsequent investigations by media and government agencies followed the movement to Guyana. The health of the movement's leader, Jim Jones, declined as he became addicted to drugs. The movement itself deteriorated as members, incited by Jones' paranoia, succumbed to fears and convictions that assaults from the outside world were inevitable. In November 1978, the arrival of a member of the United States Congress,[5] along with his staff, members of the media, and some relatives of Jonestown residents, brought the tension to a head. As the entourage was departing, the congressman was shot and killed; others were killed or wounded as well.

The Peoples Temple movement ended on 18 November 1978, when the children in Jonestown were put to death by adult members, most of whom then took their own lives. Only a handful lived to tell their story. The Temple headquarters in San Francisco were dismantled. Survivors, friends, and family members were left on their own, for the most part, to make their way in a world that offered little by way of compassion or consolation.

Most of the scholarly analysis of Peoples Temple, as well as of the movement's settlement in Guyana, has been conducted by sociologists of religion using the theoretical framework of New Religious Movements (NRMs). While most of these treatments acknowledge that the majority of the members of this movement were African American, they do not go the next step to explore in a substantive way the implications of these demographics. As noted, many of the members came from black churches; they went to Peoples Temple thinking it, too, was a church. The leadership of the Peoples Temple movement, while predominantly white, emulated Black Church culture in style and form and, to some extent, in substance. This book seeks to explore the implications of each of these circumstances, as well as of their convergence.

The first assertion that can be made is that the Peoples Temple movement cannot be treated as if it were a white movement; the second is that it cannot be treated solely within the conventional constructs of NRM theory. The editors undertook this project out of the belief that a full understanding of this movement requires its location within the disciplinary perspectives of Black Religious Studies.

The religious experience of African Americans is not the same as the religious experience of white Americans. African American Christianity—which is but one expression of African American religion—

is not the same as white American Christianity. New African American religious movements come into existence for different reasons than new white religious movements. The black religious ethos flows through a different riverbed than the white religious ethos. One must exercise caution in overlaying constructs on black religious activity that have been drawn from the study of white religious activity.

That said, Peoples Temple was in fact a racially mixed movement, which adds a whole other dimension—one might say, complication—in the interpretation of this story. The simple fact that members were both black and white (and Hispanic and Indian) says nothing, however, about integration within the movement. We do know that it was not a fully integrated movement in terms of who had power and authority. What is less clear is how "integrated" the movement was culturally. To what extent did black members respond to familiar forms of black worship without critiquing the content? To what extent did they take the social justice activism of the movement to be the proper and sufficient measure of black religiosity? To what extent did members compartmentalize the leaders' apostasy while preserving their own framework of values and religious beliefs?

Black religiosity is notable for its communalism and spirituality. The primary functions of the black religious tradition have historically been twofold: securing of survival and pursuit of freedom. Social protest and/or engagement in electoral politics toward the end of racial justice have been visible activities of black religious leaders at the national level for the past half-century and more. Which of these features were pronounced in Peoples Temple? What was the significance of the religious and/or church background of black members as they participated in this movement? In what ways did the movement contradict or compromise the goals and values of black religion?

Contrary to implicit and explicit assumptions that have shaped scholarly treatments to date, we reject the premise that African American members of Peoples Temple had no agency. Accordingly, we reject the premise that only the activity of the leadership is relevant for categorizing this or any other movement. We also reject the adequacy of the conventional categories of cult and sect for describing this multidimensional movement. If we agree, as Mary Maaga suggests, that the black and white members who joined originally were more sect-like and the young activist whites who joined after the relocation to California were more cult-like, but that the black members who joined in San Francisco represent yet a third population that is neither cult nor sect,[6] we have still not exhausted all that the movement was or may have been, for these categories do not encompass the complete dimensions of the black religious experience.

In assembling these essays, we do not presume to have arrived at the definitive category or categories. Nor are we able to provide precise answers to all the questions that arise. Rather, we are seeking here to open up the possibilities, to point to the complexity of this movement and to invite more thoughtful reflection on its many dimensions—especially its African American dimensions—than has occurred to date. In particular, we hope to bring the Peoples Temple movement home to scholars of black religion who have not heretofore regarded it as falling within their purview. Drawing on their interpretations, scholars of New Religious Movements may then gain new insights into the motives and meaning of a movement that for so many has remained an anomaly.

Anthony B. Pinn, in Chapter 1, defines the parameters of Black Religious Studies and points to the diversity of paths that practitioners of black religion have taken. By "reading" Peoples Temple through the lens of Black Religious Studies, Pinn argues, we are better able to capture and understand Peoples Temple's epistemological context as well as the theological and ritual sensibilities that members may have brought with them from various modalities of black religiosity.

Chapter 2 reprints one of the earliest treatments of Peoples Temple by scholars of black religion. Written by C. Eric Lincoln and Lawrence H. Mamiya and published in 1980, it clearly was influenced by the general sentiments of black church leaders at the time that once again African Americans had been betrayed by a white leader. Lincoln and Mamiya employ the category of "cult" in a conventional manner as they focus on the connections of the Temple leadership to an older religious movement led by Father Divine.

The essay by Archie Smith Jr. (Chapter 3), which also was published in 1980, is exceptional in that it was the first, and remains one of a handful of efforts, to discuss Peoples Temple in relation to the Black Church. Smith also provided an early profile of the racial composition of those who died in Jonestown. Those demographics are developed further in the piece by Rebecca Moore (Chapter 4). In addition to analyzing race, age, gender, and kinship relations of residents in Jonestown, Moore compares Peoples Temple with other black religious groups, and Father Divine's Peace Mission in particular.

All religion—black religion not excluded—arises out of and is lived in a particular social context. The respective essays by Tanya M. Hollis (Chapter 5) and Duchess Harris and Adam John Waterman

(Chapter 6) help us understand the social context of the movement's latter years. Hollis frames her discussion with an overview of the racial climate of San Francisco in the 1970s, then zeros in on the conflicts surrounding redevelopment in the Fillmore District where the Temple was headquartered. Harris and Waterman examine another dimension of Bay Area politics—namely the Black Panther Party—and the appropriation of the Panthers' revolutionary rhetoric by the Temple's leadership. They relate this appropriation to the larger context of postcolonial ideologies and examine how the migration of members to the settlement in Guyana reflected these currents.

Chapter 7, by Milmon F. Harrison, moves to the internal context of Peoples Temple, providing an assessment of the relative presence or absence of aspects of black religious culture as evidenced in the Temple's services—both those that were open to the public and those that were closed. Here, particular attention is given to black Christian worship style, including chanted preaching, call and response, emotive music, praise and testimony, and various forms of healing.

Chapter 8 offers a unique perspective from an individual who was personally engaged with Peoples Temple during the San Francisco years. Dr. J. Alfred Smith Sr., senior pastor of one of the most progressive black churches in the Bay Area—Allen Temple Baptist Church in Oakland—reflects on his favorable assessment of Peoples Temple during its years of activism and then reveals his change of heart following the tragedy of Jonestown. Smith's initial support was strongly contextual, arising, as it did, out of his own prophetic ministry and his strong criticism of the majority of Bay Area black churches for their passivity and inaction.

In contrast, Chapter 9 reprints a theological reflection written very soon after the Jonestown tragedy by another Baptist minister who served as director of the Black Theology Project. The late Reverend Muhammed Isaiah Kenyatta was critical of the "rush-to-judgment" that occurred following news of what had transpired in Guyana. Kenyatta found in the Peoples Temple movement a sobering commentary on American society and American churches. His prophetic call for redemption is perhaps as timely today as it was at the time of its issuance.

In the final essay of the book (Chapter 10), Mary R. Sawyer writes both as a staff member to a black politician who worked with Peoples Temple and as an activist who found personal support for her efforts from Peoples Temple members. Sawyer returns to the issue of scholarly categorization of the movement, and particularly the applicability of the category of "church." While Peoples Temple presented itself publicly as church, was perceived by the black leadership of San Francisco to be church, and embodied certain aspects of black Christianity, the only real church, Sawyer suggests, was the "church" that was preserved by black Christian members who kept the faith while the larger movement was disintegrating into something alien to the black religious tradition.

We must emphasize that this book is not intended as a definitive treatment of Peoples Temple, either as a subject for Black Religious Studies or for religious studies generally. We see this as a beginning rather than as a conclusion. We hope other scholars will respond to the challenge to enlarge our understanding of this multifaceted movement and the people who found meaning in it—first in life, and then in death.

N O T E S

1. John R. Hall, *Gone from the Promised Land: Jonestown in American Cultural History* (New Brunswick, N.J.: Transaction Publishers, 1989), 41–44, 52–54, 63–69. This book provides the most complete and compassionate history of Peoples Temple to date. See also the earlier works of Rebecca Moore. These include *A Sympathetic History of Jonestown* (Lewiston, N.Y.: Edwin Mellen Press, 1985); *The Jonestown Letters: Correspondence to the Moore Family 1970–1985* (Lewiston, N.Y.: Edwin Mellen Press, 1986); and *In Defense of Peoples Temple and Other Essays* (Lewiston, N.Y., The Edwin Mellen Press, 1988). Two edited volumes by Rebecca Moore and Fielding M. McGehee III add critical insight and perspective to the subject. These are *The Need for a Second Look at Jonestown* (Lewiston, N.Y.: Edwin Mellen Press, 1989) and *New Religious Movements, Mass Suicide, and Peoples Temple: Scholarly Perspectives on a Tragedy* (Lewiston, N.Y.: Edwin Mellen Press, 1989).

2. Hall, *Gone from the Promised Land*, 69–70.

3. The Reverend Eugene Lumpkin Jr., interview, 27 January 1998.

4. See Mary R. Sawyer, *Black Ecumenism: Implementing the Demands of Justice* (Valley Forge, Pa.: Trinity Press, 1994), 93–94.

5. The congressman was Representative Leo Ryan of California.

6. Mary McCormick Maaga, *Hearing the Voices of Jonestown* (Syracuse, N.Y.: Syracuse University Press, 1998), 75. The movement, Maaga points out, was in fact "three groups in one." For further discussion of this typology, see Chapter 10 in this volume.

Peoples Temple and Black Religion in America

1

Peoples Temple as Black Religion

Re-imagining the Contours of Black Religious Studies

ANTHONY B. PINN

Traditionally, discussions focusing on the theoretical and methodological shape of Black Religious Studies point to a problematic and narrow perception of the nature and content of black religion as a general category of experience. Take, for example, Gayraud Wilmore's framing of the field:

> The comprehensive cultural and holistic character of African American religion itself militates against the epistemological split that often characterizes much of what is called Religious Studies in the prestigious white theological schools and university departments of religion. The best religious scholarship in the Black academy is, perforce, "believing scholarship," accepting all the risk that such a position entails. It could not be otherwise. The centuries-old struggle for Black humanity in a racist environment has not encouraged the development of a dispassionate, armchair science of religion for preparing the leadership of the Black Church in North America.[1]

It is within the move from the contextual arrangements of Black Religious Studies to its content that one gets the Christianization of the field in full force. On this point Wilmore remarks: "African American Religious Studies refers to the investigation, analysis, and ordering of a wide variety of data related to the religions of persons of African descent for the purpose of an authenticating and enriching personal faith and preparing both clergy and laity for a ministry in the Black Church and community, understood in terms of competent and faithful leadership in worship, nurture, education, and corporate action in behalf of God's mission of liberation for all people."[2]

This notion of the study of black religion is further restricted by an exclusionary sense of the Black Church. This term, Black Church, does not correspond to one entity. Rather, it is a reference to a collective of denominations and communions. While widely used, including in most of my work on black religion, the term is problematic in that it is typically used to signify religious communities tied together through participation in a particular history of religious formation in the United States. And the canon of such recognized congregations and communions is typically limited to the seven largest black denominations (African Methodist Episcopal Church, African Methodist Episcopal Zion Church, Christian Methodist Episcopal Church, Church of God in Christ, National Baptist Convention USA, National Baptist Convention of America, and the Progressive National Baptist Convention). But what about black independent communities of Christian faith? Or do most also have in mind African Americans who have made their spiritual home in the Roman Catholic Church, the United Methodist Church, and so on? Additionally, there is typically presented in Black Religious Studies a bias against smaller and more theologically creative modes of religious engagement such as Peoples Temple. So conceived, traditional notions of black religion beg the question of proper study. Who, for example, should explore Peoples Temple for its religious and theological implications, and why should such a study be undertaken? While one might first lean toward New Religious Movements analysis when answering this question, this approach, I argue, does not provide the best attention to the unique dynamics of black religiosity that guided much of what defined the aesthetic (or style) and practice of Peoples Temple. Allow me to quickly provide my take on the nature of New Religious Movements scholarship as it relates to the issue at hand.

NEW RELIGIOUS MOVEMENTS BACKGROUND

Within the United States, "New Religious Movements" (NRMs) and an often corresponding anti-cult sentiment were present in the post–World War II years, but the anti-cult reaction as a generalizable movement did not materialize until the 1970s, in response to a growing trend toward Asian and occult religious practices embraced by baby boomers and others. An initial reaction against these religious communities revolved around disappointed families who did not appreciate the altered life and career plans of college-bound children, and those who were fundamentally opposed to the doctrine of these religious communities. By 1972 plans were underway to counter these

NRMs through often coercive efforts to bring family members out of "cult" communities. Government officials did not provide the assistance anti-cult groups hoped for regarding more aggressive strategies, and so attention turned to production of literature meant to counter the claims of the new movements. With events such as the Jonestown deaths, legislation was proposed, but anti-cult bills were defeated through the efforts of groups who opposed the bills as attacks on religious freedom. Groups seeking to safeguard religious tolerance and understanding marked a strategic and somewhat philosophical shift, one involving experts in these religious movements who sought to counter negative publicity through solid education and more balanced media coverage.

Much of what has been said about Peoples Temple has entailed a response to negative constructions masked by an offensive grammar of "cults" and "sects." And while important, this new conversation often misses the deep dimensions of Peoples Temple and certainly results in limited attention to the presence of African Americans in the Temple and the significance of this presence with respect to religious aesthetics, history, and cultural sensibilities. Nonetheless, one should not be surprised by this when discussions of alternative religions of the 1960s and 1970s typically present black political struggle but give little attention to the larger *religious* presence of African Americans.[3] Recognition of the latter—and Archie Smith is correct on this point—demands a radical change regarding assumptions of relevance. These assumptions are important because they determine what information and approaches of study are considered pertinent and of immediate utility and benefit. Furthermore, tied as relevance is to the scholar's agenda, it determines what "merits" investigation and what can be safely ignored. As C. Eric Lincoln notes regarding general trends in perception: "Despite the American tolerance of other ways of faith, the American understanding of the faiths we tolerate is negligible, and has a very low priority in the order of things Americans think they really need to know about. Religions are understood to the degree in which they resonate with personal beliefs, experiences, and commitments."[4] Smith argues that "the problem of relevance in studies of the new religious consciousness cannot be settled by simply adjusting Afro-American concerns within the current scope of scholarship."[5] More theoretical and methodological work i‌ required than such a simple adjustment affords. In a word, ‌larship cannot adequately address the issue of salvation and ‌m guilt in the new religious consciousness by ignoring the ‌e souls of Black folk."[6]

Perhaps, as this volume argues, what is needed is the exploration of Peoples Temple from another vantage point, that of Black Religious Studies. But the potential for such a shift raises a question: Does Black Religious Studies actually provide for a better "reading" of Peoples Temple and Jonestown? In response, I suggest it may allow for sustained attention to epistemological context—the nature of "blackness" (as a "signifier" of a certain cultural history and a certain relationship to the ramifications of undervalued flesh) as a religious resource and rationale as well as sensitivity to the theological and ritual sensibilities members of Peoples Temple may have carried over from various modalities of black religiosity. But this also points to a problem in that Peoples Temple's nature and meaning are typically discussed in reference to the Black Church, a limited conversation at best. That type of standing is strictly a matter of looking at one historical manifestation of the religious impulse versus another—the Black Church vs. Peoples Temple. This cautionary note informs what follows.

PEOPLES TEMPLE THROUGH A DIFFERENT LENS

Whereas much NRM scholarship fails to recognize the implications of blackness within various religious movements, Black Religious Studies fails to recognize the complexity of what this blackness entails. That is to say, much in the study of black religion is confined to a static sense of blackness that limits what is categorized as black religion. For example, the presence of a white religious leader, as in the case of Peoples Temple, reduces the likelihood that the latter will be explored within the standard framework of the study of black religion. And when it is examined within this context, it is often addressed as an oddity that does not really represent black religious expression and experience. Such religious developments are presented in the negative as "cults" or "sects," an aberration.[7] Several problems inform this type of study. One is the limited nature of the canon of black religion and the other is a narrow range of theoretical tools—primarily Black Theology—utilized in the examination of black religion in its current and most easily identified states.

Regarding both problems, Charles Long called for revising the study of black religion along the lines of its theory of religious experience, noting the problematic consequences of this truncated discourse. Although issued almost 30 years ago, Long's conceptual and methodological challenge has received limited attention. And so a problem remains: Black Religious Studies has carefully outlined its sources and given limited attention to method and theory, and it is clear that the religious content explored is limited primarily to the church—and a narrow depiction of the church at that. Its sensibilities and language do not extend beyond this realm. Its approach does not move beyond a discussion, usually apologetic in tone, of the Black Church, and even this is questionable, based on criticism of Black Religious Studies' real intellectual distance from said churches. So conceived, Black Religious Studies is concerned with a narrow question, considering the complexity of the black community and its religious history: What is the feeling and meaning of being black and Christian in the United States?

With this said, it is my belief that much of what is wrong with Black Religious Studies can be corrected through the theoretical challenge provided by underexplored religious traditions and communities such as Peoples Temple. In what remains of this essay, I take up the challenge to traditional Black Religious Studies engendered by critical attention to Peoples Temple with four considerations in mind: (1) the elemental nature of religious experience, or a theory of black religion; (2) the nature of black religious community; (3) the nature of transformation as religious quest; and (4) a religio-theological approach to the tragic. The purpose of this discussion is twofold. First, I seek to present a possible revision of Black Religious Studies, and related to this, I hope to provide an alternative reading of Peoples Temple.

A THEORY OF BLACK RELIGION

As should be obvious, I am troubled by the dominant theory of black religion. It is, as one might gather from the above discussion, too tied to a particular tradition—and to a limited range of this tradition's various modalities—to speak about the complexity and scope of black religious expression and experience. A great deal of our intellectual energy when it comes to black religion has revolved around attention to institutional forms, doctrines, and rituals as its basic structures. These elements are the historical "trappings" of religion, the manifestation of a much deeper and more elemental reality, and are most visible and recognized with respect to the oldest black Christian communities. That is to say, while important elements of what it means to be black and religious, these historically situated realities—church dogma, church architecture, and so on—are not all there is to religion. In fact, they represent only religion's "shell."

The elemental nature of religion has more to do with an underlying attention to meaning, an urge to make meaning. This, I believe, is what Jonathan Z. Smith has in mind when he says "what we study when we study religion is one mode of constructing worlds of meaning, worlds within which men find themselves and in which they choose to dwell. What we study is the passion and drama of man discovering the truth of what it is to be human." Historical realities, historical materials, are, he continues,

> the framework within whose perimeters those human expressions, activities and intentionalities that we call "religious" occur. Religion is the quest, within the bounds of the human, historical condition, for the power to manipulate and negotiate one's "situation" so as to have "space" in which to meaningfully dwell.[8]

We move toward the central concern, the *center* of religion, to use Mircea Eliade's terminology. This center, I argue, entails a quest for complex subjectivity, a wrestling with history for the development of a fuller sense of humanity as the prize, to develop a profound conviction that "one's existence matters."[9] In short, this complex subjectivity is a seeking for full humanity, a push for status as a subject of history as opposed to the racist manner in which those of African descent have been projected as objects of history. It is the quest for a better utilization of human potential and creativity. Conceived this way, religion entails a mode of experience through which we seek to keep open and in creative tension a multitude of spaces of fulfillment.

This process began for those of African descent in the United States during the period of slavery, as black bodies rebelled against the existential and ontological construction of Africans as subhuman. Physical space—church buildings—and written affirmations are more recent developments, having emerged sometime after the first one hundred years of an African presence in North America. Hence a uniquely religious experience in the context of North America begins not with verbal articulation, but with the body itself. In an ironic sense, the defining characteristics and justification for their enslavement—the body—was also the loci of their religiosity or quest for subjectivity. It is this element and its display and placement, appreciation, and "protection" that marks the similarity among the various traditions housed in black communities—the Black Church, United House of Prayer for All People, Oyotunji African Village, Peoples Temple, and so on. The complexity and importance of various manifestations of this underlying impulse—this push for greater humanity or subjectivity—should not be measured only by numerical participation. Doing so has been one of the problems with Black Religious Studies.

It involves a reaction against practices that are not part of numerically significant communities and that are not representative of the major black denominations and their "accepted" offshoots.

Scholars such as James Evans sense this underlying impulse, this quest for full humanity, but mistakenly limit its expression to the recognized Christian faith housed in the major black denominations:

> Black religion attempts to help African-American Christians to sense the world as God senses it. A second hermeneutical task of black religion is to dismantle the misinterpretations of themselves and the world that undergirds American Christianity. That is, black religion is a protest against those portrayals of African-Americans as less than human or outside the providential care of God. . . . Black religion attempts to provide a self-knowledge for African-American Christians by helping them to see themselves as God sees them.[10]

But surely there is more to black religion than this. One begins to debunk this false assumption—black Christianity as the only important mode of black religious experience—by recognizing that this quest for complex subjectivity predates the Black Church because it did not rely on the church structures but rather first developed in and through the body.

Religion is experience, perhaps a category of experience defined by a quest for *"MORE."* It is shaped by social context and contact, involving a fighting against absurdity and devaluation. An example is provided by one member of Peoples Temple who reported that she "found something she had never found in the United States. For the first time, she believed she had found a society free of sexism and racism and one in which she experienced full acceptance as a Black woman. She had a cause to live for. American society had never given her that."[11] This much I have learned from historian of religions Charles H. Long: religion has something to do with the development of "more authentic forms of community," which entail a recognition of the value and "authenticity of all persons."[12] Put another way, the system—Nation of Islam, Black Church, Voodoo, Peoples Temple, and so on—is the historically conditioned manifestation of the quest or feeling for complex subjectivity. Herein religion retains some of its early meaning—to bind together—but in this case it is a nourishing and binding together of various strands of existential and ontological possibility.

Mindful of this black Christian bias of Black Religious Studies, one gets a sense of why Peoples Temple is foreign terrain for most in Black Religious Studies, with the exceptions of Lawrence Mamiya, C. Eric

Lincoln, Archie Smith Jr., Muhammed Isaiah Kenyatta, and Mary Sawyer. But only Sawyer thinks about Peoples Temple as black religion in ways that do not render it some type of odd or grotesque development. Yet Sawyer approaches Peoples Temple as black religion within the confines of the Black Church. While her work is invaluable, it holds the potential to fix one's gaze on the most visible "trappings" of black religion at the expense of deeper commonalities between Peoples Temple and other modes of black religion that cannot be explained in terms of worship style or cultural leanings, but instead deal with a shared connection to the elemental nature of religion.

THINKING ABOUT BLACK RELIGIOUS COMMUNITY

The failures noted above and found within the limited scholarship on Peoples Temple generated within Black Religious Studies are tied to a wrongheaded theory of involvement, a kind of elitism or Black Church chauvinism. Archie Smith, for example, noted shortly after the tragedy of Jonestown that the psychoanalytical perspective on Jonestown and Peoples Temple suggests persons drawn to such "cults" are weak-minded and dependent, without clear vision and self-consciousness because they are "in search for a surrogate parent or authority figures. In other words, the prime targets for recruitment into such movements as the Peoples Temple were the oppressed, especially poor Blacks, the lonely, dependent and insecure who welcome the message of egalitarianism."[13] (It must be noted that Smith rejects the psychoanalytical perspective in that it fails to take into consideration the quest for social equality.) While I agree that the "message of egalitarianism" as Smith explains it is attractive, the underlying impetus for involvement is a quest for complex subjectivity having to do with more than socioeconomic goods. Instead it revolves around a much more substantive concern centered on greater status as fully human within a religious community whose particular ethos—aesthetic qualities, doctrine, and relationship networks—is more attractive to some than to others. Hence, participation in Peoples Temple is not a matter of socioeconomic or psychological "flaws." It is not a matter of psychological weakness or shortcomings. Rather, it stems from the manner in which Peoples Temple's approach to subjectivity, that is full humanity, spoke to the existential condition and epistemological sensitivities of some. To think otherwise says more about the researcher's personal leanings than about the nature of Peoples Temple's community and praxis.

Muhammed Kenyatta turns the psychological approach on its

head by pointing out the flaws and weaknesses in the society which drove Peoples Temple members to Jonestown and which prevented them from returning to the United States. Kenyatta goes further, however, when he claims that the members of Peoples Temple attempted to create something new. "We know that the Peoples Temple became, in part, a pilgrim church," he writes. "It set out to a frontier place in the hopes of better perfecting the practice of its faith."[14]

What I want to highlight is Kenyatta and Smith's effort to point out the deep yearning for full humanity that motivated the participation of African Americans. I find this more promising; yet there is a problem with the manner in which Black Religious Studies—if Smith (and I would add C. Eric Lincoln and Lawrence Mamiya) is representative—frames the conversation. G. K. Chesterton once remarked that the United States was a "nation with the soul of the church," and in like manner, Black Religious Studies has all too often been a field of study "with the soul" of the Black Church.[15] Resulting from this is an assumption that participation in Peoples Temple and other religious communities must entail, finally, not the value of these communities for their members but a shortcoming with respect to the Black Church that pushes people away. As noted by Lincoln and Mamiya: "[T]hat the proliferation of exotic white or 'international' cults attractive to blacks may seriously threaten the historic black preference for traditional in-group religious affiliation is not lost upon the more alert leadership of the Black Church."[16]

I suggest the criteria for an interpretation of Peoples Temple must be altered, recognizing instead the nature of the experience within that community without the Black Church as the litmus test for authenticity of religious encounters. Furthermore, to pinpoint for scrutiny the ethical and epistemological shortcomings of Peoples Temple's leadership and membership, as is commonly the case, challenges "recognized" modes of black religion by begging the question of similar shortcomings in the Black Church, the Nation of Islam, and so on. While Smith, on the one hand, notes the value of Peoples Temple, he points out its flaws in a way that raises questions concerning the possibility of similar shortcomings within more easily and commonly noted modalities of black religion:

> Many black people originally responded positively to Peoples Temple because it was a movement that provided psychic support and linked it with a program of social/communal outreach. . . . By breaking with the insularity and seemingly irrelevant style of traditional Black Church worship, many thought they had found in the

Peoples Temple a form of church involvement that spoke more directly to the issue of spiritual uplift, justice, social change and communal empowerment. Their vision of a new social order was not wrong. It was expressive of the relational paradigm. It was a vision broader than that found in many of the black churches they left. But their vision was not enough. It lacked a self-critical dimension that would have enabled them to discern the false claims of Jim Jones towards ego deification. Black people's involvement in Peoples Temple and Jonestown is difficult to explain in light of the Black Power and Black Theology of liberation movements and developing Black nationalism of the 1960s, and the African roots phenomenon of the 1970s. It appears as an anomaly.[17]

Black Religious Studies has been reluctant to condemn its recognized modalities of black religion on the basis of the "indiscretions" or "misdeeds" of some leaders, arguing instead that the movement and its value, the people and their project are much greater than any particular leader. One need only think in terms of Adam Clayton Powell Jr., Martin Luther King Jr., and Jesse Jackson to understand this point. Should not this same hermeneutic of the group be utilized with respect to Jim Jones and Peoples Temple? Can Black Religious Studies really define Peoples Temple strictly in terms of its leadership? Are there not lessons to be learned from Cheryl Townsend Gilkes' work on alternate modes of "authority" and more complex ways to define religious community?[18] Furthermore, outside the realm of sociology of religion, a careful reading of Black Theology points out the importance of thinking about liberation beyond the scope of individual personalities and what they can achieve. This appears to be the lesson learned through observation of Latin American base communities as the incubator for organic and communally derived modes of leadership premised upon a central mantra—"God's preferential option for the poor"—and the recognition that humans are fallible creatures.

In light of Smith's commentary, I ask several questions. Is it proper to assume participation in Peoples Temple stems from the failure of the Black Church to live out its principles? Is there not the possibility that African Americans participated in Peoples Temple, forged community around Peoples Temple, because of its creative approach to the development of life meaning? Must we think about the movement of African Americans into Peoples Temple as a negative statement about the Black Church, thereby maintaining the supremacy of traditional black Christianity, rather than as a positive statement concerning Peoples Temple's vision for complex subjectivity?

In all fairness, I think the theoretical and epistemological issues lodged in this dilemma are large and deeply rooted. Perhaps, and I want to exercise some caution here, there is strong significance to the manner in which Lincoln and Mamiya see the connection between African American "other-ness" and "odd" religious traditions. In Lincoln's words:

> [I]t was not until a peculiar interplay of social and economic factors produced a series of exotic religious movements in the urban black ghettos of the post–World War I era that "cult" took on its distinctive, conventional meaning. Such colorful hierophants (with equally colorful titles) as Father Divine, Daddy Grace, Honorable Elijah Muhammad, Rabbi Cherry and others caught the imagination of an America which, having harbored a historic suspicion about the spiritual adequacy of black religion, was now prepared to accept the black cult as visible documentation of what had always been suspected. In consequence, alternately romanticized and ridiculed in the press, such groups . . . came to represent to most Americans what was meant by "cult." . . . Inevitably, the association of cult with the more exotic expressions of black religion encouraged the distension of the term into a convenient appellation eventually applied in popular usage to most, if not all, organized black worship.[19]

While there is probably a great deal of truth to this—the merging of "marginal elements" in the popular imagination—the response to it on the part of Black Religious Studies is problematic. It appears that Black Religious Studies, following the lead of early critics such as Arthur Huff Fauset, sought to correct for this by safeguarding and distinguishing its prized religious institutions from marginal communities.[20]

With this in mind, Smith, and Lincoln and Mamiya, at the very least, imply a tying of authentic black religion to a certain strain of black consciousness, marked by what is often referred to as ontological blackness (i.e., linking inclusion in the black community with a certain perspective on and grasp of racial markers such as specified cultural sensibilities, social leanings, and approved relationships). Regarding this practice, Victor Anderson wisely notes in his volume *Beyond Ontological Blackness* that Black Religious Studies reifies blackness and holds it as the measure of fit with the Black Religious tradition. Hence, Black Religious Studies, particularly black and womanist theologies, have unwittingly supported forms of essentialism in ways that actually counter the struggle for a liberated existence.[21] Think, for example, of Black Theology's early, almost exclusive focus on liberation against racism from the male perspective. This preoccupation of necessity, for example, meant little attention was given to the sexism implicitly accepted by black male theologians and the churches they claimed to represent. In addition to the manner in which this essentialized sense of blackness shapes and limits understandings of oppression, it also restricts the nature and scope of the black religious community.

To be authentically black comes to imply participation (or at least nominal appreciation for) the Black Church tradition as exemplified by black-founded and black-run denominations. A strong epistemological link, if not an ontological one, is thereby forged between the Black (run) Church and black communities. To emphasize this point I turn to a passage I have quoted often because of the continuing relevance of its assumptions regarding true black religion as exclusively Black Church religion:

> In the beginning was the black church, and the black church was with the black community, and *the black church was the black community. The black church was in the beginning with the black people; all things were made through the black church, and without the black church was not anything made that was made.* In the black church was life, and the life was the light of the black people. The black church still shines in the darkness, and the darkness has not overcome it [italics added].[22]

Efforts have been made to break free of this limited depiction of black religious communities, and by extension the contours of what it means to be black and religious. This, however, is not a theoretical battle that is waged once. Rather, it requires continued effort to explode the canon of black religion and to problematize myopic definitions. This is not to say that the links between Peoples Temple and the Black Church tradition are of no importance. Rather, my concern is that we look not only at the ways in which the Black Church tradition informs Peoples Temple's theology, aesthetics, and praxis, but also at the manner in which Peoples Temple might inform the canon of black religion and Black Religious Studies.

On this point, serious engagement with Peoples Temple and the effort of scholars to think about it with respect to its "Black Church" dimension raise an interesting question: What and where is the *black* in black religion? This question first surfaced with respect to the presence of African Americans in the Roman Catholic Church, the United Methodist Church, and other predominantly white denominations. And implied in this question was a critique of black involvement with institutions that were not developed for and by African Americans. Bluntly stated, how could churches premised upon "white" religious sensibilities, with a history of questionable engagement with African Americans, help the once-despised develop life-meaning and orientation? What becomes evident through this line of questioning is the manner in which the "proper" loci of black religiosity are defined in terms of numerical strength—where most black folk are found. Nonetheless, this does not explain the reluctance of those in Black Religious Studies to give attention, for example, to Peoples Temple, a community that was roughly 80 to 90 percent African American after African Americans began to join in significant numbers during the early 1970s. This is not to say that the African American presence in Peoples Temple is completely lost on all scholars.

Mary Maaga and Mary Sawyer provide important insights into the involvement of African Americans and the ways in which it shaped Peoples Temple.[23] They do so by introducing the hermeneutical category of "Black Church" as a way of exploring and explaining the manner in which a certain constituency within Peoples Temple drew on black Christian aesthetics, theology, and culture. Regardless of such efforts, as important as they are, it strikes me that there is much to be gained by thinking through Peoples Temple as a modality of black religion, as the Black Church and the Nation of Islam are modalities of black religion. For Sawyer the question of whether Peoples Temple was a "real church" requires a yes or no response.[24] In her book, Maaga argues Peoples Temple's structure to be composed of "three groups in one." The third of these three is the "urban Black Church." While some disagree with this assessment, I believe Maaga suggests that Peoples Temple and Jonestown provided an opportunity to maintain the best elements of traditional black Christian practice and mixed them with an aggressive concern for sociopolitical activism. This is not to say that Peoples Temple kept all the "best" elements of black Christian practice. That level of certainty is not possible. Rather, I believe there is in Maaga's depiction the presence of sensibilities and leanings in Peoples Temple that made the maintenance of certain black Christian aesthetics and practices a possibility because Peoples Temple was not theologically and ideologically opposed to either black Christian aesthetics or practices. In her words:

> Most of the three thousand and the majority of those who moved with Peoples Temple to Jonestown, Guyana, were yet a third type of Peoples Temple member. They were primarily black and lived in urban California, particularly San Francisco and Los Angeles. The attraction of Peoples Temple for these former and current church members was the ability to bridge the gap between the other-worldly

preaching of many black spiritualist church traditions and the concrete political activism of the black power political movements.[25]

This is not to suggest that Sawyer and Maaga argue for an understanding of Peoples Temple as Black Church. Making such an interpretation of their work would be misleading. Instead they suggest that certain segments of Peoples Temple can be related to elements of Black Church tradition, and that attention to these intersections are important components of study. I agree with Sawyer and Maaga that there were certainly black Christians involved in Peoples Temple and Jonestown. However, I believe there are benefits to a more general paradigm for investigation—black religion as an elemental category of religious experience that relates to the Black Church but also to all other modalities of religious expression in African American communities. Using this general paradigm raises an important question: Were all the blacks Christian?

Moving in this direction—Peoples Temple as a theory of black religion in addition to discussion of segments of Peoples Temple as they might or might not relate to or in some ways correspond to elements of the Black Church tradition—allows for the inclusion of a variety of sensibilities that influenced Peoples Temple, at least early in its development. This does not negate the strong Christian sensibilities of some members; rather, it simply exhibits Christian sensibilities within a larger arena of religious commitments and perspectives. One should note, for instance, that thinking about segments of Peoples Temple in terms of possible correlations with the Black Church tradition does not necessarily entail a discussion of the manner in which Jim Jones borrowed from Father Divine in thinking about the nature of community. "Like the Peace Mission," John R. Hall remarks, "Peoples Temple was to become an extended family that offered its communal fellowship as a shelter from the uncertain world beyond. In turn, Jones used the organization of Peoples Temple as a springboard to social action, establishing care homes for the elderly, running a free restaurant to feed the hungry, maintaining a social service center to help people," and so on.[26]

Of greater controversy and importance in light of recent studies on the Black Church is the issue of nontheism in Peoples Temple. It is on this issue that those holding Peoples Temple to include, as one of its internal groups, a manifestation of black religion stumble over the same issue of theological normalcy as do those in the study of black religion I critiqued earlier. Black religion may be theistic or even polytheistic, but never atheistic. Such an assumption, from my vantage point, is based on selective historical memory. But when African American cultural history is viewed based on a hermeneutic of theodicy, for example, the logic of the theism norm is proven faulty. From the antebellum period to the present, African Americans have maintained an important presence in humanist and atheist circles. Keep in mind, for instance, the presence of African Americans in the Communist Party during the 1920s who critiqued the idea of God and promoted a human-centered perspective on life, or workers in the Civil Rights struggle such as James Foreman who rejected God and embraced human potential. In fact, he wrote:

> It is that leap of faith which I now refuse to make. I reject the existence of God. He is not all-powerful, all-knowing, and everywhere. He is not just or unjust because he does not exist. God is a myth; churches are institutions designed to perpetuate this myth and thereby keep people in subjugation. When a people who are poor, suffering with disease and sickness, accept the fact that God has ordained for them to be this way—then they will never do anything about their human condition. In other words, the belief in a supreme being or God weakens the will of a people to change conditions themselves.[27]

Examples of this perspective abound, and many have been collected in anthologies, monographs, and articles dealing with the nature and meaning of African American humanism.[28] When one considers the manner in which intellectual and more popular explorations have unearthed a humanist tradition within African American communities, there is no reason from my perspective to assume African American members were of necessity outside the more humanistic turns present at points in Peoples Temple's history. This is particularly true when one takes into consideration that the increase in African American converts in the early 1970s coincided with Peoples Temple's move away from theological Christianity (while maintaining an affiliation with the Disciples of Christ). There is, I believe, some philosophical and theological significance in this.[29]

Does this growing presence support the notion that a human-centered gospel troubles African Americans? While some argue Jim Jones may have provided competing messages—atheistic communism for some and a theistic communalism for others—and there is something to this, one should not dismiss the complexity of black religious opinion and expression as it is manifest in both theistic and nontheistic ways.[30] It seems unlikely that African Americans would remain in Peoples Temple and Jonestown if bothered by the humanist teachings simply because they did not want to appear to be "traitors." For some this may have been the case, but it is also plausible that for others the humanist teachings rang true. Such a connection to non-supernatural orientation would not run contrary to black religion but, as I have argued numerous times, would amount to another nontheistic trajectory or modality of black religion. Furthermore, and outside the humanist critique, Jones' presentation of himself as a "savior" or "messiah," while strange to some, would not have meant a complete contradiction to the Black Religious tradition that was familiar, I would imagine, to many who joined Peoples Temple, in that various black leaders have made similar claims. One example is the depiction of Master Fard Muhammad within the Nation of Islam. According to the official teachings of the Nation, as expressed first by the Honorable Elijah Muhammad, Master Fard is the Great Mahdi:

> One of the main things that one must learn is to distinguish between the history of Jesus two thousand years ago and the prophecy of the Jesus 2,000 years ago, which often proves to be that of the Great Mahdi, the Restorer of the Kingdom of Peace on Earth, who came to America in 1930 under the name of Mr. W. D. Fard. Later, he'd admitted that he was Mr. Wallace Fard Muhammad, the One Whom the world has been looking for to come for the past 2,000 years. According to the Holy Qur'an's chapter and verse which we have under discussion [Chapters 3:41, 42, 44, 46], the name Messiah, the meaning, fits that of the Mahdi more than any other man.[31]

Such claims may appear fantastic, yet there is a notable tradition of such assertions within black religion that would make similar claims by Jim Jones theologically plausible for some within various African American communities.

THE NATURE OF TRANSFORMATION AS RELIGIOUS QUEST

The notion of movement, no doubt first derived as a category of thought from what remained of cultural and social memory related to the Middle Passage and slave auctions, has played a significant role in the language and aesthetics of black religion, hence of Black Religious Studies. It was and remains a powerful signifier of transformation, of a reconstituted self and community, bound together through a shared vision. In particular, "exodus" and "exile" language and imagery have functioned as powerful paradigms, serving to shape epistemologically, culturally, and historically dominant understandings of black religious development within the context of North

America and the African diaspora in more general terms. Early Black Church theology highlights the perception of African Americans as an exilic community confined to the harsh social terrain of North America as a modern "Babylon," and numerous preachers have raised the question in countless sermons regarding the angst that marks black life: "How can we sing the Lord's song in a strange Land?" It was also understood, however, that this exile was a temporary arrangement, often a matter of theodical and providential significance perceived in terms of merited punishment for disobedience to God or refinement necessary for a great work ahead. In either case, it was understood within black religion, and Black Religious Studies highlights this, that exile was of necessity followed by exodus into better circumstances.

For some, this exodus involved a nationalistic appeal to emigration—a movement back to Africa.[32] Entailing an often heated debate within Black Church circles, prominent figures such as African Methodist Episcopal Church bishop Henry McNeal Turner and Presbyterian minister Alexander Crummell presented emigration as a providential exodus by which Africa would be redeemed. This theological position was in keeping with a metaphorical adaptation of Psalm 68: 31: "Let bronze be brought from Egypt; let Ethiopia hasten to stretch out her hands to God." This religious nationalism is expressed in altered form by communities such as the Nation of Islam that seek to establish African Americans as a "nation within a nation," separated from whites, as blacks—godlike beings—prepare themselves for their great destiny. Some who embraced Judaism (often combining it with African American religious aesthetics), such as the Hebrew Israelites, expressed the significance of movement or exodus through relocation to Israel.[33] Many members of black communities, including some who might have become members of Peoples Temple, embraced the "Back-to-Africa" philosophy as espoused by Marcus Garvey, the leader of the largest movement of African Americans in the history of the United States.[34]

In addition to the significance of emigration as a religious and theological expression of exodus and exile language, Black Religious Studies highlights the importance of movement within the context of the United States as an important religious paradigm. For example, Milton Sernett's work on the Great Migration—the mass movement of African Americans into southern and northern cities shortly after the Civil War through much of the twentieth century—details the manner in which such movement is existentially and culturally linked to major institutional, aesthetic, and doctrinal developments within black religion.[35] When the connotations of movement are noted, one gains a better sense of the religious diversity of black communities in that during this period of migration the Nation of Islam develops; the Church of God in Christ emerges; national Baptist conventions form; modalities of black Judaism spring forth. All are committed to the placement of God's chosen in a better socioeconomic, political, and religious place.

Theological and doctrinal alterations partially connected to institutional transitions and developments are also noteworthy in that it is during this period that the Black Church is dominated by an "other-worldly" orientation. According to Gayraud Wilmore, this involves a shift away from a focus on a social Christianity marked by a muscular interaction with pressing socioeconomic and political issues facing blacks, to a preoccupation with a type of radical individualism expressed in terms of individual salvation over against social transformation.[36]

This theologically informed passivity was broken only by the Civil Rights movement and the involvement of black religious communions in struggle, connoting a profound engagement with movement or exodus as signifier of social transformation. Dr. Martin Luther King Jr. makes frequent use of the language of movement to express this point. One only need think, for example, of his response to those who argued that blacks were "moving too fast" for a sense of the argument made here. King argued that the plight of the oppressed required, and God demanded, action. Subtly pointing to the progress of Africa, to the development of the continent that figures such as Turner and Crummell had hoped for, King looks back to the United States and sees a need for action defined in terms of the movement of black bodies:

> The American Negro saw, in the land from which he had been snatched and thrown into slavery, a great pageant of political progress. He realized that just thirty years ago there were only three independent nations in the whole of Africa. He knew that by 1963 more than thirty-four African nations had risen from colonial bondage. The Negro saw black statesmen voting on vital issues in the United Nations—and knew that in many cities of his own land he was not permitted to take that significant walk to the ballot box. . . . Witnessing the drama of Negro progress elsewhere in the world, witnessing a level of conspicuous consumption at home exceeding anything in our history, it was natural that by 1963 Negroes would rise with resolution and demand a share of governing power, and living conditions measured by American standards rather than by the standards of colonial impoverishment. *An additional and decisive fact con-*

fronted the Negro and helped to bring him out of the houses, into the street,
out of the trenches and into the front lines. This was his recognition that
one hundred years had passed since emancipation, with no profound
effect on his plight [italics added].[37]

From the spirituals and blues, to early church leaders and the faithful
of other traditions, to King and the present diasporic struggle for
equality, Black Religious Studies has described and analyzed black
religion using the language of movement (most typically the meta-
phors of exodus and exile) and has preferred to speak about African
Americans through a grammar of "chosen-ness." However, this has
usually been done in ways that do not problematize the liberative
effects of movement. That is to say, little attention has been given to
religious communities for whom the language of movement is significant but for whom it does not necessarily generate the type of praxis
that traditional formulations of ethics would sanction. As a result, we
have missed an opportunity to enhance the theoretical framework that
informs Black Religious Studies. I suggest Peoples Temple is a case in
point.

Peoples Temple's theological framework shares with other modalities of black religion a concern with exodus and exile as paradigms
of transformation. As Maaga notes, "These were people who had internalized Marcus Garvey's Back-to-Africa movement during the
1920s; almost half of the elderly residents of Jonestown had already
migrated once from the American South to California in search of a
more just society."[38] The very movement from the United States to
Jonestown marked the continuation of flight to better circumstances.
What we must remember from this is the importance of "space" for
the unpacking of visions regarding social transformation. The system
of ethics advocated by Peoples Temple was concerned with the creation of space in which the development of complex identity or multidimensional subjectivity could be worked out. In other words, "We
are always in negotiation, not with a single set of oppositions that
place us always in the same relation to others, but with a series of
different positionalities. Each has for us its point of profound subjec-
tive identification."[39]

The measuring of one's commitment to this norm, this process of
more liberated identity, is understood in terms of fidelity, a faithful-
ness to the creation of this "safe" space. What Ira G. Zepp Jr. says
concerning communal "ritual or ceremonial centers" is pertinent here.
The space in which communities such as Peoples Temple live and
"have their being" is the *axis mundi*, the "axle or pole around which"

their collective and individual identity turn "and without which [their] world would collapse."[40] Furthermore, the blind tenacity with which the "threat" to Jonestown from external forces and assumed internal "traitors" was fought speaks to the importance of this center because, again borrowing a concept from Zepp, "as humans we have a profound need to repudiate, if not escape, the disorder and broken-ness of life, and to establish islands of stability as a counterpoint to chaos. The reaction of a center is usually the way people resist dis-order."[41] In this space believers feel a sense of ease, of purpose and order that is defended fiercely because the structure of reality that marks Peoples Temple and other religious communities is dependent upon it for the reconstitution of socioeconomic, political, cultural, and "spiritual" being.

This is the nature of religious space and community, yet it becomes dangerous when protection of physical and metaphorical space is so consuming that it requires a compromise of the very principles that sparked its initial creation, when the welfare of the individual mem-bers of the community is sacrificed for the preservation of "space." What this involves is a failure to heed the metaphorical value of Jon-athan Z. Smith's warning: "Map is not territory."[42] That is to say, the content of religious vision must not be forgotten, and meaning must be gathered, not simply imposed. To simply impose meaning upon history exposes one to risk and to the tendency to engage in a warped vision of purpose that is superficial and ideological in the negative sense of the word. As Smith notes, "For a given group at a given time to choose this or that mode of interpreting their tradition is to opt for a particular way of relating themselves to their historical past and social present."[43] However, this balancing of past and present can be-come misguided and perverted, resulting in the forgetting of the initial motivations for the tradition. Moving back to the concepts with which I started this section, the significance and meaning of exodus is trans-muted into a paranoid sense of exile in that the "promised land" does not deliver all that was promised. In the haunting words of Jim Jones just prior to the mass suicide and murders: "We can't go back; they won't leave us alone. They're now going back to tell more lies, which means more congressmen. And there's no way, no way we can sur-vive."[44]

The symbols and social structures used to express and explain uto-pian visions fracture under the strain when *communitas* in its fullness is not found, and these visions lose their significance in light of per-sistent "evil." That which maintained the logic or epistemological co-hesiveness of the community is compromised and questioned. Does not such a move at least in part speak to the failings of Peoples Temple's vision for renewed life in Guyana? In an odd twist, Jonestown entailed a desire to "disappear," to be left alone to live in "peace," yet near the end it also entailed a deep paranoia over invisibility—a fear that the community's successes and merit would be denied by the outside world. In other words, African Americans and others were drawn to Peoples Temple and were willing to embrace the Jonestown project because the Temple helped them attack and subdue modes of false consciousness, whether defined in terms of the demonic system of capitalism or racism.[45] Yet this community would ultimately succumb, in a Guyana jungle, to a new modality of false consciousness, one that would prove all too deadly.

A RELIGIO-THEOLOGICAL APPROACH TO THE TRAGIC

I am attentive to a seldom-discussed statement made by theologian James Cone because of its importance for our understanding of truth and revelation. He says:

> When people ask me, "How do you know that what you say is true?" my reply is: "Ultimately, I don't know and neither does anybody else." We are creatures of history, not divine beings. I cannot claim infinite knowledge. What I can do is to bear witness to my story, to tell it and live it, as the story grips my life and pulls me out of the nothingness into being. However, I am not imprisoned within my story. Indeed, when I understand truth as story, I am more likely to be open to other people's truth stories. As I listen to other stories, I am invited to move out of the subjectivity of my own story into another realm of thinking and acting.[46]

In light of Cone's words, Jonestown reinforces something of epistemological worth, lessons learned throughout the various moments of black religious development: truth (i.e., the rightness of one's story) is not discovered, it is formed, made. We should have learned this much from the religious history of the United States, which was created from economic concerns and demonic theological formulations in which "truthful" statements or stories asserted the inferiority of some and the superiority of others. Sad, but this is the process. The Black Church, as one form of black religion, has fought to make this not so, but it has remained the case. Efforts have been made by members of the Nation of Islam and by black humanists, with similar results. Truth is forged by human hands for human purposes, and to fulfill human needs. There is no "truth," just resonating claims and assertions that hopefully serve the improvement of life options. This being the case, "truth" is revisable. Are the claims acceptable based upon the existing human condition and need? The ethical requirement is simple: religious claims and truths should be tested in the arena of human experience, that is, how they "wear" on the human body.

We should gather from the tragedy of 18 November 1978 a more critical understanding and interpretation of ethics of social transformation, perhaps based on a hermeneutic of creative tension, measuring the "rightness" of actions by a synergy between individual desire and group good. Such a stance seeks to monitor the individual's perspective based upon the cultural and historical memory of the group, providing a corrective for misguided critiques and warped practices. This type of life in and between community is not a limitation on the self's quest for meaning, rather it is an extension of that quest; in some respects, it is the culmination of that quest in that it brings into a healthy tension community and the individual. With respect to accomplishing this, ethicist Sharon Welch is correct in asserting that activity is risky and there is no method for the production of moral vision that is free from risk.[47] There is no way, as Jonestown teaches us, to guarantee that humans will always operate in morally and ethically enriching ways, that the vision for transformation will maintain its integrity. As many scholars have noted, Jonestown in part expressed an effort to maintain a rigid distinction between good and evil, with both camps—Jonestown's residents and their opponents—claiming the former. But within such a struggle, the traditional dualism of "good" and "evil" is unreliable and problematic. Sharp distinctions like this tend to foster disillusionment when those assumed "good" are found guilty of participation in "moral evil." This absolutist distinction between these two—good and evil—does not allow for the recognition that all humanity is capable of both, and, what is more, is guilty of both.[48]

Catherine Wessinger and others are quite clear with respect to the importance of community above all else advocated by Jonestown. In fact,

> the ultimate concern for the Jonestown residents was to preserve their community. Loyalty to the collective was the primary value. . . . Rebecca Moore has argued that the members of Peoples Temple, and especially the residents of Jonestown, were bonded together by their shared participation in the life of the community, which increasingly included participation in rituals of violence.[49]

Or, as Mary Maaga notes, public meetings at Jonestown provided community leaders the opportunity to create

> consensus within the community and for Jones to convey a sense of the special importance of the enterprise in which they were engaged. Occasionally, educational exercises were practiced in which people were asked to write about their understanding of socialist ideology and about their willingness to sacrifice for the survival of Jonestown.[50]

Jonestown's final days involved a sacrifice first of "enemies" and "traitors" at a remote air strip, but this was considered an incomplete sacrifice, unable to keep the community and safeguard its vision of "apostolic socialism." There was a call for a more complete sacrifice, an act of violence through which the community regrettably would seek to preserve the vision through the sacrifice of itself.[51]

This does not mean that effort should not be maintained to work for transformation, but it must be based on a creative tension as the desires of individuals are measured and corrected by the demands of community. This is, I believe, what Christine Miller attempted to impress upon Jim Jones at the last community meeting during the murders and suicides—a requirement to maintain perspective with respect to the nature of sacrifice (reflecting some elements of René Girard's discussion of the subject): "I still think, as an individual, I have a right to say what I think, what I feel. And I think we all have a right to our own destiny as individuals. And I think I have a right to choose mine, and everybody else has a right to choose theirs."[52]

Who is properly scapegoated?[53] Peoples Temple, whether in Indiana or California, relied for much of its history on the ability to locate, isolate, and name evil and evildoers. This ability, however, diminished in a substantial way in Jonestown and even before. Lines of opposition were to some extent blurred: Enemies within the gates? Enemies at the gates? Let us extend this line of inquiry. What happens when one thinks about issues of psychological norms and the tragic through the lens of religious warriors such as Nat Turner, whose religious vision and sensibilities drew commentary similar to the idea of "oddities" implied above? The theory of "oddities"—some leaders can be dismissed and their deeds explained away by labeling them odd—must be approached with caution when one thinks of heroes of Black Religious Studies such as Turner, or Denmark Vesey, or Gabriel Posser. Caution is necessary because of the unpredictable manner in which "inspiration" flows within black religion and the manner in which "contact" between the cosmic and the mundane is made manifest. It is, I believe, a mistake to think about involvement in religious communities or the embrace of religiously motivated ideals simply in terms of outcomes or end products. Can one fully understand the involvement of African Americans in Peoples Temple simply through attention to "Jonestown in 1978"? Or can one fully appreciate the religious convictions of Nat Turner by simply focusing on his death? Likewise, can the value of the Black Church be measured simply in the persistence of sexism, classism, heterosexism, and homophobia within black churches? While outcomes have some importance, when taken alone they do not provide the best way to access the logic of involvement.

Part of the tragedy experienced after Jonestown is the forgetting of the humanity of those involved. By so doing, scholars ultimately deny those who sought complex subjectivity—a life full of meaning— the significance and scope of this quest. Clearly, attention to Peoples Temple within the study of black religion (or Black Religious Studies), particularly its transmutation into Jonestown, pushes Black Religious Studies in challenging ways. It forces a rethinking of the nature of tragedy, deliverance, redemption, and the existentially absurd. This rethinking entails a reconstitution of the theological meaning of and social space for transformation, and in this way it raises questions concerning the texture of *communitas*. Ultimately, it raises a strong theodical question, a theodicy with no satisfying answer but one for which silence is all too inappropriate.

NOTES

1. Gayraud S. Wilmore, "Introduction," in *African American Religious Studies: An Interdisciplinary Anthology* (Durham, N.C.: Duke University Press, 1989), xii.

2. Wilmore, *African American Religious Studies*, xii–xiii.

3. For example, Robert S. Ellwood, *The Sixties Spiritual Awakening: American Religion Moving from Modern to Postmodern* (New Brunswick, N.J.: Rutgers University Press, 1994). I also point to this omission in a review essay dealing with *Christian Responses to the New Age Movement: A Critical Assessment*, by John A. Saliba, and *New Religious Movements: Challenge and Response*, by Bryan Wilson and Jamie Cresswell, in *Reviews in Religion and Theology* 7, no. 2 (April 2000): 145–150.

4. C. Eric Lincoln and Lawrence H. Mamiya, "Daddy Jones and Father Divine: The Cult as Political Religion," in this volume. Originally published in *Religion in Life* 49 (1980): 6–23.

5. Archie Smith Jr., "Black Reflections on the Study of New Religious Consciousness," in *Understanding the New Religions*, ed. Jacob Needleman and George Baker (New York: Seabury Press, 1978), 211.

6. Archie Smith Jr., "Black Reflections on the Study of New Religious Consciousness," 215.

7. I have in mind, for example, Arthur Huff Fauset's *Black Gods of the Metropolis: Negro Religious Cults of the Urban North* (Philadelphia: University of Pennsylvania Press, 1971).

8. Jonathan Z. Smith, *Map Is Not Territory* (Chicago: University of Chicago Press, 1993), 290–291.

9. Jonathan Z. Smith, *Map Is Not Territory*, 291.

10. James H. Evans Jr., *We Have Been Believers: An African-American Systematic Theology* (Minneapolis: Fortress Press, 1992), 23–24.

11. Archie Smith Jr., "We Need to Press Forward: Black Religion and Jonestown, Twenty Years Later," *Alternative Considerations of Jonestown and Peoples Temple*, <http://jonestown.sdsu.edu>, accessed 11 July 2003.

12. Charles Long, "The Oppressive Elements in Religion and the Religions of the Oppressed," in *Significations: Signs, Symbols, and Images in the Interpretation of Religion* (Minneapolis: Fortress Press, 1986), 170.

13. Archie Smith Jr., "An Interpretation of the Peoples Temple and Jonestown: Implications for the Black Church," this volume; originally published in *PSR Bulletin: Occasional Papers* 58, no. 2 (February 1980), 1. Mary R. Sawyer provides an important critique of this perspective in " 'My Lord, What a Mourning': Twenty Years Since Jonestown," *Alternative Considerations of Jonestown and Peoples Temple*, <http://jonestown.sdsu.edu>, accessed 11 July 2003.

14. Muhammed Isaiah Kenyatta, "America Was Not Hard to Find," in this volume, originally in *The Other Side* 93 (June 1979): 34–42.

15. Quoted in Ellwood, *The Sixties Spiritual Awakening*, 19.

16. Lincoln and Mamiya, "Daddy Jones and Father Divine," 9. It is interesting to note that some members of Peoples Temple also maintained membership in black denominations.

17. Archie Smith Jr., "We Need to Press Forward," 3.

18. Cheryl Townsend Gilkes, *If It Wasn't for the Women: Black Women's Experience and Womanist Culture in Church and Community* (Maryknoll, N.Y.: Orbis Books, 2000).

19. Lincoln and Mamiya, "Daddy Jones and Father Divine," 7–8. Mary McCormick Maaga marks the development of non-tolerance at a later time. Hence, "in contemporary religious studies [I would suggest the more focused study of new religious movements] there is 'before Jonestown' and 'after Jonestown.' The deaths of more than nine hundred people in a jungle commune, the vast majority of whom died by ingesting a cyanide-laced beverage, signaled the end of an era of relative religious tolerance in America and the beginning of a time of cynicism, paranoia, and fear about nonmainstream religions, variously referred to as cults, sects, alternate religions or new religious movements." Mary McCormick Maaga, *Hearing the Voices of Jonestown* (Syracuse, N.Y.: Syracuse University Press, 1998), 1.

20. Fauset, *Black Gods of the Metropolis*.

21. Victor Anderson, *Beyond Ontological Blackness* (New York: Continuum Publishing Group, 1995).

22. Joseph Washington, "How Black Is Black Religion?" in *Quest for a Black Theology*, ed. James J. Gardiner and J. Deotis Roberts, Sr. (Philadelphia: Pilgrim Press, 1971), 28.

23. Other noteworthy studies seeking a related humanization of Peoples Temple include the insightful volumes by Rebecca Moore. See, for example: *In Defense of Peoples Temple and Other Essays* (Lewiston, N.Y.: Edwin Mellen Press, 1988); *A Sympathetic History of Jonestown: The Moore Family Involvement in Peoples Temple* (Lewiston, N.Y.: Edwin Mellen Press, 1985); *The Jonestown Letters: Correspondence of the Moore Family, 1970–1985* (Lewiston, N.Y.: Edwin Mellen Press, 1986).

24. This perspective is presented in Sawyer's chapter in this book. I am grateful for Sawyer's response (e-mail message on 8 August 2002) to an early version of my essay in which she clarified her perspective on Peoples Temple as noted in the section of the essay corresponding to this note.

25. Maaga, *Hearing the Voices of Jonestown,* 81. Maaga's mention of black spiritual church traditions is interesting in that it raises a host of questions. Most important to me at this stage is the manner in which it opens the possibility of traditional African religious practices. That is to say, to the extent black spiritual churches draw on traditions such as voodoo (some of the black spiritual churches in New Orleans are a prime example of this), it is possible some members of Peoples Temple were also influenced by such practices. At the very least, this possibility merits additional attention.

26. John R. Hall, "Peoples Temple," in *America's Alternative Religions,* ed. Timothy Miller (Albany: State University of New York Press, 1995), 305.

27. James Foreman, "God Is Dead: A Question of Power," reprinted in *By These Hands: A Documentary History of African American Humanism,* ed. Anthony B. Pinn (New York: New York University Press, 2001), 272–273.

28. In addition to the volume noted in endnote 27, see for other examples of this work: Norm Allen Jr., *African American Humanism: An Anthology* (Buffalo, N.Y.: Prometheus Books, 1991); idem, *The Black Humanist Experience: An Alternative to Religion* (Buffalo, N.Y.: Prometheus Books, 2002); William R. Jones, *Is God a White Racist? A Preamble to Black Theology* (Boston: Beacon Press, 1999); Anthony B. Pinn, *Varieties of African American Religious Experience* (Minneapolis: Fortress Press, 1998), chapter 4; idem, *Why Lord? Suffering and Evil in Black Theology* (New York: Continuum, 1995).

29. Catherine Wessinger describes this humanist perspective as follows: "Jim Jones taught that the ultimate reality, the true God, was 'principle' or 'Divine Principle.' Principle was equated with 'love,' and love was equated with 'socialism.' Jones derided traditional Christianity as 'fly away religion,' and rejected the Bible, particularly the influential King James Version, as being written by white men to justify the subordination of women and the oppression and enslavement of people of color. According to Jones, the Bible only contained beliefs about a 'sky God' or 'buzzard God,' who was no God at all." Catherine Wessinger, *How the Millennium Comes Violently: From Jonestown to Heaven's Gate* (New York: Seven Bridges Press, 2000), 37.

30. On this point see Judith Mary Weightman, *Making Sense of the Jonestown Suicides: A Sociological History of Peoples Temple* (Lewiston, N.Y.: Edwin Mellen Press, 1983), 79–84.

31. The Honorable Elijah Muhammad, *The True History of Master Fard Muhammad, Allah (God) In Person* (Atlanta: MEMPS Publications, 1996), 50.

32. Eddie Glaude's *Exodus! Religion, Race, and Nation in Early Nineteenth-Century Black America* (Chicago: University of Chicago Press, 2000) is an important text related to the religious significance of exodus language for African Americans. For additional information on the Back-to-Africa Movement, see Edwin Redkey, *Black Exodus: Black Nationalist and Back-to-Africa Movements,*

1890–1910 (New Haven, Conn.: Yale University Press, 1969); and Sylvia Jacobs, ed., *Black Americans and the Missionary Movement in Africa* (Westport, Conn.: Greenwood Press, 1982). Interesting primary materials include: Wilson Jeremiah Moses, ed., *Liberian Dreams: Back-To-Africa Narratives from the 1850s* (University Park: Pennsylvania State University Press, 1998); Edwin Redkey, ed., *Respect Black: The Writings and Speeches of Henry McNeal Turner* (New York: Arno Press, 1971); and Wilson Jeremiah Moses, ed., *Destiny and Race: Selected Writings from Alexander Crummell, 1840–1898* (Amherst: University of Massachusetts Press, 1992).

33. See Ethan Michaeli, "Another Exodus: The Hebrew Israelites from Chicago to Dimona," in *Black Zion: African American Religious Encounters with Judaism,* ed. Yvonne Chireau and Nathaniel Deutsch (New York: Oxford University Press, 2000), 73–87.

34. Maaga, *Hearing the Voices of Jonestown,* 10–11.

35. Milton Sernett, *Bound for the Promised Land: African American Religion and the Great Migration* (Durham, N.C.: Duke University Press, 1997).

36. Gayraud S. Wilmore, *Black Religion and Black Radicalism* (Maryknoll, N.Y.: Orbis Books, 1983).

37. Excerpt from Martin L. King Jr., *Why We Can't Wait,* found in James M. Washington, ed., *A Testament of Hope: The Essential Writings of Martin Luther King, Jr.* (New York: Harper & Row, Publishers, 1986), 523.

38. Maaga, *Hearing the Voices of Jonestown,* 10–11.

39. Stuart Hall, "What Is This 'Black' in Black Popular Culture?" in *Black Popular Culture,* ed. Gina Dent (New York: New Press, 1999), 29, 30.

40. Ira G. Zepp Jr., *The New Religious Image of Urban America: The Shopping Mall as Ceremonial Center* (Niwot: University Press of Colorado, 1997), 35.

41. Zepp, *The New Religious Image of Urban America,* 50.

42. This is the title to his book published by the University of Chicago Press in 1993.

43. Jonathan Z. Smith, *Map Is Not Territory,* xi.

44. Printed in Appendix B to Maaga, *Hearing the Voices of Jonestown,* 148.

45. I draw on Charles Long and his analysis of Friedrich Schleiermacher for my depiction of false consciousness. Charles Long, "Interpretations of Black Religion in America," in *Significations* (Minneapolis: Fortress Press, 1986), 136–138.

46. James Cone, *God of the Oppressed* (New York: Seabury, 1975), 102–103.

47. See Sharon Welch, *A Feminist Ethic of Risk* (Minneapolis: Fortress Press, 1990).

48. This is Sharon Welch's point in "Frustration and Righteous Anger Do Not a Politics Make," in *Sweet Dreams in America* (New York: Routledge, 1999), 27–29.

49. Wessinger, *How the Millennium Comes Violently,* 45, 47.

50. Maaga, *Hearing the Voices of Jonestown,* 8.

51. See Maaga, *Hearing the Voices of Jonestown,* Appendix B—"Suicide Tape Transcript."

52. Maaga, *Hearing the Voices of Jonestown,* Appendix B, 153.

53. René Girard, *Violence and the Sacred,* trans. Patrick Gregory (Baltimore: Johns Hopkins University Press, 1997); idem, *Things Hidden Since the Foundation of the World* (Stanford, Calif.: Stanford University Press, 1987).

2

Daddy Jones and Father Divine

The Cult as Political Religion

C. ERIC LINCOLN AND LAWRENCE H. MAMIYA

On a tragic afternoon in the fall of 1978, in a protracted orgy of coercive suicide, nearly a thousand Americans died in a bizarre expression of religious commitment. Although the event took place in the far-off jungles of Guyana, the history, composition, and the publicly expressed ideology of the so-called Jonestown cult all reflected an apparently irreconcilable conflict or culture crisis its membership had experienced in America[1]—hence their expatriation. Despite their physical removal from the United States, the "crisis" they experienced at home was apparently aggravated by the arrival in Jonestown of Congressman Leo Ryan, accompanied by members of his staff and by newsmen. Unfortunately, all these "intruders" from the United States, i.e., "the government" and "the press," were symbols of the very problems the Jones people had fled to the jungles of South America to escape.

There is no parallel in American religious history for the final act of mass suicide in which hundreds of Jonestown believers participated, some of their own volition.[2] Yet there is a certain irony in the fact that the escalation of religious deviancy—or, if you prefer, the proliferation of alternative religious understandings in conventional American religious life—should have its most unfortunate expression in Guyana, an "undeveloped" community scarcely heard of in America. Certainly America was hardly prepared to accept mass corporate ritual suicide at the behest of a self-appointed savior as a likely pos-

Originally published in *Religion in Life* 49 (1980): 6–23. Reprinted by permission.

sibility in America. In the conventional American mind, such happenings could conceivably occur, of course, but they belonged to those back pages of the news routinely devoted to "exotic" behaviors in less sophisticated societies.

Nevertheless, geography notwithstanding, the Jonestown happening was American—as American as Mother Ann Lee, or Elijah Muhammad, or Billy Graham. The problem is that while we undoubtedly have the most widely variegated religious nonconformity of any nation on earth and the most elaborate safeguards for the protection of nonconformism, Americans as a whole remain conceptually naive about most religious behavior. We understand Methodists and Baptists best of all, of course, and Congregationalists and Presbyterians almost as well. We know a little more about Catholics than we did 50 years ago, and a little more about Jews. Universalists-Unitarians and Quakers are considerably more elusive, and remain for the most part in the uncertain shadows of anecdote. Black religion, a new term for an old tradition, remains a puzzlement ("why would anybody . . . ?" [ellipses in original]); and those sects without clear, familiar denominational identification, and all cults whatever, are simply beyond the conventional interest. In short, despite the American tolerance of other ways of faith, the American understanding of the faiths we tolerate is negligible, and has a very low priority in the order of things Americans think they really need to know about. Religions are understood to the degree in which they resonate with personal beliefs, experiences, or commitments. The lower the degree of resonance, the more likely are alien religions to be dismissed from the level of consciousness at which meaningful decisions are made. Only when a Malcolm X, or a Charles Manson, or a Sun Myung Moon, or a Jim Jones rips the myopic veil with an obtrusion of perceived threat or outrage does an unfamiliar religion assume significance.

THE CULT AND BLACK RELIGION

The deluge of new religions now flooding the spiritual plain in America suggests two things, at minimum: (1) the culture crises or dislocations which afflict our society are many—and continuing; and (2), while we may never see another Jonestown (N'shah Allah),[3] enlightened self-interest may compel us to learn a lot more about the beliefs and commitments of religious out-groups than we have known in the past.

The "cult," which is furthest removed from conventional religious experience and therefore least understood, is by no means a new phenomenon in America, having been one of the earliest expressions of nonconformity testing the American dedication to religious pluralism. Cult-type organizations by whatever name flourished in the eighteenth and nineteenth centuries; but it was not until a peculiar interplay of social and economic factors produced a series of exotic religious movements in the urban black ghettos of the post–World War I era that "cult" took on its distinctive, conventional meaning. Such colorful hierophants (with equally colorful titles) as Father Divine, Daddy Grace, Honorable Elijah Muhammad, Rabbi Cherry, and others caught the imagination of an America which, having harbored a historic suspicion about the spiritual adequacy of black religion, was now prepared to accept the black cult as visible documentation of what had always been suspected. In consequence, alternately romanticized and ridiculed in the press, such groups as the Black Muslims, Black Jews, and the celestials inhabiting the terrestrial heavens of Father Divine soon came to represent to most Americans what was meant by "cult."

Inevitably, the association of cult with the more exotic expressions of black religion encouraged the distension of the term into a convenient appellation eventually applied in popular usage to most, if not all, organized black worship. "Negro cults" (a term often used interchangeably with "Negro sects") became a familiar designation intended to distinguish black corporate religion from white denominations. This practice remained in vogue until an emergent black consciousness defined black religion as the superlative ethnic enterprise and disassociated it from conventional pejorative connotations. Unlike the more conservative Negro Church of the past, which considered the black cults an embarrassment, the contemporary Black Church assumes its liberation from white constructs of Christian doctrine and ritual propriety to include liberation from the need to feel guilty about whatever the black experience in religion includes. This would seem a reasonable conclusion, particularly if it is determined that the escapist spiritual paranoia of the black cults was in large measure a tragic, spiritual *modus vivendi* aimed at transcending *in this world* the crippling evils of racial suppression.[4]

In spite of its sense of liberation to be itself, the Black Church was shaken by the Jonestown affair, as is evident by the numerous formal and informal conventions called to address the situation. Most disturbing was the feeling that the news media tried to make it appear that Peoples Temple was a black cult, when in fact an undetermined number of its members, the cult leader himself, and his top lieutenants were all white. Black churchmen complained bitterly about the close-up treatment the television cameras and the newspaper photographers gave the grotesque clumps of bloated black bodies rotting on the jungle commons where they fell after celebrating their final communion with Kool-Aid and cyanide. Irrespective of its guilt or innocence, the impatience with the press undoubtedly functioned to ease the frustration engendered by the enormity of the events at Jonestown. Nevertheless, the press revelations forced into focus the critical question of why, in this era of black consciousness and black liberation (in which the Black Church figures so prominently), so many black people did in fact give their allegiance, their money, and finally their lives to Jim Jones, a white, self-proclaimed apostle to America's disinherited.

Our present task is not addressed to either the discovery or the analysis of possible causal factors within the Black Church which may have contributed to the apparent attractiveness Jim Jones' cult had for its black followers. That the attraction was more than casual seems well documented by the statistics of the final holocaust, by the subsequent surfacing of surviving relatives and loved ones and their recurrent stories of how their deceased friends or members of their families (and sometimes they themselves) had been skillfully recruited into the movement. Many of these survivors are members of the Black Church, as indeed had been most of those who joined and remained with the movement until its tragic implosion.

The black congregations who lost members to Jones' recruitment are located principally in the Midwest and on the West Coast; but the possibility that the Jones movement may be a prelude of things to come, and that the proliferation of exotic white or "international" cults attractive to blacks may seriously threaten the historic black preference for traditional in-group religious affiliation, is not lost upon the more alert leadership of the Black Church. The perceived status value of holding at least nominal membership in white congregations of the mainline denominations is already a factor of increasing ambivalence among the developing cadre of upwardly mobile young blacks who are the principal beneficiaries of the Civil Rights struggle of the 1950s and 1960s. The formula which has proved most successful for them is characteristically conservative, warning them away from "far-out" associations at any level.

Nevertheless, the attractiveness of the cults to the white youth of the upper middle class (who are more readily forgiven for their experiential indiscretions) offers a persistent challenge to those young blacks who are tempted to measure their own reception in terms of the acceptability of their participation in what they perceive as peer activities. The problem is exacerbated by the veritable deluge of new religions and the confused status of their legitimacy. Whether in fact there is a growing public acceptance of contemporary cults, or whether there is mere public resignation in the face of their apparent legal right to exist, the cult phenomenon seems well on the way to becoming a commonplace response to the uncommon spectrum of anxieties, frustrations, and yearnings which illustrate our times. Practically all the new religions are white—or perhaps it is more accurate to say that practically none of them are black. Whatever their origin, they seem principally attractive to the white middle class which comprises the predominant membership and, in most cases, the local leadership and/or lieutenancy.

The scientific study of these new religions is still in the process of development, but some of the cults appear to be considerably more grotesque in both doctrine and ritual than any of the flamboyant black cults around which the term crystallized a generation or so ago. This undoubtedly accounts for some membership restraint on the part of middle-class blacks, but we are reminded that while the Jones cult attracted an inner core of middle-class whites, the majority of blacks who followed the Indianapolis preacher were impoverished and déclassé. Just what attracted these least advantaged blacks who bypassed the traditional black churches to identify with Jim Jones is perhaps implicit in the very nature of the cult and cult leadership factors we intend to examine in some detail. While there is no evidence that Jim Jones' Peoples Temple or any similar cults have made any significant numerical inroads on this traditional preserve of the Black Church to date, the evidence that the black poor and the indigent as well as the avant-garde of the black middle class could now be considered "susceptible" raises a double specter of possible things to come.

THE ANATOMY OF A CULT

The principal contribution to conceptual understanding of religious affiliation and behavior has been the typologies designed by German scholars Ernst Troeltsch and Max Weber[5] in the early days of sociological understanding and modified from time to time by American investigative scholarship.[6] The problem is that the refinements and modifications have not matched the pace of our spiritual inventiveness. The result is that, relatively speaking, the science of the sociology of religion and conventional understanding find themselves in a similar predicament: both suffer from want of precise definitions of the religious modalities encountered in contemporary experience.

In consequence, the church-sect-cult typology has become a kind of Procrustean bed, and some of the new religious entities made to lie on it in the interest of scientific analysis have to be stretched, lopped, or levered in all directions in what is usually a vain effort to make them fit. This is particularly true of some of the exotic cult types which could hardly have been anticipated when the church-sect-cult typology was invented. The Jones cult is a case in point, and in attempting to understand and interpret its less obvious ramifications a resort to the traditional typological distinctions must still be made, but the risk can be justified if it is recognized in advance that an element of "procrusteanism" is probably inherent to the task and if a clearer conceptualization is the ultimate result.

Institutional religion has been conveniently divided among "denominations" and "cults," with the denomination or "church" referred to as that constituency whose predominantly middle-class, birthright members are in essential peace and harmony with society and the political order, which has a stake in the material success of its membership, and which looks primarily to the grace of God and the atonement of Jesus Christ for salvation. In the church all mankind is considered salvageable, and expulsion from membership is extremely rare. On the other hand, the sect begins typically as a fragment of some denomination which has become alienated over issues of doctrine, ritual, or behavior. The sect is usually predominantly (or wholly) lower-class, has a strong suspicion of the social order, rejects the notion of birthright membership, and does not hesitate to excommunicate whoever is not in harmony with its precepts. It is characteristically ascetic and millenarian in posture, avoids the contamination of the "unsaved," and features personal holiness or sanctification as the surest route to salvation. As the generations go by, the sect membership moves up the socioeconomic ladder, its alienation declines, and its posture is progressively modified in the direction of the church type from which it originally derived.

THE CULT LEADER

Although there is no unanimity of opinion on the precise nature and function of charisma in the cult enterprise, most observers do agree that it is a critical quality contributing significantly to effective leadership and group maintenance. This is an observation well substantiated by our own studies of the Black Muslims and other groups.[7] The charismatic leader is typically a man of uncanny sensitivity. He has a near clairvoyant ability to sense out and give dramatic verbalization to the most private yearnings of his followers, sometimes before even they themselves are fully conscious of what it is they want or need to enhance their lives with accomplishment or meaning. Here the father image is authenticated by the leader's prior knowledge of the needs of his flock and his identification with them. "Father" Divine, or "Daddy" Grace, or "Daddy" Jones knows what his children need to make them happy, and what is more he, and probably he alone, can bring it about. The "father's" uniqueness and power derive from his unique possession of some essential truth or some esoteric knowledge which is never shared with even his closest disciples. We suggest that this unique "knowledge" or insight, this peculiar access to the "occult," may in fact be the critical element of the charismatic leader. Certainly it is the critical distinction which sets him apart from all others and provides him with sources of power they neither share nor understand.

In consequence of his peculiar knowledge or power the charismatic leader is unaffected by the fears and anxieties of ordinary individuals. Because he is privy to the future, he is contemptuous of the present. Even at the height of his accomplishments the person is never more than a way station to an even more glorious future, and the powers which control the person are the inevitable obstacles to the realization of what is promised. It follows that whomever or whatever the supersight of the leader identifies as an impediment to the coming of the cultic kingdom is either a devil or the work of the devil(s). Hence the devil and his works are the legitimate targets, indeed the required targets, for the wrath of the faithful, and the peculiar energy of a cult movement derives largely from the consuming commitment to the destruction of the devil and his evil doings. The true believer must therefore have an uninhibited capacity to hate "the devil" and to hate "evil"—and become an instrument (living or dead) of their eradication.

The leader's conviction that ultimate success will reward the dedication of the faithful comes through as unshakable and unassailable. For his followers it is a matter of knowledge, the fundamental challenge of his leadership is to be able to inculcate the group with what he *knows* so successfully that it is internalized by the cult as what they *believe*. To the degree that this can be accomplished, the unity and integrity of the cult are assured. That is why the leader may go out of his way on occasion to defy or to antagonize "authority" (or other devils), for in so doing he accents his own indomitability while demonstrating the vulnerability of the opposition. Those whose belief in his unique superiority is most convincing, and who clearly derive unusual inspirational adrenaline from the leader's teachings or behavior, become his lieutenants, and they are rewarded by distinctive regalia or responsibilities which reflect the leader's confidence in their commitment and ability.[8]

The person and the office of the leader are of course inviolate—even sacrosanct. The primary allegiance of his followers is not to his teachings or to his ideology, but to himself. What he teaches and what he does take on significance only in the context of who he is—not vice versa. Neither the office nor the movement makes the man. It is the man who invents the movement, invests it with significance (derived from his own persona), and creates the office he holds as the protective instrument of his authority. The leader is always conscious of his own uniqueness. However, he may on occasion deliberately adopt a stage role of abject humility or identification with the least of his followers, as expedience may demand. But this *ritual* is never misconstrued by those inside the movement. His venerability is never in question, whatever the style the leader chooses to adopt. He may choose to live like an ascetic or like a prince. In either case it is *his* option, and he is free to pursue it or to change it in accordance with his interest or convenience.

Because of his independent, superior insight, the leader is characteristically impatient with the contrary opinions of others. He is above criticism, which is at best no more than an illustration of the ignorance of his enemies and at worst a transparent strategy of the devils who oppose him.[9] Nor is the leader bound by the conventions of truth or reason. It is the end that counts. The realization of the goals of the movement is the sole criterion by which behavior is to be judged. Truth is what the faithful *believe* to be true. This is the only truth that overcomes. In any case, it is not so much *what* is said that matters as it is by *whom* it was said, and *how*. Hence the style and manner of the leader in his public role are of utmost importance. The defiant gesture, the arrogant posture—in short, the histrionics of delivery may accomplish the desired response where logic and truth never would. What is more, since only the leader is possessed of the truth, his communication is most often in terms of prophecy or revelation, neither of which can be tested. A doctrine that is understood or a proposition that can be tested is useless as an instrument of control.

All conventional moral observances are transcended by the office of the leader. They simply do not apply. While he may choose to set certain examples of moral behavior for his followers, this is not to be construed as his own submission to (or need for) normative constraints. Inside the cult this is patently understood. Outside the leader may project an image of deception, unfairness, and the presumption of inordinate privileges, especially in regard to material comforts and sex. Within the cult his apparent arrogance is more likely a function of maintenance designed to protect his uniqueness and make certain that the prerequisite distance between leader and followers is observed. In any case, it is rare indeed that the prerogatives of the leader ever surface *within the cult* as the subject of complaints.[10]

THE PRIVATE COSMOS

The characteristic cult leadership makes an extraordinary effort to isolate the cult from the contaminating influences of the enveloping society. This isolation may be of three kinds:

1) *Communicative isolation.* Members are taught to dissimulate, to be evasive, to be secretive or claim ignorance about cult activities. They may also utilize esoteric phrases or code words, or any similar means to avoid revealing anything of importance about themselves or their leaders. There is apt to be a certain pride in the private nature of the "business" of the cult which is symbolized by the popular aphorism: "Those who say, don't know; and those who know, don't say!"

2) *Social isolation.* Members keep to themselves whenever possible. Cult responsibilities such as meetings, fund raising, etc., reduce the time available for extracult contacts, which are considered potentially contaminating. Members travel together in groups, thus providing their own "approved" social environment whenever possible. Commitment is thus constantly reinforced, and challenge is buffered by corporate unanimity.

3) *Physical isolation.* Living in dormitories, communes, settlements, etc., provides continuous physical isolation for those not required to work in the outside world.

The ultimate goal is complete isolation—the maintenance of a *private cosmos* capable of avoiding most unapproved contact with the outside world, or so filtering such contact as to render it innocuous to the interests of the cult. This was Jones' signal achievement in Guyana. The more isolated the cult, the more tentative is the retention of a larger reality for both leader and follower. In a completely private cosmos reality is reconstructed in terms of the visions of the leader as they are reinforced by the affirmations of the faithful. This may well set the stage for a sustained corporate relationship so at variance with the real world outside as to encourage, if not in fact to ensure and produce, an extreme paranoia for all concerned.

It is quite probable that the self-image of the believer is already substantially blurred when he enters the cult. A negotiable identity is a construct of self-perception reinforced by the communicated perception, of others who are important to the self-perceived. To put it another way, one may be what he perceives himself to be, but only to the degree that other significant and respected perceivers are in reasonable agreement. In a closed cosmos, identity (and reality) are determined by the individual and his peers in the cult, and more significantly by the superior wisdom and revelations of the leader. In the early Muslim movement, Fard gave names to his followers on the prior knowledge of their paternity, no matter what the official birth certificate or the parents had to say.[11] The more perfect the isolation, the more compelling becomes the leader's assessment of reality, as he alone has access to any input or knowledge beyond the confines of the world he has created for himself and his followers.

Reinforcement between the leader and the led is mutual and constant. Initially the leader's assumption of prerogatives or titles or other scarce values may be little more than an arrogant gesture or the simple exploitation of his followers. But in a closed cosmos where he is the supreme, indeed the *only,* power the constant obeisance of all those in his private world may well become a source of increasing megalomania, to the end that the leader comes to accept as right and proper not only the prerogatives he has claimed, but the implications of those prerogatives. In short, his once tentative claims—now readily and routinely honored by the faithful—take on the quality of divine rights and become an intrinsic part of the ideological structure which defines the cult, as well as its protocol of means.

Such seem to be the dynamics of the cult experience, and if they have been accurately interpreted, the mystery of the Jonestown holocaust should be considerably less obscure.

WHO JOINS THE CULT?

Who are the members of the typical cult? They vary of course as do all other religious devotees, but there are some characteristics which may be useful indicators. The common dismissal is that cult membership comes almost exclusively from the ranks of the discontented. While this is probably true, so saying is not saying quite enough. They may have been dissatisfied with their lives but cult members are not typically drawn from the ranks of those who are without hope. Rather they are individuals whose despair of relief has become increasingly pronounced and whose search for deliverance has turned from "rational" or conventional resources (which have been unavailing) to the challenge of possibilities which lie outside the normal pattern of social or ideological experience. The more urgent the perceived need for relief or fulfillment, the more miraculous or the more potent are the resources required to overcome the situation of drift or stagnancy, or the pain of being a self that for whatever reason has remained inconsequential. Hence the cult member is self-perceived either in context of progressive meaninglessness or in danger of being bypassed by the conventional values by which "successful living" is commonly measured.

Religion is one means of dealing with the problems of anxiety and scarce values, but religion differs from other ways of coping in that the anxieties and the values to which it is principally addressed are in the category of the ultimate—i.e., the anxieties of total dimension and the values above which and beyond which there are none.

In short, the end sought by religion is "the pearl of great price," the highest possible level of fulfillment. In the pursuit of that value the religionist may prefer to make his witness with those of his own family, or of his own class, or of his own race, or with those of his own denomination. Such preferences represent values which may be both legitimate and pragmatic, but they are in no sense ultimate. They are preferred means to an end which is itself transcendent of all such preferences. In consequence, it can be said of the blacks who followed Jones, and the thousands of white middle-class youth who attach themselves to one or the other of the currently popular cults of Oriental import, their common conviction is that they have finally found a way where there was no way. Now, touched with the healing wand of the long-sought agent-saviors, they look back with pity and disdain upon their conventional-minded parents and pastors who failed them in their need and desperation.

For those who join the cult in search of personal rebirth or escape from an unacceptable identity, the old unappreciated self is abandoned and the image of the believer is merged into the image of the cult. The individual self becomes significant because the cult has a significant identity. If the cult is respected, every member participates in that respect. Hence, the new member may have no purpose and no goal beyond his assimilation into the group and his identification with the cult and its values; and life itself, i.e. physical existence, may become no more than an instrument for the realization of the values of the cult.

FATHER DIVINE AND DADDY JONES

For all its flamboyance, the ideal model of contemporary religious cult has been that of Father Divine. Divine's cult not only contained many of the sociological characteristics described previously, but more importantly it left a deep imprint in recent American history; hundreds of thousands of Americans, both black and white, were held spellbound by this charismatic figure for several decades. Father Divine was as much, or even more, a media event than Jim Jones and Jonestown. While the press has usually elevated the exotic and flamboyant characteristics of Divine's cult, the powerful political influence which this diminutive figure wielded has often gone unnoticed. Nonetheless, the political dimension of the modern religious cult may be of critical importance in understanding contemporary cultic phenomena, and the very interesting parallels and comparisons which may be observed between Jones' cult and that of Father Divine may be particularly illuminating.

From the *New York Times* accounts of Jones' earlier ministry it becomes apparent that the only religious model which significantly affected him was that of Father Divine.[12] In the 1950s he attended a service in Philadelphia conducted by Father Divine and left thoroughly impressed. This experience had a lasting influence on Jones' style of ministry and his organization. One of his aides, Ross E. Case, said, "He was always talking about sex or Father Divine or Daddy Grace, and was envious of how they were adored by their people and the absolute loyalty they got. Jim wanted all that affection and loyalty for himself."[13] From watching the examples of Father Divine or the Reverend Adam Clayton Powell, Jones realized the importance of a large religious congregation as a political power base.

Like Father Divine, Jones urged his parishioners in Indianapolis to call him "Father" or "Dad." This use of paternalistic terminology is of course not unusual in the Christian tradition where "father" or some synonymous term is a common designation for "pastor." In the black religious tradition, counterpart terminology may also be applied to the wife of the leader—especially if he himself is highly venerated and if she is considered properly complementary. Impressed by the co-regency of "Mother Divine" in Father Divine's movement, Jim Jones encouraged his followers to refer to his wife Marceline, as "Mother Jones." In the black cults a leader who became Father or Daddy was more than a mere pastor. He represented absolute authority and commanded absolute obedience. It was this power of the black cult leader which fascinated Jones and which he determined to emulate.

Both Father Divine and Daddy Jones had their greatest impact in times of social upheaval in American society. The depression of the 1930s provided the soil for Divine's movement, while the chaos and turmoil of the Civil Rights–Vietnam era, particularly the late 1960s and early 1970s, undoubtedly added to the numbers of Jones' followers. Both men were known for good works. They fed and housed the poor. For 15 or 20 cents the destitute could eat a banquet-like meal at one of Father Divine's restaurants, or sleep in one of his clean hostels for 50 cents a night. Similarly Jones' Peoples Temple fed thousands of poor people daily in its soup kitchen. Jones' followers lived in communal houses, while Father Divine called his hostels "heavens," but both leaders required their disciples to contribute their entire economic holdings to the central organization in return for food, shelter, a variable "need-stipend," and the security of inclusion.

During the times when it was not popular to do so, both cult leaders held to an ideological goal of interracial harmony, blacks and whites together, and even the turn toward "Black Power" in the late 1960s did not deter Jim Jones from his vision of creating an integrated cosmos. Of course, for Father Divine, whose movement antedated Jones' Temple by more than a generation, the very idea of an interracial community was novel and much more difficult to implement, even in the liberal North. The racial caste system was more rigidly drawn and the racial taboos more strictly enforced in the 1930s, and these conditions probably influenced Divine's doctrine of sexual abstinence among his followers, for the anti-miscegenation laws in many states were political realities no successful movement, religious or secular, could afford to ignore.

Unlike many charismatic leaders who tend to shy away from bureaucratic structures, both Jones and Divine were good, effective organizers. They knew how to reach and mobilize the masses and how to create institutions. At the peak of his power Jim Jones had an estimated twenty thousand followers, while Father Divine claimed a following in the hundreds of thousands. Jones undoubtedly copied some of the organizational features of Divine's movement. For example, the members in the innermost organization of the four-tiered structure of Peoples Temple were called "angels," a term certainly borrowed from Divine. However, Jones lacked Divine's imagination in naming his celestial company. Angels like Sister Heavenly Delight had no counterparts in the Jones cult. Where two-thirds of Jones' leadership hierarchy was composed of whites, Divine's angels were equally divided between the races. In the black cults, faith healing and miracles, preaching and music, were the common techniques of the cult evangelists. The evidence suggests that Jones tried conscientiously to mold himself in the black preaching tradition but never quite succeeded. He envied the articulateness of a Martin Luther King Jr. or a Malcolm X, and the masterful control of a Father Divine. His dependency on showmanship (e.g. the hiring of gospel choirs, bands, etc.) was a rather obvious attempt to make up in community circuses what he himself lacked in style.

Finally, on the major issue of mass suicide, there is an interesting footnote to the relationship between Father Divine and Jim Jones and their movements. Toward the end of his career Daddy Jones and his followers practiced the ritual of mass suicide by drinking potions which turned out to be placebos. He called these terrifying evening rehearsals "white nights" (to avoid offending his black followers by identifying death and evil with blackness, as is usually done in Western tradition). Sara Harris, who did a careful study of Father Divine's movement, in one of her earliest writings, predicted a mass suicide among his followers upon Divine's death. She wrote: "If Father Divine were to die, mass suicides among the Negroes in his movement could certainly result. They would be rooted deep, not alone in Father's relationship with his followers but also in America's relationship with its Negro citizens. This would be the shame of America."[14]

There is no known instance of any kind of mass suicides among Divine's followers. Nevertheless, the prediction by a careful student of the movement that such a catastrophe could take place attests to the power of the cult leader. It also raises the intriguing question of whether Jim Jones may have come by more substantive information on this subject during his informal (but nonetheless protracted and intense) study of Divine than may have been available earlier to Sara Harris. But if there was a doctrine of suicide within the ideological lathwork of the Divine cult, it does not appear in any of the extant literature of the movement.

On the other hand, Jones learned what he knew about the Divine ideology from face-to-face contact with the membership, and it is at least possible that the germ of the idea may have been come by in this way. Yet this seems refuted as a probability, because there appears to be no oral tradition in the surviving membership of the Divine movement which in any way substantiates a Divine call to mass suicide. What seems more likely is that Jones' pursuit of information about Father Divine led him to Sara Harris' study, where her prediction of mass suicide was offered as a kind of *obiter dictum* to her research. Fascinated by the idea, Jones apparently made it the cardinal event of his ritual procedures. Its gruesome effectiveness is suggested by the determined allegiance of hundreds who accepted the cyanide cocktails without complaint and without objection. A witness to the scene noted "the smiles, the failure of more members to flee, the dying with arms linked ... A survivor recalls one woman objecting only to be shouted down with cries of 'traitor.' "[15]

THE JONES CULT AS POLITICAL RELIGION

How does one make sense of Jonestown, mass suicide, and Jim Jones? Is it religion? Is it politics? Or is it merely mass hysteria—another incidence of the Harlem-type cults or those crazies in the Bay area "at it" again?

The idea of "political religion" is probably one of the more helpful analytical categories in making sense of the diverse and multifaceted dimensions of Daddy Jones' movement. David Apter and Robert Bellah have defined political religion as an attempt to turn the state, regime, or movement into an ultimate concern, to turn what is finite into something ultimately meaningful and valuable.[16] Political religion means that an institution or a person takes on the characteristics of the sacred in symbols, rituals, language, beliefs, etc. Expressions of nationalism or nationalist movements often take on religious form. Hitler's movement of National Socialism is an example of a modern political religion par excellence. His charismatic energy and speeches, the staging of massive parades and pageantry, the use of the swastika (an ancient Germanic religious symbol for the sun) contributed to the impact. Other examples of political religions include Maoism and the Red Book in China, and Kwame Nkrumah's Convention People's Party in Ghana. This analytical category can illuminate the religio-political nature of Jones' Peoples Temple in several ways.

First, political religion reveals the "this-worldly activism" of Jones' group, the intense quest for social justice and socialist utopia, which permeated their worldview. Jones believed in "apostolic socialism" as a form of "this-worldly" salvation.[17] Jonestown was to be a fulfillment of this vision, and political religion makes it possible to understand the motivation of some members who joined the group for nonreligious reasons. Some of the white radicals felt like Deborah Layton Blakey, who claimed that "by joining the Peoples Temple, I hoped to help others and in the process, to bring structure and self-discipline to my own life."[18]

Second, political religion helps to make sense of seemingly contradictory statements by Jones and his followers on the subject of religion. His wife is reported to have said in an interview that "Jim has used religion to try to get some people out of the opiate of religion."[19] When Congressman Leo Ryan visited the Peoples Temple headquarters in Georgetown, Guyana, he was puzzled at the lack of outward religious trappings and lack of references to God in his conversations with members. Jones himself claimed to be a Marxist, yet he also claimed that his movement was religious. Obviously there is a strong element of pragmatism and manipulation in Jones' political religion. As one reporter noted, "To the religious he offered religion; to the ideological he offered politics; to the ignorant and gullible he offered miracles."[20]

Third, the idea of political religion helps to demystify the ritual of mass suicide and to uncover the elements of the demonic in the movement. Ritual actions are rehearsed events which provide a controlled direction for human impulses. The ritual of mass suicide in the purview of Jones' political religion is to be understood as "revolutionary suicide" or "suicide for socialism."[21] The closed cosmos of Jonestown produced a "siege mentality" among its inhabitants. The deaths of Congressman Ryan and several others had sealed its fate, and the dress rehearsals of "white nights" were to become a reality; the enemy was already here. In this sense the suicides of Jonestown are similar to those of the Jewish Masada and to the Japanese Kamikaze pilots who died for the emperor, the head of another political religion.[22] The real tragedy of Jonestown is the political innocents whose spiritual quest made them pawns in a fanatical/political ritual of suicide and murder.

Every political religion is infected with elements of the demonic in the sheer grasping for power. The visions of the good life and the good society, the considerable acts of human kindness and mercy, and the courage to attack the problems of an unjust society all begin to fade before the power of the demonic. William James in his classic study, *The Varieties of Religious Experience,* has coined the term "diabolical mysticism" to describe those charismatic personalities who fall prey to the demonic. Jim Jones fits the description of a diabolical mystic, as do Hitler and Idi Amin. The combination of political power and religious energy often contributes to a megalomania which ordains in its private cosmos the fantasies denied it in the real world.

Jim Jones' political religion differs from the usual secular variety in that his movement began as a religious interest which took on more and more political characteristics. In contrast, Hitler's movement began as a secular political party and developed religious dimensions.

Nevertheless, the analytical category is helpful in examining the combination of Jones' Marxist-socialist rhetoric with fundamentalistic Christian beliefs, for this peculiar syncretism also explains how Jones was able to penetrate the black community in San Francisco. He used his religious base to attract the masses and his political connections to obtain power and resources. Just as Fiorello LaGuardia found it expedient to journey to Harlem to pay his respects to Father Divine, the political kingmaker during his campaign for mayor of New York City, Jim Jones was similarly courted by the political elite of California. He played a crucial role in the election of the late George Moscone as mayor of San Francisco, and his hand was prominent in the political successes of well-known public figures. Jones' success in the political arena was based on what he had learned from figures like Father Divine no less than on his own uncanny instincts.

Political religions, like charismatic leaders, come in all shapes and sizes. The fact that the tall, handsome Daddy Jones had only a relatively small following compared to Father Divine or Mao Tse-tung at the peak of their respective careers should not be a factor to discount Jones' cult from consideration as an important political religion. The size of the group may not be as important as the qualitative expressions of intense loyalty and commitment which are raised to ultimate levels in its interests. It is not to be forgotten that Hitler's Nazi movement began with a small group of discontented workers and soldiers in the beer halls of Munich. The chaotic social conditions of a country, widespread discontent, and the resonance of the charismatic's message are factors which may determine the movement's potential despite the size of its following. Fortunately, America in the mid-1970s was returning to a calmer period. If the Vietnam War and its accompanying dislocations had been allowed to continue, Jones' following would probably have swollen to enormous proportions with unpredictable results. His rhetoric and behavior—a mix of humanitarian idealism, radical Marxism, biblical fundamentalism, and Christian social action—would have had an extraordinary appeal, something for everyone. He also knew, and exploited, the propagandist's art—it is not what you say but how you say it that counts.

Politics and religion were curiously intertwined in the cult of Daddy Jones. Political religion illuminates the major value and themes of Jones' life as well as the motivations of his followers. In spite of the doctrine of the separation of church and state and the differentiation of spheres in modern industrial societies, modern cults like Jones' have consciously attempted to incorporate politics into religion. It is this reintegration of previously differentiated spheres into one total worldview that is unique about the present-day cults, and perhaps their most alarming aspect. The possibilities of critical perspective are lost when pluralism is dissolved. Only the word of the leader is left—to be obeyed, as was Daddy Jones', unto death.

NOTES

1. See Allan W. Eister, who argues that such crises or "dislocations" occur whenever conventional belief systems, meanings, and orientations are disturbed, and that the provocation of cult interest or activity may ensue in consequence. "An Outline of a Structural Theory of Cults," *Journal for the Scientific Study of Religion* (1972): 319–333.

2. Accounts vary, but the presence of a coercive element, both psychological and physical, seems reliably established.

3. "If God wills it"—a popular Muslim expression.

4. All the prominent black cults, including those led by Father Divine, Daddy Grace, Rabbi Cherry, and Elijah Muhammad, were "escapist" in the sense that they originated as a response to severe racially determined limitations imposed on "Negroes."

5. Weber's church-sect typology was first refined and popularized by his student Ernst Troeltsch in *The Social Teachings of the Christian Churches* (New York, 1931). Weber's *Sociology of Religion* was first published in Germany in 1922.

6. See, for example, H. Richard Niebuhr, *The Social Sources of Denominationalism* (New York, 1929); Milton J. Yinger, *Religion, Society and the Individual* (New York, 1957); Benton Johnson, "On Church and Sect," *American Sociological Review* (1963): 539–549.

7. See C. Eric Lincoln, *The Black Muslims in America* (Boston, 1960).

8. See Eric Hoffer, *The True Believer* (New York, 1951).

9. "The harder you hit the devil," explained Malcolm X, "the louder he will holler." Private interview with C. Eric Lincoln, 1959.

10. In an interview which touched on his alleged dalliance with certain of his female secretaries, Elijah Muhammad impatiently dismissed the subject with a wave of his hand and a cryptic reference to his divinity. While there is no evidence that the man who called himself "The Messenger" thought of himself as divine in the sense of being a god or being immortal, there was a definite implication that he considered himself distinctly different from his followers, and that this distinction meant superior prerogatives and superior responsibilities. Such notions, however defined, are commonly accepted by most cults and by some sects as well; and in such instances sexual intercourse with the leader may be ritualized and interpreted as a means of leavening what is merely human (i.e., profane) with a touch of divinity (i.e., the sacred). Hence, such activity may be considered by the faithful to be a demonstration of pastoral love and responsibility rather than the exploitation of privilege.

The minister of a sect-type church in North Carolina excoriated a weeping young husband who discovered the cleric in bed with his wife with the reminder that it was he, the "unsaved" husband, who was corrupting the young woman and making the pastor's work of "sanctification" quite difficult. "After all," the clergyman explained, "it takes a stomp-down clean sheet to cover one that's stained!"

11. Lincoln, *Black Muslims in America.*

12. Robert Lindsey, "Jim Jones—From Poverty to Power Over Many Lives," *New York Times,* 26 November 1976.

13. Lindsey, "Jim Jones."

14. Sara Harris, *Father Divine* (New York, 1971 reprint; originally published in 1953), 351–352.

15. *Washington Post* reporter Charles A. Krause's *Guyana Massacre* (New York, 1978).

16. David E. Apter, "Political Religion in the New Nations," in *Old Societies and New States,* ed. Clifford Geertz (New York, 1965). Apter uses Robert Bellah's definition of religion. Also see Bellah's classic essay on "Civil Religion in America" as a form of political religion in a modern industrial society. Although Apter applies the term "political religion" to nationalist movements in Third World countries, we are extending the usage to include cults like Jim Jones' Peoples Temple in modern industrial societies.

17. Charles Krause coined the apt term "apostolic socialism" to describe Peoples Temple. *Guyana Massacre,* 33. [Ed. note: Jones himself used the term "apostolic socialism" in many of his sermons.]

18. Affidavit of Deborah Layton Blakey regarding "The Threat and Possibility of Suicide by Members of the Peoples Temple," given 15 June 1978, in San Francisco. Appendix D in Krause, *Guyana Massacre,* 187–194.

19. Krause, *Guyana Massacre,* 33.

20. Krause, *Guyana Massacre,* 34. Compare with Muhammed Kenyatta, who observed that the Jones cult "had all the right things going for it ... an anti-capitalist bias, commitment to cooperative ownership, multi-racial composition, and a profession of Christian communalism." *The Other Side* (June, 1979): 37 [reprinted in this volume].

21. Krause, *Guyana Massacre,* 121, 193.

22. Krause, *Guyana Massacre,* 112. At Masada 1,000 Jewish defenders killed themselves on 15 April AD 73 rather than be captured by the besieging Romans. Although the tendency of most scholars has been to raise the Masada event to the level of heroism and to denigrate Jonestown, there are similar social and psychological dynamics present. The "siege mentality" in particular must be understood to make sense of Jonestown.

3

An Interpretation of Peoples Temple and Jonestown

Implications for the Black Church

ARCHIE SMITH JR.

In this paper I shall (1) consider two theories which emerged to "explain" Jonestown; (2) identify secularism as a central theme; (3) relate this central theme to a plausibility crisis in Black Church religion and the appeal of Peoples Temple; and (4) suggest some implications for the Black Church and its ministry in the light of Peoples Temple and the Jonestown holocaust.

EXPLANATORY NARRATIVES

It is important to consider the social science interpretations that emerged to "explain" the so-called mass murders-suicides at Jonestown, Guyana. Social scientists are in a particularly strategic position to influence our definition of reality, the role of religion in the lives of black people as well as influence our understanding of what happened at Jonestown.

The "Psychoanalytically Oriented Worldview" Explanation

One of the major paradigms or worldviews that emerged to explain Jonestown I call the "psychoanalytically oriented worldview" explanation. This explanatory framework has its roots in secularism

This essay was first presented as a paper by Dr. Archie M. Smith Jr. at the annual meeting of the Association for the Sociology of Religion in Boston on 27 August 1979. It was first printed as an "Occasional Paper" in the *PSR Bulletin* 58, no. 2 (February 1980), a publication of the Pacific School of Religion, in Berkeley, California. It is reprinted here by permission.

and contributes towards a plausibility crisis in traditional understandings of religion.

The bottom line in this worldview is that religious phenomena are based upon an illusion—perhaps the oldest, strongest, and most persistent illusion of humankind. Religion is perceived as an inadequate attempt to deal with the reality demands of civilization. Religious cults, formed around a charismatic leader, have their origins in the sociopathic make-up of the leader. Persons who are drawn to religious cults and take up membership in them tend to be passive-dependent types in search for a surrogate parent or authority figure. In other words, the prime targets for recruitment into such movements as Peoples Temple were the oppressed, especially poor blacks, the lonely, dependent, and insecure who welcomed the message of egalitarianism.

According to this worldview, such persons had little or no sense of inner value, sought direction from a paranoid charismatic leader, and in the process took on his developing psychosis and messianic hopes. A fusion or total and fatal identification was made with the charismatic leader in the isolated jungles of Jonestown, Guyana. He and the group had become one. When the leader made the decision to commit suicide, he took the entire group with him.

This general worldview was one of the explanations that emerged to give meaning to the mass murders-suicides at Jonestown. This particular worldview sought to locate the origins of the holocaust of Jonestown within the psychological framework—i.e., the thinking processes and mindset of Jim Jones and his followers.

"Audience corruption" is a term used to identify the interaction between the leader and his followers. Followers learn to give the responses the leader wants them to learn; they feed them back to the leader on cue, who in turn believes even more in the power and rightness of his leadership. When he announces that he is God, the followers feed back the supporting behavior, and the leader soon comes to believe unquestionably in his own deification. In turn his unquestioned assent to divinity is believed by the followers. Absorbed in the immediate crises, the present is the only reality, and the sole authority within that closed cosmos is the leader, who is deemed beyond challenge.

This, in brief form, is the essence of the psychoanalytically oriented view of religion. Religious cults, from this perspective, are a form of psychosis, a break with reality. In Marxism, it is a source of error, a false consciousness incapable of correctly diagnosing reality as it actually exists. The psychoanalytic worldview has helped persons to understand some of the inner forces that move individual men and women, but it has not enabled a social critique of personal life or a critique of the evolving social order. And it has not been decisive for understanding the social or relational character of our existence.

The "Only in California" Explanation

The other explanation I wish to consider is the one that suggests that Jonestown could only have come out of California. This I call the "Only in California" explanation.

California is perceived as propagator of the bizarre. California gave the nation Richard M. Nixon. It was where Robert Kennedy was assassinated. It was the home of the Charles Manson Family; Aimee Semple McPherson, and her Four Square Gospel Church; Father William Riker's church of the Perfect Christian Divine Way; the Zebra Murders; the Symbionese Liberation Army; Synanon; the Free Speech Movement; est; Bakke; and Proposition 13.

The idea behind the "Only in California" thesis is the notion that California represents individualistic hedonism, a retreat from reality, a playground, or perhaps it is the insane ward; that out west a peculiar ethos of normlessness has emerged which puts certain groups and kinds of folk at high risk for all kinds of exploitative adventures.

San Francisco, as Howard Thurman once observed, is the most secular of U.S. cities. But I cannot accept the idea that Jonestown could have emerged *only* from the soil and social ethos of the San Francisco Bay Area and nowhere else, that Jonestown is solely the product of California culture.

The meaning of Peoples Temple and Jonestown must be set within the context of the twentieth century. By suggesting this context, I am implying that explanations of Peoples Temple and Jonestown, as event, cannot be reduced to the personality of one man, or to the uniqueness of California culture (nor to the regressive nature of black religion, which I do not address here).

We are much the wiser to understand Jonestown, not as an anomaly, but as a product of a culture which attempts to repress and trivialize the essentially religious impulse.

THE CHALLENGE OF SECULARISM

Secularism is the dominant cultural theme. By secularism I mean the erosion of traditional religious symbols of orientation and meaning centered around a compelling belief in one ultimate reality, and the increasing openness to a plurality of competing beliefs—all of which claim to be equally ultimate and meaningful. Secularism as a molding power of modern consciousness is easily underestimated. It does not stand alone but is supported by pluralism and privatism.

Each of these forces creates problems for the Black Church and a challenge to its ministry. In other words, we are facing a plausibility crisis in the Black Church which cannot be adequately appreciated apart from an adequate grasp of the meaning of secularism. Secularism has contributed to individualistic and privatized understandings of religious commitment and evangelism. The underlying assumption is that the way to improve social or communal life is through the saving or salvaging of individual souls (or psyches).

Such attempts woefully ignore critical reflection upon existing power arrangements which create hardships and contribute to social dislocation and alienation. Individual salvation has been the pervasive theme in Black Church religion on the West Coast in recent times. It is true that during the nineteenth century, and during the Civil Rights and Black Power movements of the 1960s, the pressure was on the Black Church to be at the forefront of black liberation and social transformation, and indeed it was. But this emphasis was and continues to be resisted by many.

Secularism is and has been a long-term social-historical process that has permeated institutions of our society, including the Black Church, and has affected our psychological and social outlook. The end result is a secularized conscience, closed to the claims of religious truths. The cunning feature of this process is that it happens without our conscious recognition of it. In short, we are deeply embedded in a cultural and historical process that tends to obscure the relational character of our existence.

RELATIONALITY

As an alternative to an individualistic and privatized approach to the church's ministry, I wish to suggest a conceptual basis for ministry, one that is consistent with the historic role of Black Church religion in the nineteenth century and one that perceives the connection between personal liberation and social transformation; political impotence and personal disintegration. The key concept here is *relationality*.

Relationality is perhaps best captured in the old Zulu proverb: "umuntu ungumuntu ngabanye abantu" (a person is thus, because of other persons). He or she is there because there are other people with him, before him and after him. Relationality suggests that the black community and the Black Church, though interdependent, are constitutive elements, each in the life of the other. They are mutually bound together in a common enterprise, and they share a common destiny. The Black Church, therefore, cannot realize its historic role of liberation and empowerment in the present situation apart from black culture and the black community as a whole. And the black community cannot exist as a viable community and culture in a racist society by denying or destroying the key institutions that have enabled it to survive.

Nineteenth-century black religious leaders in California, as well as throughout the United States, had a relational vision which predated the social gospel movement and enabled them to lend personal responsibility to issues of social justice. Their vision embraced the liberation struggles of the whole black community, religious and secular.

Many black people originally responded positively to Peoples Temple because it was a movement that provided psychic support and linked it with a program of social/communal outreach. Hence, black people's involvement in the Peoples Temple movement can be seen as an attempt to make black religion relevant to their social, political, and economic condition. By breaking with the insularity and seemingly irrelevant style of traditional Black Church worship, many thought they had found in Peoples Temple a form of church involvement that spoke more directly to the issues of spiritual uplift, justice, social change, and communal empowerment.

Their vision of a new social order was not wrong. It was expressive of the relational paradigm. It was a vision broader than that found in many of the black churches they left. But their vision was not enough. It lacked a self-critical dimension that would have enabled them to discern the false claims of Jim Jones towards ego deification.

Black people's involvement in Peoples Temple and Jonestown is difficult to explain in light of the Black Power and Black Theology liberation movements and developing black nationalism of the 1960s, and the African roots phenomenon of the 1970s. It appears as an anomaly.

However, the relative success of the Peoples Temple movement in San Francisco and Jonestown is not difficult to explain when we consider that the influence of these movements of the 1960s did not take significant hold in established black religious institutions and consciousness of the majority of black churches in the San Francisco Bay Area. What Peoples Temple was able to offer black people was a social-political economic program linked with a tangible cause, an authoritative charismatic leader and a vision of a new social order.

The Fillmore District of San Francisco has one of the most comprehensive mental health and social service networks to be found anywhere. Although Peoples Temple was not formally identified as a part of this network, it did have a strong working relationship with it. This network and Peoples Temple developed a kind of ideal working relationship that many activists and socially concerned church people (who work with poor people) desired and were drawn to.

The appeal of Peoples Temple was not only its charismatic leader but its interpretation of religion, its sense of family and social outreach programs. Peoples Temple was concerned with black unemployment, problems of poverty, juvenile delinquency, criminal justice, welfare dependency, alcoholism, drug addiction, and related social problems.

The ability of Peoples Temple to influence structures of power gave folk a sense of "somebodiness," a sense of belonging to a great cause. In order to appreciate its appeal, we must see it amidst an enclave of the relatively conservative, status-conscious, privatized religious orientation of many black churches which had an inward religious orientation but without the outward thrust of significant social action programs or political involvement.

Even after the Jonestown tragedy, one embittered person who was a participant in Peoples Temple put it to me this way:

> Most black churches do not even want to be bothered with understanding or framing a response to Guyana. Peoples Temple emerged out of a need and filled a vacuum in the black community; a need that was missed by the black churches. Peoples Temple ministered to the unchurched, the black elderly, the addicted and alcoholic, welfare dependents, juvenile delinquents, the lonely and the alienated of all sorts.

It is small wonder, then, that many found in the Peoples Temple movement a place to belong, an outlet for their religious and political aspirations, a social program, and a cause to which they could give themselves.

New West magazine reported on 18 December 1978, that Jim Jones (with his 2,000-member congregation) was the only political leader in San Francisco who could completely control the way his followers would vote.

He moved into the heart of the Fillmore District, took over the lives of young black men, old women, mothers and babies. According to news reports, he infiltrated black organizations and diluted their effective counter moves. He took hundreds of poor and black people with him into the isolated jungles of Guyana and in time ordered suicide or murder. In the interim, he did much to give people hope and a vision of a new society.

There were critical voices in the black religious community, but these few voices alone were not organized and strong enough to counter the effects of Jones and his movement. Can this happen again, or in other American cities? And, if so, then what kind of structures or mechanisms are necessary to counter such moves before they escalate into strong politically and financially backed movements on the scale of Peoples Temple? Would such a movement have gotten as far as it did if the chief victims were not the disposable people—black youth (some of whom were wards of the State and juvenile delinquents), elderly black women on Social Security, drug addicts, and left wing social activists?

IMPLICATIONS FOR THE PASTORAL CARE
MINISTRY OF BLACK CHURCHES

In the wake of Jonestown, the temptation will be strong on the part of Black Church leadership not only to denounce Jim Jones and Peoples Temple, and write it off as the work of the devil, but there will also be the attempt to avoid legitimate guilt, remove oneself from hearing appropriate criticism, and to deny responsibility in what happened. In a society as interdependent as ours, no one can walk away clean. Such denial would be unfortunate if it is used to justify no change in the way the Black Church sees its mission and ministry. If this is the case, then Jonestown would be a message that fell on deaf ears!

It will be important to remember the positive and heroic things done by Peoples Temple which somewhere, somehow need to be continued. The official closing of the Temple on 31 December 1978 created a vacuum that other groups may not be able to fill as successfully or very fast. Peoples Temple has already demonstrated the need for a ministry that will reach those for whom no one else seemed to care.

Black churches are challenged to consider the possibilities of a multifaceted, cooperative outreach and social change ministry, shared by a number of black clergy and lay people, and to combine such efforts with other community resources. No one church or clergyperson ought to try to fill this vacuum alone. To go it alone tilts in the direction of messianism and egomania.

The idea of relationality suggests a cooperative enterprise, a shared ministry. This is a challenge, because it is often difficult for the clergy to share authority and leadership roles or to acknowledge their own limitations. We have our own ego problems, which often get in the way of fashioning creative and cooperative responses to social issues.

On the other hand, the community and our congregants sometimes expect miracles from us—things that they do not expect from other professionals. The potential for audience corruption, self-deception or collusion is always present. The seduction is that our congregants often look to us to provide answers to problems that are too great for any one person to solve. No one can possibly answer or fill the void in someone else's life, nor can any one person (or church) alone transform the social order. To attempt such creates false hopes and false dependency, and thwarts the necessary development of communal efforts to fashion responses for creative social change. The tendency towards messianism is just as real for the rest of us as it was for Jim Jones. We all participate in the same structure of finitude that Jim Jones knew.

Here, in brief, are further implications for the church's ministry derived from this presentation:

1. *Interpretive.* The Black Church as a witness to the presence of the living God has an interpretive role to play, as well as being a gathering place for worship. This role includes: interpreting to the people as clearly as it can the events that mark and circumscribe their existence in ways that can enable them to link their faith with responsible involvement in the world; interpretations that bring to bear the Biblical Word and mediate the active caring of God's presence in our time. The church's interpretive role ought to enable us to identify our social location, give insight concerning the nature of the social structures under which we labor, and prepare us to fashion creative responses as persons of faith and agents of change.

2. *Communal Empowerment and Interdependence.* The Black Church must once again assert itself as a communal church, seeking to heal, empower and undergird black families, support the alienated, psychically distraught and socially abandoned, and feed the spiritually hungry. The church cannot do this alone, but must see itself as a part of a social network.

We are still challenged to reject the ideological rationale and behavior that support our enslavement. As in the past, when slaves asserted their own rights as humans against the teachings of slave-owner religion, the Black Church is challenged today to play a similar role in the lives of black families and single persons who face new forms of alienation and spiritual bondage to materialistic values. Of central importance here are processes of victimization in black male-female relationships.

3. *Social Action.* Interpretation and healing must incorporate social action aimed at systemic change. Interpretation must be linked to praxis and reflection. Social action must seek to comprehend and transform the process and social arrangements which maintain and legitimate structures of oppression.

In the words of the 6 August 1977, National Conference of the Black Theology Project in Atlanta, the Black Church "must come out from behind its stained glass walls and dwell where mothers are crying, children are hungry, and fathers are jobless." Social action ministries must be open to the critical perspectives of others as the church and community continue to evolve the praxis of caring, emancipation and social transformation.

4. *Prophetic.* The Black Church in the United States has often played a prophetic role when it has proclaimed the power of the gospel in judgment upon an exploitative economic and social system which ensures structural inequality and insidious forms of racism and sexism. The role was expressed in the witness of Harriet Tubman, Sojourner Truth, Richard Allen, Jeremiah B. Sanderson, Martin Luther King Jr., and a host of other witnesses. The prophetic role of the church must continue to evolve an alternative perspective consistent with its interpretive task and social action ministry.

CONCLUSION

Secularism found expression in the dominant theoretical explanation that emerged from social science about Peoples Temple and Jonestown. Yet, this theory, which I called the "psychoanalytically oriented worldview" explanation, was incapable of diagnosing the larger social world that produced Jonestown, and it failed to enable a critical analysis of the social structure, even if it did help to explain some of the inner forces that may have motivated persons to join Peoples Temple and its move to Jonestown.

Finally, I have attempted to frame an adequate response from a broadened perspective of black pastoral care. Within this perspective individual liberation and social transformation are linked. I have tried to point out that emancipatory struggle must seek to strengthen awareness of the connection and interdependence of human life, and must continually involve a social and self-critical dimension enjoined with faith in the One who underlies and struggles through the efforts of black people to be free, and who struggles through conditions of oppression and tragedy everywhere. Genuine social emancipation is inseparable from the emancipation of the human self and mind. These are a part of the same dialectic which is at work in the community of the oppressed on this side of Jonestown.

4

Demographics and the Black Religious Culture of Peoples Temple

REBECCA MOORE

The Peoples Temple agricultural project in Jonestown, Guyana, was a racially black community in a number of key respects. A large group of African Americans who migrated from the southern U.S. to California made up a sizeable contingent of those living in Guyana. African Americans had long supported the Temple with contributions, tithes, and wages while living in California, but in Jonestown it was clear that the Social Security checks of black senior citizens made up the primary source of income for almost a year. Finally, the majority of Jonestown's residents were black, and African Americans held key leadership positions in the jungle outpost.

Was the community in Jonestown culturally black as well?[1] By "racially black" we are referring only to an individual's or a group's racial or ethnic classification, that is, their skin color. By "culturally black" we mean a condition in which an individual identifies with a host of values, problems, strengths, and concerns associated with the fact of being black in the United States. The former is generally a matter of birth, while the latter is usually a matter of socialization. Thus, "blackness" is not always self-evident. We might look at certain prison populations or particular school districts, for example, and say that racially the group comprises a black majority, even though culturally the group's values or structures may reflect the values of the dominant society. Or in contrast, European slaveowners instituted chattel slavery, but within that white-created institution of slavery, a black counterculture emerged.

We would like to argue that Peoples Temple was a culturally as well as racially black movement. It shared characteristics with other undeniably black religious groups, most notably the Peace Mission of Father Divine, which Jim Jones, the group's white leader, used as a model. Some common characteristics included similar racial profiles in terms of membership and leadership, similar worship styles and practices, and, most importantly, a profound commitment to over-coming racial inequality. This commitment can be seen in the pro-gressive practices in which the Temple engaged, as described else-where in this book, as well as in the renunciation of privilege white Temple members made. Peoples Temple could not entirely transcend its roots in America's racist past, and so its reality is a mass of con-tradictions: good will and bad faith combined. Nevertheless, the em-igration of the group from the United States in order to create a hate-free society abroad indicates the depth of its members' desire for justice.

This article expands upon previous demographic studies of Jones-town which documented the project's predominantly black member-ship. We attempt to further the discussion of Peoples Temple by con-sidering that black membership with additional data unavailable to previous studies. In addition, we look at elements of the Temple's religious culture within the context of black religious experience. This framework helps to illuminate and clarify practices within the move-ment.

PREVIOUS DEMOGRAPHIC ANALYSES

While the news media and the public, especially people in the San Francisco Bay Area, considered Peoples Temple a black activist church with a charismatic white pastor, it wasn't until 1982 that the full extent of black involvement began to be appreciated. Archie Smith Jr. compiled State Department data on Jonestown victims and pub-lished two tables in his book *The Relational Self*, which indicated not just a black majority of victims in Jonestown (71%), but a black female near-majority overall (49%).[2] Moreover, almost a quarter of those liv-ing in Jonestown (22%) were black women over the age of 51. Smith argued that while the black members of Peoples Temple saw the group providing real services to the community and creating an alternative to the status quo, their vision "was not broad or critical enough to perceive the barriers of class, sex, age, and race in the social structure of the organization itself."[3] He referred to the continuing superior-inferior relationships perpetuated in the movement as racism.

In his 1987 book *Gone from the Promised Land*, John R. Hall provided estimates of the racial composition of Peoples Temple at various points in the group's 25-year history. Hall wrote that of the families that migrated from Indiana to California in 1965, half were black and half were white.[4] Hall said that the largest proportion of members who went to Jonestown (40%) were middle-aged and elderly blacks from the U.S. South, along with their families.[5] Hall's overall population of African Americans in Jonestown totaled 70%, which corresponded to Smith's figures.[6]

Mary Maaga provided perhaps the most extensive demographic survey in *Hearing the Voices of Jonestown* (1998). Building upon Hall's work, she highlighted the problem of considering members of Peoples Temple in a uniform mass. She identified three distinct groups which existed side-by-side in the organization. They included a group of white and black families who had joined in Indiana; younger whites who joined in California; and a population of urban blacks drawn from churches in the San Francisco Bay Area and in Los Angeles.[7] Using documents generated by Peoples Temple—recovered from Jonestown by U.S. troops and housed in the California Historical Society—Maaga prepared a profile on every Jonestown resident she could identify. Building upon Smith's finding that the majority of black residents were female, Maaga examined family relations, marital status, work experience and training, and age at the time of death in Jonestown, focusing in particular on the role women played in the organization.

METHODOLOGY AND SOURCES

Maaga's thumbnail sketches served as one source in developing a database of all Peoples Temple members living in Jonestown and Georgetown, Guyana.[8] We began with this cohort, rather than with *all* Temple members, because of the accessibility of records and the volume of material which is available, although we hope eventually to generate a database which includes Temple members who were living in Redwood Valley, San Francisco, and Los Angeles at the time of the deaths in Jonestown. Thus, this study is limited to Temple residents in Guyana, and conclusions may not be drawn concerning Peoples Temple as it existed in California.

Our starting point was a roster of those who died which was published by the U.S. Department of State on 17 December 1978.[9] This document served as the basis for the list which has appeared on the website *Alternative Considerations of Jonestown and Peoples Temple* since 1998.[10] The initial list grew and was corrected and amended by family members who pointed out errors to the website manager.

The accuracy and completeness of the cohort of Temple residents of Guyana jumped tremendously with the release of papers from the FBI in 2002 pursuant to a Freedom of Information Act lawsuit, *McGehee et al. v. U.S. Department of Justice*. Additional sources include reports and censuses generated by Peoples Temple, such as a listing of people planning to go to Guyana and monthly head counts of people living in Jonestown.[11] A collection of passport and other photographs of Temple members at the California Historical Society helped with some identifications when there was a question of race or gender, but this method was not foolproof. Finally, the assistance of former Temple members, including Laura Johnston Kohl, Grace Stoen Jones, and Stephan Jones, greatly helped in the identification of family members, names, and so on.

We created a record on each individual in the FileMaker database program which included the following information:

Given Name	Last Name
AKAs (Also Known As)	Better Known As
Photo Availability	Date of Birth
Age at Death	U.S. Residence Before Moving to Guyana
Date of Entry into Guyana	Date of Death
Place of Death	Race
Gender	Occupation outside Peoples Temple
Occupation in Jonestown	Government Income
Mother	Father
Spouse/Partner	Siblings
Children	Sources of Information for Record

We then sorted the records by field to determine various combinations, such as age, gender, and race. It is important to note, as we do in the following tables, that occasionally one or two individuals may be double-counted. Because the numbers of Latinas/Latinos, Native Americans, Asians, and those of unknown race and ethnicity were so small, we collapsed these figures into a single category called "Other." In addition, we wanted to highlight mixed-race individuals and families, and so we set those figures apart in a "Mixed" category.

THE FINDINGS

We began with a larger cohort than previous studies: namely, *all* Temple members living in Guyana on 18 November 1978 rather

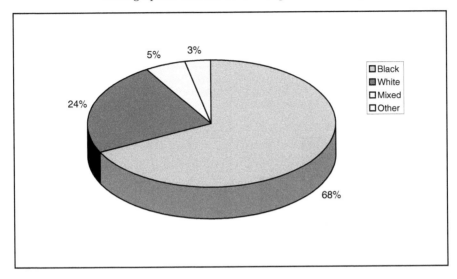

Figure 1. Temple Members Living in Guyana

than just those who died in Jonestown. Nevertheless, the number of African Americans making up the group tops two-thirds, at 68% (Figure 1). Black membership thus dominated Temple life in Guyana by a substantial majority, but by a slightly smaller margin (2%) than in earlier studies. It seems likely that the percentage of black members to total members was greater in California than in Guyana, although this conclusion is anecdotal and based on the observation of hundreds of photographs of stateside members of Peoples Temple.[12]

We calculate that approximately 1020 members of Peoples Temple were living in Guyana as of 18 November 1978. We estimate that 122 people survived the tragedy, but this figure is fluid.[13] The news media frequently reported that 918 people died in Jonestown. This number includes four members of Congressman Leo Ryan's party—including Ryan himself—and one Temple member who were killed at the Port Kaituma airstrip outside Jonestown, and four Temple members who died in Georgetown. We have come up with names of 900 individuals who we are fairly certain died, though many of these are children, never identified, who we presumed died because the custodial parent also died in Jonestown. Despite the shortfall, we do not dispute the official figures, but rather have tried to give names to as many people as we possibly can.

Almost twice as many females as males lived in Jonestown, which

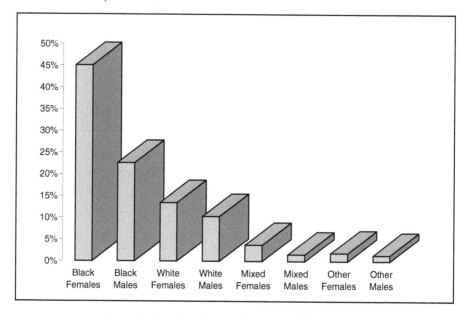

Figure 2. Membership by Gender and Race

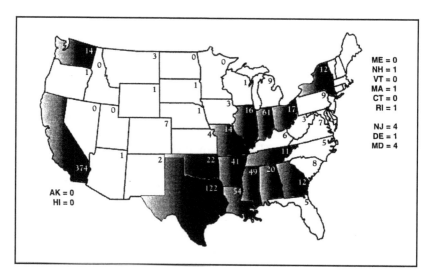

Figure 3. Distribution of Birthplaces
for Jonestown Residents

Table 1. States of Origin (more than ten members)

	Blacks	Whites	Mixed	Other	Total
California	232	106	29	7	374
South					
Texas	113	5	2	2	122
Louisiana	53	1			54
Mississippi	48			1	49
Arkansas	39		2		41
Oklahoma	19	2		1	22
Alabama	19			1	20
Missouri	10	3	1		14
Georgia	9		3		12
Tennessee	11				11
Total					345
Others					
Indiana	23	36	1	1	61
Ohio	2	15			17
Illinois	12	2	2		16
Washington	5	9			14
New York	4	7		1	12
Total					120

becomes significant when we look at leadership patterns in the community (below). Black females made up the largest group of residents of Jonestown (45%), with white females making up 13%. Black males made up over one-fifth (23%), with white males making up a tenth, and the remainder falling in the Mixed or Other categories (Figure 2). Clearly women played an important role in the community, both numerically and organizationally, as Mary Maaga indicated in her book.

The geographical distribution of where people were born indicates a strong southern black presence, as Hall observed. The U.S. map (Figure 3) indicates from which states 10 or more members of Peoples Temple originated. California, of course, is the largest as the Temple's base of operations (374), with Indiana ranking third (61), as its place of origin. But the chart shows that 345 came from nine southern or border states, with 93% of these members being African American.

Many of these African Americans died on 18 November 1978. The

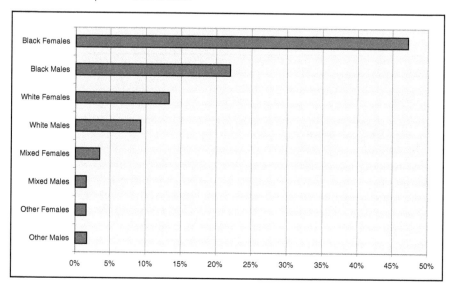

Figure 4. Percentages of Deceased, by Race and Gender

proportion of blacks who died (69%) does not differ significantly from the proportion who lived in Guyana (68%). Figure 4 shows that almost half of those who died in Jonestown were black females (47%), corresponding to their presence in the community (45%), while black males also died in the same proportion as their presence (22%).

The gender-race distribution shifts when we consider who survived the tragedy by either being in Georgetown, the capital, or by leaving Jonestown on 18 November (Figure 5). Only one-third of the 122 survivors were black females. About one-quarter of the survivors were black males, several of whom were members of the community's basketball team, in Georgetown that day for a championship basketball game. In fact, almost a tenth (9%) of the male survivors belonged to the basketball team. Fourteen percent (14%) of the survivors were white females, but the percentage of white male survivors surpasses their presence in the community (19% as opposed to 10% overall). Only 30 children under the age of 19 survived, only 14 of whom were under age 10.

The numbers show two age bumps for those living in Guyana: namely a large number of children under 20, as well as those in their twenties; and a secondary group of senior citizens (Figure 6). One hundred thirty-one (131) children were under the age of 10; 234 were between the ages of 10 and 19; and 186 were in their 20s. This means

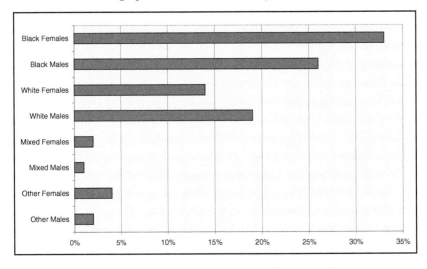

Figure 5. Percentages of Survivors, by Race and Gender

that more than one-half of the residents were under 30, and more than one-third were under 20. While many teenagers worked in Jonestown to support the project, these figures nevertheless reveal a relatively large non-productive population. Two hundred eleven (211) people were 60 and older, with three-fourths of this segment being black females.

While the number of seniors may indicate a sizable non-productive work force in the community, they nevertheless played an important role in supporting Jonestown through their monthly Social Security checks. We took a snapshot of Social Security income for the month of September 1978, since we had the greatest amount of information for that month.[14] Because there was public concern about Social Security fraud, the U.S. Department of Health, Education and Welfare provided a list of the beneficiaries and the checks which had been recovered from Jonestown. In that month, 173 beneficiaries received a total of $36,548.30 in checks which were recovered—uncashed—at the site of the tragedy.[15] Of those 173 beneficiaries, 157 were black, 15 were white, and 1 was Native American. But if we add to that figure those who had received Social Security income in other months, the number of blacks jumps to 182, the number of whites to 18, with a single Native American recipient, and a single Latino (Table 2). Thus, African Americans, particularly the elderly, were helping to finance the community in Guyana.

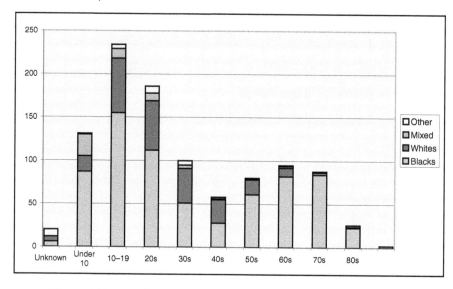

Figure 6. Race and Age of Temple Members Living in Guyana

We also looked at family groupings in Jonestown and discovered a large number of affective ties. Only 256 people who died in Jonestown, or 20% of the total, had no apparent family connections with anyone else present. Within the 80% remaining, we identified 182 family units, with a family unit being defined as at least one parent and at least one child.[16] Three-quarters of these family units consisted of three or more members (Figure 7). One hundred family units combined to make up 43 extended families, which we grouped by blood ties or by adoption, e.g., grandparents, parents, children; aunts, uncles, cousins (Figure 8). This means that about half of the 182 family units which existed in Jonestown had additional family ties with each other.

We found further connections between family units and extended

Table 2. Social Security Recipients Living in Guyana

	Black	White	Native American	Latino	Total
Sept. Checks	157	15	1		173
Add'l SSA	25	3		1	29
Total	182	18	1	1	202

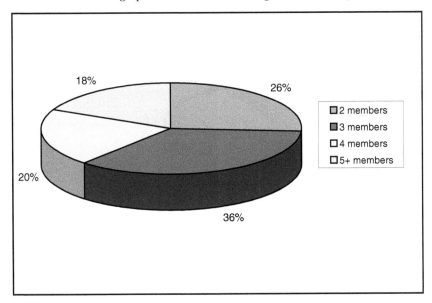

Figure 7. Family Units in Jonestown

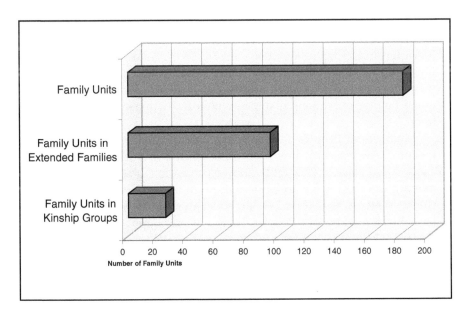

Figure 8. Family Groupings

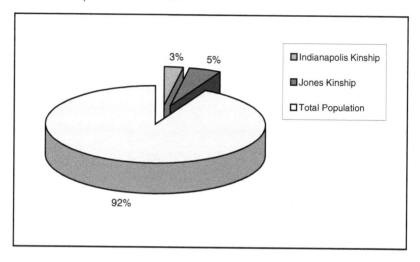

Figure 9. Kinship Groups

families in the form of kinship groups, which linked extended families through marriage. We identified two main kinship groups in Jonestown, which we called the Indianapolis group and the Jones group. These two groups accounted for six extended families, 25 family units and 84 individuals; that is, they constituted 8% of the total population in Guyana (Figure 9). When we look more closely, we see that the Jones kinship group alone makes up 5% of the total. This means that Jim Jones not only acted as the group's leader, but he was also intimately connected to a large number of residents. Clearly he had as much family investment as did the other individuals living in Jonestown.

Members of Peoples Temple came from a variety of jobs and professions. The majority, however, came from the working classes, as Table 3 indicates.[17] This table shows professions people held *before* moving to Jonestown.[18] In light of these figures, it does not seem accurate to assert, as C. Eric Lincoln and Lawrence H. Mamiya do, that most black members of Peoples Temple were "impoverished and déclassé."[19] Although whites are disproportionately represented in the fields of education and law, blacks clearly dominate all of the professions listed, in keeping with the Temple's racial profile.

Jobs and responsibilities shifted at the agricultural project, with many more people working in agriculture, food preparation, and mechanical and building trades in order to support the community. Some

Table 3. Professions of Peoples Temple Members

Occupation	Black	White	Mixed	Other	Total
Medical	104	45	5	1	155
Clerical (secretaries, clerks, tellers, sales)	60	34	4	4	102
Food/Cooks/Wait Staff	90	9	3	2	104
Farm/Agricultural	65	9	1	2	77
Domestics/Housekeeping	73	1	2		76
Building Trades (Elec., Plumb., Const.)	27	16			43
Mechanics	24	14	1	2	41
Education	20	19	2	1	42
Custodian/Maintenance/ Laborer	28	11		3	42
Finance (Accounting, Bookkeeping)	6	14	1		21
Management (Store, Office, Care Home)	11	7		1	19
Law	1	3			4

people moved up in terms of responsibilities, especially in terms of managing agricultural production. Some moved laterally, shifting from cooking or domestic work in the United States to similar occupations in Jonestown. Some moved down the social ladder, exchanging professional responsibilities for manual labor.

When we turn to leadership roles in Jonestown, we get some evidence of racism, as noted by others.[20] The Planning Commission (PC) was Jim Jones' personal advisory group, his closest associates and decision-makers. Only 6 of the 37 members of the PC were black, or one-sixth.[21] While this figure seems low, it may indicate class or occupational differences in which blacks have been historically underrepresented.[22] If we look at the individual names on the list, we see that fifteen PC members came from Indiana, and thus were some of the institution's longest and most devoted followers. Almost twice as many women as men (25 to 12) made up the PC, with five of those men coming from Indianapolis. The high proportion of females indicates Jones' preference for, and trust in, women over and against men. At least a half-dozen women on the list were those with whom Jones had had sexual relations.

The PC seemed to wield enormous power as long as Peoples Temple was based in California. Upon the move to Guyana, however, authority seemed to decentralize among a larger, more diverse body, as an organizational chart recovered from Jonestown reveals (Figure 10). Fifteen department heads or their assistants were white, while 24 heads or assistants were black, with the remaining three being Native American, Latina, and unknown. African Americans headed six departments—Public Utilities, Production, Businesses, Education and Child Care, Entertainment and Public Relations, and the "Administrative Triumvarite [sic]"—and served as assistants in all other committees except for Legal and Accounting (note: the Legal Department was composed of three lawyers). The two staff members of the triumvirate were black. As with the Planning Commission, more females appear on the chart than do males.

As egalitarian as this organizational chart appears, the reality was that power and authority in Jonestown rested in the Planning Commission and remained with Jim Jones rather than in a decentralized leadership system. Although a piece of paper affixed to the chart is dated 12 July 1978, we do not know the exact date the chart was prepared. It seems likely that it was fabricated for the benefit of Leo Ryan's trip to Jonestown in November.[23] The organizational chart reveals a number of errors and omissions, such as listing one of the lawyers as Gene Wagner rather than Gene Chaikin. There are other problems with the chart.[24] For example, the security team is not identified; responsibility for the work crew—those in charge of community discipline—is not listed. What can be said, however, is that the chart correctly identifies a number of black leaders in Jonestown, though it may not accurately represent the level of authority they actually had.

Matching Jonestown's racial profile more closely was the project's security team. It is important to note here that this is the most anecdotal compilation of names used in this study, as well as the most sensational. These names were provided by survivors returning from Guyana—including defectors and apostates as well as loyalists in the first stages of grief—who were questioned by the FBI upon their arrival in the United States.[25] In other words, traumatized individuals at their most vulnerable either volunteered or were coerced into naming names. Of the 67 people named as Security, 58% were black, while 39% were white. Only five females were identified as being part of Security. We believe that security figures are somewhat inflated, since some informants identified all members of the basketball team and the archery team as part of Security.

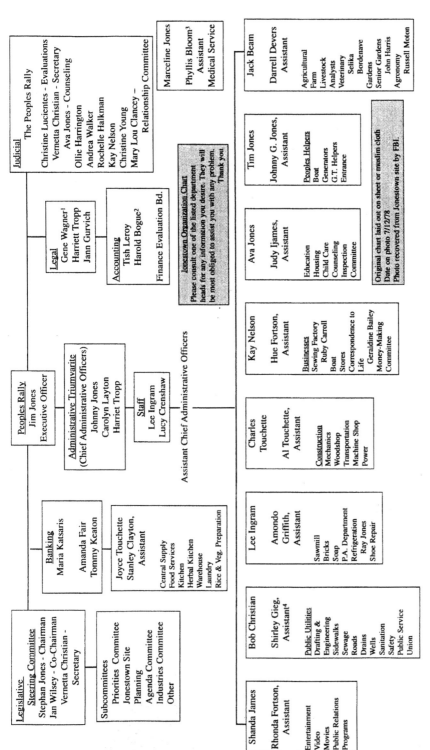

Figure 10. Jonestown Organizational Chart

1. No such person; probably Gene Chaikin.
2. No such person; probably Harold Cordell.
3. No such person; probably Phyllis Houston.
4. No such person; no one close to that name who might reasonably substitute.

ANALYSIS AND IMPLICATIONS

These figures show that Peoples Temple's agricultural project in Jonestown, Guyana, can appropriately be identified as a primarily black community in racial terms for a number of reasons. First, the majority of Temple members and Jonestown residents were black. As noted at the beginning of this chapter, numbers alone do not necessarily indicate the cultural blackness of an institution in terms of its values, goals, and purposes. But the high percentages of black involvement in the Temple's Guyana operations do point to its existence as a racially black group.

Second, the southern origins of Peoples Temple members also reveal the black roots of the organization. Several authors have noted that southern blacks who moved north or west looking for work and safety during the migrations of the 1930s and World War II found established black churches too "fine, fashionable and formal," and thus turned to black "cults."[26] Joseph Washington wrote that these black religions provided "a creative, imaginative and indigenous (if insufficient) response to the failure of churches and society to satisfy the immediate needs of black people."[27] We can see that the experiences of southern black members of Peoples Temple may well have paralleled those who joined Washington's black "cults." The involvement of southern blacks in the movement strongly suggests a black racial and cultural identity.

Third, elderly African Americans provided many of the day-to-day financial resources for the project by donating their Social Security income. In return they received health care, housing, food, and other basic necessities. Although one surviving black senior citizen, Hyacinth Thrash, described an inadequate diet in Jonestown, she did add that:

> One thing you can say for Jim—he didn't deny medical care when they needed it. . . . We all had our blood pressure checked regular, Indians too. . . . Jim had real fine caring nurses too, both black and white.[28]

Many seniors had signed life-care agreements with non-profit corporations created by Peoples Temple in exchange for their Social Security income, much as senior citizens sign up for life care with centers in the United States. Their financial contributions were crucial to the maintenance of Jonestown, and the fact that September Social Security checks had not been cashed as of 18 November may point to the existence of a suicide plan as early as September, if not before.

Finally, although African Americans made up only a minority of Jones' personal leadership group, they did make up the majority of department heads and assistants in Jonestown. They also dominated the Jonestown security force, a contradictory position in which blacks may have been both feared and hated, as well as trusted and responsible. Nevertheless, it is clear that African Americans played a number of significant leadership roles in the Jonestown community.

We see a similar racial imbalance in Father Divine's leadership group for the Peace Mission, another black movement dedicated to racial justice and empowerment. "The sole potentially troublesome inequality was the disproportion of white disciples holding positions of responsibility, a situation that obtained in Harlem as well as California," wrote Robert Weisbrot of Father Divine's Peace Mission movement.[29] Weisbrot went on to say that this situation did not disturb most of the followers, who continued to believe that the Peace Mission was dedicated to racial equality both in practice as well as in theory.

Although Lincoln and Mamiya saw discontinuity between Jones and Divine, the numbers show more similarities than differences. Jones deliberately emulated many elements of Father Divine's movement, even going so far as attempting to take over the Peace Mission after Divine's death. Father Divine relied on a core group of about 12 personal secretaries, most of middle-class background, most of them female. Nearly all of Father Divine's secretaries in the 1930s were white, as were most of the lawyers, according to Weisbrot, although Lincoln and Mamiya claim that Father Divine's leadership group was equally divided between the races. Weisbrot concluded that "the high representation of whites in leadership roles did not reflect a deeper intent to establish or regulate any racial hierarchy."[30] Thus, from Weisbrot's perspective, a predominantly white advisory group did not indicate racism in the Peace Mission, because Father Divine himself was black. Moreover, the presence of white leadership at the Peace Mission has not distinguished the group as a white religious movement in the minds of scholars of black religion.

Peoples Temple and the Peace Mission appear to be remarkably similar in several additional respects. Some similarities were genetic, and not coincidental, since Jones modeled himself and the Temple after Divine and the Peace Mission, right down to having members call him "Father." Other similarities, however, highlight the racial and cultural elements constitutive of black religious movements. The majority of Father Divine's followers—from three-fourths to nine-tenths—were female, just as in Jonestown, where they made up two-thirds of the membership. Most were poor black women, often widowed or

divorced. Many writers have noted disproportionate female membership in New Religious Movements (NRMs), especially in black "cults"
or alternative religions arising from the black community.[31] We see
disproportionately high numbers of females in most mainline religions
in the United States. In the Peace Mission, as in Peoples Temple, both
genders lived communally in the United States, pooling their resources to support the movement and to save money.

The two groups shared cultural values as well. Both were committed to complete racial integration, though one through celibacy
(Divine) and the other through intermarriage and biracial births
(Jones). Both sought financial independence through businesses and
members' income. Both provided communal housing so that resources
could be pooled and shared. And both sought economic, social, and
political justice. If we call Father Divine's Peace Mission a black religious group, can we not call Jim Jones' Peoples Temple one as well?

Though the two groups did differ in several important ways, Peoples Temple nevertheless shared many more similarities with the
Peace Mission—a black religious group—than it did with the typical
NRMs emerging from the 1960s and 70s counterculture.[32] Those
groups were predominantly made up of white, middle-class, educated
young people, the very cohort which Maaga defines as a "new religious movement" *within* Peoples Temple.[33] Eileen Barker notes that
those who have joined the better-known alternative religious groups
in the West, such as Children of God, International Society for Krishna
Consciousness, or the Unification Church, have been disproportionately white and from the educated middle classes, with the exception
of Peoples Temple and the Branch Davidians.[34] Speaking in 1977, Archie Smith Jr. noted that a conference on "new religious consciousness" held in Berkeley "was largely treated . . . as a universal affecting
young people in general, i.e., W.A.S.P., rather than youth from certain
ethnic backgrounds and particular social strata." He continued:

> Recruits to the new religious movements tend to be urban white
> youth, well-educated and from middle- and upper-class families.
> Their disaffection is with the inability of established white religious
> traditions and materialistic strivings of family life to yield depth of
> meaning in living.[35]

He argued that by ignoring the problem of race, scholars make white
experience normative, and thus give only a partial glimpse of the to-
tality of religious experience in a pluralistic society. His words seem
prophetic in light of subsequent analyses of Jonestown.

If we examine Peoples Temple within a framework which considers black religious experience normative in terms of racial and cultural identification, however, we emerge with a better understanding of the movement. We begin to understand the supposedly peculiar practices of the Temple in light of W. E. B. Du Bois' description of the black church in America:

> The Negro church of to-day is the social centre of Negro life in the United States, and the most characteristic expression of African character. . . . This building is the central club-house of a community of a thousand or more Negroes. Various organizations meet here—the church proper, the Sunday-school, two or three insurance societies, women's societies, secret societies, and mass meetings of various kinds.

Du Bois goes on to list the various "entertainments, suppers, and lectures" which are held in addition to the five or six weekly religious services. "Considerable sums of money are collected and expended here, employment is found for the idle, strangers are introduced, news is disseminated and charity distributed."[36] Within the context outlined by Du Bois, the endless meetings, offerings, services, "entertainments, suppers, and lectures," which both Temple members and Temple apostates describe, no longer appear as efforts to control people's lives—as explained in traditional anti-cult or psychological analyses of NRMs—but rather are efforts to liberate people from the oppressive society in which they live. The communalism of Peoples Temple, which culminated in the move to Guyana, is something with which Du Bois would have felt comfortable, since he considered the church a "communistic institution," which expresses "the inner ethical life of a people in a sense seldom true elsewhere."[37]

If we continue to consider black experience normative, then Du Bois' description of the black pastor fits Jim Jones like a glove. He called the pastor a medicine-man, healer, interpreter of the Unknown, a comforter of those who are sorrowing, the supernatural avenger of wrong, bard, physician, judge, priest, "and the one who rudely but picturesquely expressed the longing, disappointment, and resentment of a stolen and oppressed people."[38] Jones was all of those things, and of course much more. The "crazed charismatic cultist" depiction of Jones fails to recognize his debt to Black Church traditions and mores.

The intimate relationship between leader and followers, however, can lead to what Archie Smith called audience corruption. "Followers learn to give the responses the leader wants them to learn; they feed it back to the leader on cue. He in turn believes even more in the power of the rightness of his leadership."[39] Although Lincoln and Mamiya claimed that Jones' ultimate goal was the creation of his own private cosmos in Jonestown, in which control was absolute, we don't have to go to the jungle to see a similar dynamic between pastor and people, preacher and congregation. The isolation in Guyana prevented critical reflection on the process of audience corruption; nonetheless, the pattern of congregational elevation of the pastor, the cult of personality which existed in the 1970s, continues to exist in the twenty-first century in black churches in the San Francisco Bay Area, and indeed, in many churches throughout the nation.

Arthur Huff Fauset's differentiation between worldly and other-worldly black groups also helps illuminate the dynamic at work in Peoples Temple. Fauset concluded his survey of black cults in the 1930s by comparing those groups which focused on social and economic change and those which focused on the Bible. "There is an indication that as American Negro cults become more intent upon social, economic, and political problems," he wrote, "the literal adherence to the Bible as a book of reference diminishes."[40] Those cults which rigidly adhered to the Bible tend to be apolitical, while those emphasizing "original economic, social, and political programs tend to develop their own set of rules, even going so far as to discard the Bible entirely." We certainly see the abandonment of the Bible with the move to Jonestown, if not before, and a growing secular emphasis within the community. Moreover, we have Jones' own critique of biblical contradictions and the Bible's justification of oppression in "The Letter Killeth," a booklet which lists page after page of political and social problems that Jones had with the good book.[41]

If we continue to look at Peoples Temple within the normativity of black experience rather than white, we then understand that the move to Guyana—far from being aberrant or indicating isolationist tendencies in traditional NRMs—reflects the exodus to the Promised Land which has characterized black religion in America. Charles Long identified Africa, and the longing for home, as one of the key elements of black religion, because African Americans are a "landless people."[42] Members of Peoples Temple called Jonestown the Promised Land. They looked forward with anticipation to having their own land, free of the problems of urban life: crime, drugs, unemployment. While the longing for the Promised Land is often spiritualized into an other-worldly hope in the Black Church, Jonestown realized that hope in the here-and-now.

When my parents visited Jonestown in May 1978, my father observed the enthusiasm with which an elderly woman with a speech impediment was arriving along with them. He noticed her swaying to the music that night in the community center. He saw old people tending crops, and he wrote of his experience:

> I have never been anyplace where I saw the older people so much a part of the community. . . . One woman was out hoeing her own little garden. Others had picket fences around their houses. . . . When I saw the woman hoeing I thought of Micah's words: ". . . They shall sit every one under his vine and under his fig tree, and none shall make them afraid. . . ." The fears that are a part of city life are gone.[43]

Jonestown signified a homecoming that occurred in the historical present rather than in an eschatological future. The years of wandering were ended. John Moore's reflections again indicate this mood:

> I had a feeling that everybody was somebody. I thought of Israel's understanding of herself, and later the church's self-understanding: "We who were nobody are now God's people."[44]

More work remains to be done on Peoples Temple in order to fully grasp its nature as a black organization, particularly an analysis of the group and its composition as it existed in California. Additional comparative studies that examine unquestionably black institutions also will help clarify or solidify the understanding of the Temple as a black movement. For example, to what extent, if any, does Peoples Temple fit into Hans A. Baer and Merrill Singer's typology of black religious groups?[45] While the group seems to meet at least one of Charles Long's three criteria for studying African American religion in the United States, does it meet the other two? How does the movement compare with the five groups Arthur Fauset examined in the 1930s?[46] In light of Weisbrot, Fauset, and others' discussion of Father Divine's Peace Mission, what is Jim Jones' debt to Father Divine?[47] These and other questions deserve due examination in order to more fully understand the Temple's place in black religion in America.

In the meantime, the significant contributions that African Americans made to Peoples Temple, particularly to its agricultural project in Guyana, make it clear that Peoples Temple was a black religious group, both racially and culturally. Numbers alone do not tell the whole story. They do, however, provide the rationale for considering Peoples Temple and Jonestown within the context of black experience and black religion in America. In combination with cultural analyses, the numbers go a long way to providing the framework for future studies. That should be the starting point, and the presupposition, for further work on Peoples Temple and Jonestown.

NOTES

This essay could not have been written without the extensive contributions of Fielding M. McGehee III, who loaded raw information into a database, identified who lived and who died in Jonestown, and helped compile the statistics on which the analyses are based. For this reason, I will be using "we" throughout to indicate our collaboration on the research process. I also appreciate the extensive comments made by my co-editors as well as those extended by John R. Hall.

1. We are differentiating between Peoples Temple and Jonestown to reflect the changes that existed within the organization once it moved from the United States to Guyana.

2. Archie Smith Jr., *The Relational Self: Ethics and Therapy from a Black Church Perspective* (Nashville, Tenn.: Abingdon, 1982), 229–231.

3. Smith, *The Relational Self*, 197.

4. John R. Hall, *Gone from the Promised Land: Jonestown in American Cultural History* (New Brunswick, N.J.: Transaction Books, 1987).

5. Hall, *Gone from the Promised Land*, 72.

6. In works from the 1990s, Benjamin Beit-Hallahmi also presents racial and gender profiles of those who died in Jonestown. See Beit-Hallahmi, with Michael Argyle, *The Psychology of Religious Behavior, Belief and Experience* (London and New York: Routledge, 1997); and in the *Illustrated Encyclopedia of Active New Religions, Sects, and Cults* (New York: Rosen, 1993, 1998).

7. Mary McCormick Maaga, *Hearing the Voices of Jonestown* (Syracuse, N.Y.: Syracuse University Press, 1998), 75.

8. Dr. Maaga's data are available through the California Historical Society.

9. *The Assassination of Representative Leo J. Ryan and the Jonestown, Guyana Tragedy. Report of a Staff Investigative Group to the Committee on Foreign Affairs, U.S. House of Representatives*. 96th Congress, 1st Session, 15 May 1979 (Washington, D.C.: U.S. Government Printing Office, 1979), 112–126.

10. *Alternative Considerations of Jonestown and Peoples Temple*, <http://jonestown.sdsu.edu>, accessed 11 July 2003. The lists of those who died and those who survived were extensively corrected and updated in May 2003.

11. These documents come primarily from Peoples Temple Records, California Historical Society, MS 3800.

12. More than 90% of the passport and membership photos of Temple members depict black men, women, and children.

13. This figure overestimates the number of survivors because we chose to err on the side of presuming people were alive rather than dead.

14. *The Assassination of Representative Leo J. Ryan*, 720–774. This information is available online at <http://jonestown.sdsu.edu>, accessed 11 July 2003.

15. Sixteen beneficiaries received two checks, either for cost of living increases or for dependent minors.

16. We also noted 20 sibling groups comprising two or more siblings, with no other family present.

17. Occupational Records, Peoples Temple Records, California Historical Society, MS 3800.

18. Maaga, *Hearing the Voices of Jonestown*, Appendix A, 145.

19. C. Eric Lincoln and Lawrence H. Mamiya, "Daddy Jones and Father Divine: The Cult as Political Religion," in this volume. Maaga critiques the deprivation theory as an explanation for Peoples Temple's appeal for African American members, *Hearing the Voices of Jonestown*, 81–82.

20. See Lincoln and Mamiya, and Archie Smith Jr., in this volume, and Smith's Chapter VIII in *The Relational Self.*

21. The list of Planning Commission members was generated primarily from FBI documents RYMUR 89-4286-1207 and 89-4286-1557. RYMUR is the FBI's acronym for "Ryan Murder Investigation."

22. Thanks go to John R. Hall for making this point.

23. We appreciate Laura Johnston Kohl's help in assessing the validity of this organizational chart.

24. If the chart had genuinely been valid as of 12 July 1978, the name of either Debby Layton or Teri Buford would have been listed as a financial officer. Debby Layton defected in May 1978, and Teri left in October, which might explain their absence, especially if the chart had been created in November. The names of other of Jim Jones' trusted advisers—including Mike Prokes and Karen Layton—are also missing. Dick Tropp, whose voice appears on several Jonestown tapes, does not appear on this chart. Neither Tim nor Mike Carter, who were spared from the deaths at Jonestown in order to smuggle a briefcase full of cash to the Soviet Embassy in Georgetown, are on this chart.

25. These names appear in FBI documents RYMUR 89-4286-1557, -1207, -1681, -1552, and -1562.

26. Miles Mark Fischer, "Organized Religion and Cults," in *African American Religious History: A Documentary Witness*, 2d ed., ed. Milton C. Sernett (Durham, N.C.: Duke University Press, 1999), 464–472, here 469; Arthur Huff Fauset, *Black Gods of the Metropolis: Negro Religious Cults of the Urban North* (Philadelphia: University of Pennsylvania Press, 1944), 80–81; and Melvin D. Williams, *Community in a Black Pentecostal Church: An Anthropological Study* (Pittsburgh, Pa.: University of Pittsburgh Press, 1974), 5–13.

27. Joseph R. Washington Jr., *Black Sects and Cults* (Garden City, N.J.: Doubleday, 1972), 17.

28. Catherine (Hyacinth) Thrash, as told to Marian K. Towne, *The Onliest One Alive: Surviving Jonestown, Guyana* (Indianapolis: M. Towne, 1995), 90–91.

29. Robert Weisbrot, *Father Divine and the Struggle for Racial Equality* (Urbana: University of Illinois Press, 1983), 77.

30. Weisbrot, *Father Divine and the Struggle for Racial Equality*, 78.

31. See, for example, Fischer and Fauset.

32. The Peace Mission movement was turned outward toward the general society, while Peoples Temple grew progressively more inward, eventually abandoning U.S. society in the move to Guyana. Moreover, Jim Jones espoused socialist economics, while Father Divine promoted black capitalism. See Hall, *Gone from the Promised Land*, 73.

33. Figure 6 shows what a tiny percentage this young white group was in comparison to the total population. Yet it was influential beyond its numbers, since those young whites helped black and white underclass members through the social service system as "clients."

34. Eileen Barker, "New Religious Movements: Their Incidence and Sig-

nificance," in *New Religious Movements: Challenge and Response*, ed. Bryan Wilson and Jamie Cresswell (London and New York: Routledge, 1999), 15–31.

35. Archie Smith Jr., "Black Reflections on the Study of New Religious Consciousness," in *Understanding the New Religions*, ed. Jacob Needleman and George Baker (New York: Seabury Press, 1978), 212.

36. W. E. B. Du Bois, *The Souls of Black Folk*, ed. David W. Blight and Robert Gooding-Williams (New York: Bedford Books, 1997), 152.

37. Du Bois, *The Souls of Black Folk*, 153.

38. Du Bois, *The Souls of Black Folk*, 152.

39. Smith, Chapter 3 in this volume.

40. Fauset, *Black Gods of the Metropolis*, 108.

41. Jim Jones, "The Letter Killeth," online at <http://jonestown.sdsu.edu>, accessed 11 July 2003.

42. Charles H. Long, "Perspectives for a Study of African-American Religion in the United States," in *Significations: Signs, Symbols, and Images in the Interpretation of Religion* (Philadelphia: Fortress Press, 1986), 173–184.

43. Rebecca Moore, *The Jonestown Letters: Correspondence of the Moore Family 1970–1985* (Lewiston, N.Y.: Edwin Mellen Press, 1986), 245.

44. Moore, *The Jonestown Letters*, 247.

45. Hans A. Baer and Merrill Singer, *African-American Religion: Varieties of Protest and Accommodation*, 2d ed. (Knoxville: University of Tennessee Press, 2002).

46. Fauset studied Mt. Sinai Holy Church of America, United House of Prayer for All People, Church of God, Moorish Science Temple of America, and the Peace Mission Movement.

47. Tim Reiterman and John Jacobs have made a start in *Raven: The Untold Story of the Rev. Jim Jones and His People* (New York: Dutton, 1982), as has John R. Hall. More needs to be done.

5

Peoples Temple and Housing Politics in San Francisco

TANYA M. HOLLIS

In 1999, the public television station KQED aired a documentary entitled *The Fillmore* on the history of the San Francisco district surrounding Fillmore Street in the area known as the Western Addition.[1] The program traces this history through the area's early days as a largely Jewish neighborhood, the 1906 earthquake and fire, the settlement and dislocation of Japanese Americans, and the influx of African American wartime workers during World War II. It explores the wartime and postwar rise of jazz clubs, restaurants, and a busy commercial district that made the Fillmore one of the most exciting and closely knit neighborhoods in San Francisco. The focus of the film then shifts, depicting the district's decline during the late 1940s and 1950s and the subsequent urban renewal projects that devastated the entire Western Addition, the area immediately west of the civic center of the city, with the Fillmore District at its center. Interviews with community leaders and advocates recall the shift from a vibrant, largely black community in its heyday to a neighborhood under siege, fighting for survival and organizing against powerful enemies that included real estate developers, corporate downtown interests, politicians, and bureaucratic agencies of the city and federal governments. As the film progresses through the 1970s, just as the dust begins to settle, the mass murders and suicides at Jonestown occur in 1978. The Reverend Hannibal Williams, leader and founding member of the Western Addition Community Organization (WACO), viewed the Jonestown tragedy as the end result of a chain of causality that began with redevelopment and its cataclysmic destruction. He stated in a speech:

The times were right to produce a man like Jim Jones. The circumstances of a community that is broken up, when the relationships that bind people together fall apart, the time is always right for a religious scoundrel to take advantage of our credibility. Justin Herman [executive director of the San Francisco Redevelopment Agency] literally destroyed the neighborhood and in the process he made the neighborhood ripe for anybody with any kind of solution. People were desperate for solutions, something to follow. Jim Jones was another solution. He had a charismatic personality that won the hearts and souls of people. And people followed him to hell. That's where Jim Jones went. That's where he took the people who followed him.[2]

What was the "solution" that Jim Jones, pastor of Peoples Temple, offered? What particular problems did the community of the Fillmore face, and how were those problems being addressed by existing community institutions? Popular theories hold that escalating poverty and continued racism in the largely black community fed Peoples Temple, and that these conditions eventually caused African Americans to abandon their churches, homes, and families and follow a white man to a communal agricultural project in Guyana. However, scholars have rarely explored the destruction of the community, the residents' struggle for self-determination, and the radical transformations urban renewal brought to the Fillmore in the years before Peoples Temple came to San Francisco. Such a history would focus on the already embattled African American community that had fought and won a landmark case against the San Francisco Redevelopment Agency (SFRA) and its powerful allies. At the time of the arrival of Peoples Temple, this community was still in an intense period of political activity, struggling to hold the SFRA to its requirement of community input and its pledge to discontinue removing the citizens of the Fillmore from their homes and using the land for other purposes.[3]

This chapter seeks to expand the historical perspective on Peoples Temple in San Francisco. It presents the Fillmore District as a community that had recently mobilized against outside aggressors seeking to displace it when the Temple moved into the neighborhood in 1972. This historical survey, which begins in the nineteenth century, may provide a new perspective on the Temple's entrance into the Fillmore, its response to the community's need for social services, and its eventual engagement with issues of housing in the city of San Francisco. This involvement at the local level helped meet the community's need for political "intermediaries" and for a social network of support in the recently depopulated Fillmore. Attention to this purely secular aspect of the Temple may paradoxically provide a new context within which to account for the features that marked it as a specifically black religious institution despite its white leadership. The Temple's social and political projects and stances thus need to be read against the background of calls issued by black communities both in San Francisco and elsewhere for an activist response by black churches and religious institutions to the material struggles of African Americans, as well as their spiritual needs.

THE FILLMORE

Prior to World War II, San Francisco's black population numbered around 5,000.[4] In terms of overall San Francisco demographics, this represented a fairly small enclave, but one that traced its roots to the earliest pioneers to the Pacific Coast. Drawn by the Gold Rush and the chance for economic advancement, many African Americans came west from slave states after California joined the Union as a free state in 1850. Many settled in the cities of San Francisco, Sacramento, and later Los Angeles, and began to build churches, community organizations, and social networks that continued to draw relatives, friends, and family members to the West, largely from the rural South. However, the population of blacks in California remained relatively small until the mid-twentieth century.[5]

World War II prompted a massive migration of African Americans west to California with the promise of employment in the shipyards and other war-related industrial jobs in San Francisco and several East Bay cities, as well as in Los Angeles. Between 1940 and 1950, the black population of San Francisco increased 800 percent, going from 4,846 (0.8 percent of the population) to 43,502 (5.6 percent of the population).[6] In 1940, 3,000 African Americans, nearly two-thirds of San Francisco's black population, lived in the Western Addition, the area immediately west of the city's civic center. The Western Addition also included almost the entire population of Japanese Americans in San Francisco in the area known as Japantown along Geary between Laguna and Fillmore Streets.[7] In 1942, the Western Addition was rapidly emptied as Japanese Americans were forced by Executive Order 9066 to leave their homes for internment camps throughout the country. Arriving black workers began to move into the newly available housing, mainly as renters, concentrating in the Fillmore District, and clubs, hotels, and retail shops owned by blacks in the community replaced the Japanese American businesses. After the war, returning Japanese American internees attempted to move back into the neighborhood, but many were forced to move from the area altogether due to the lack of housing.[8] By 1950, the number of African Americans in the Fillmore had increased to the point that, in the words of Brian Godfrey, "they had fatally ruptured the area's previous ethnic structure, leading to a massive and self-reinforcing 'white flight.' . . . By 1960, the core of the Western Addition was solidly black."[9]

This concentration was not entirely a matter of choice, however. Blacks seeking housing in San Francisco were largely unable to rent or purchase homes in areas other than the Fillmore and Bayview neighborhoods. According to Charles S. Johnson in *The Negro War Worker in San Francisco*, written in 1944, "that a concerted effort is being made by neighborhood groups, merchant associations and improvement clubs to restrict the area of living for Negro families to the present boundaries of the Fillmore district . . . seems fairly evident."[10] Although a forced community, it was a productive and active one. Black-owned businesses, professional services, and community organizations dominated the neighborhood. The number of black churches also increased radically, with full congregations. Describing the Fillmore, former resident Charles Collins recalls:

> I had a complete cadre of African American doctors to take care of my body. We had religious institutions, cultural institutions that gave the community a sense of cohesiveness. We had black lending institutions. All of that stuff instills in a person a tremendous sense of confidence about what could become of you and who you are.[11]

In the decade following the war, conditions of overcrowding and rising unemployment, combined with absentee landlords, a decline in city services such as garbage and policing, and increasing drug use led to further degrading of available housing. And although many attempted to leave the neighborhood and purchase homes in suburban areas, they were again confronted with the racism that had brought them to the Fillmore in the first place. As Douglas Henry Daniels states:

> Racist attitudes, restrictive covenants, and the sudden influx of Black migrants created the ghettos near the San Francisco shipyards at Hunter's Point and along Fillmore Street. . . . After occupying the crowded, dilapidated, or temporary structures, Negroes found it more difficult than other Americans to find suitable housing in desirable locations.[12]

However, there were other enclaves of African Americans in San Francisco, such as the Ingleside District in southwestern San Francisco, and

Hunters Point and the adjacent Bayview District in the southeastern part of the city, which were more than 50 percent black by 1950. While the Fillmore and Bayview/Hunters Point remained low-income areas for the most part, middle-class blacks, working mainly in the recently opened blue-collar, professional, and city employment sectors, formed the community in the Ingleside District after the war.[13]

URBAN RENEWAL

In the same decade, the economy of San Francisco was in a state of flux, "retooling" itself away from wartime production to a professional and financial service–oriented economy, employing workers in what were mainly upper- and middle-class jobs in sectors such as real estate, insurance, retail, and other office work.[14] The shift precipitated a widening of the gap between rich and poor, as lower level jobs moved from the industrial sector into the service sector. It also meant that more middle- and upper-income housing became necessary. This need, combined with the continued loss of tax revenue as property values declined in the Western Addition, encouraged the city of San Francisco to embark on a radical course of urban renewal. To begin the process, the city designated a large portion of the Western Addition, with the Fillmore at its center, a "blight" zone.[15] In project documentation for Project Area 2, the San Francisco Redevelopment Agency defined blight as "residential buildings unfit and unsafe for occupancy; mixed and shifting uses; overcrowded dwelling units; inadequate provision for ventilation, light, sanitation, and open spaces; obsolete platting; economic dislocation; and depressed property values." The existence of blight, it was argued,

> contributed substantially and increasingly to the problems of, and necessitated disproportionate expenditures for preservation of public health and safety, adequate police protection, crime prevention, correction, prosecution and punishment, treatment of juvenile delinquency, fire and accident prevention, and other public services and facilities.[16]

Perhaps a more trenchant definition is offered by Lawrence Friedman, a Stanford University professor of law:

> Finding blight . . . merely means defining an area that cannot effectively fight back, but which is either an eyesore or is well-located for some particular construction that important interests wish to

build. . . . Urban renewal takes sides; it uproots and evicts some for the benefit of others.[17]

In 1949 the U.S. Congress passed the Housing Act, which gave local agencies the authority to use the power of eminent domain to claim buildings in areas the city designated as blighted (defined as having a loss of revenue). In anticipation of the passage of the federal Housing Act, San Francisco created the San Francisco Redevelopment Agency (SFRA) in August 1948, and the city soon applied for and received multiple redevelopment grants. During the term of Mayor Elmer Robinson (1952–1955), the SFRA was largely understaffed and moved slowly on the new projects, but under Mayor George Christopher, the agency changed radically. Initially "wary of massive renewal schemes," he became deeply involved in the reorganization of the agency; as Chester Hartman states:

> Christopher simply could not ignore the urging of the city's corporate representatives, especially at election time. Another factor was the changing face of San Francisco into a "city of color," with an increasing Black, Asian, Latino, and Filipino population. It was becoming apparent that urban renewal could be used to displace the city's minorities and recapture the centrally located residential areas they had inherited after whites moved out, an opportunity not lost on Christopher, who reflected the attitudes of the city's Anglo-European politicians and small businessmen.[18]

In 1959, Mayor Christopher hired M. Justin Herman (the former regional administrator of the Housing and Home Finance Agency, which controlled federal funding for redevelopment) to be the new executive director of the San Francisco Redevelopment Agency, a position he occupied from 1959 to 1971 under Mayors Christopher, John F. Shelley, and Joseph Alioto. Descriptions of Herman vary according to what side of the bulldozer one was on, according to Chester Hartman:

> In the downtown highrise office buildings, banks, and City Hall he was Saint Justin, while in the prisonlike housing projects of Western Addition and the streets of the Mission barrio he was the "white devil." "Negroes and the other victims of a low income generally regard him [Herman] as the arch villain in the black depopulation of the city," wrote the Sun-Reporter, the Fillmore-based newspaper of the city's Black community, in 1965.[19]

A HUD official, quoted in Ira Nowinski's *No Vacancy*, a collection of photographs of former residents of hotels in the downtown district of Yerba Buena displaced by redevelopment, states that "Herman was one of the men responsible for getting urban renewal named 'the federal bulldozer.' . . . He could move rapidly on renewal—demolition or construction—because he was absolutely confident that he was doing what the power structure wanted as far as the poor and the minorities were concerned."[20]

In 1956, the SFRA embarked on the redevelopment of Project Area 1 (A-1) in the Western Addition. The A-1 project goals included widening Geary Street into an eight-lane Geary Boulevard, constructing office buildings and middle-income housing, and building a Japanese Cultural and Trade Center. With the SFRA invoking the power of eminent domain, redevelopment funds were used to purchase homes and buildings, relocate families into "equal or better" housing, and demolish many of the existing structures. Private developers were offered incentives in the form of grants and subsidized loans from the federal government. Most of the new construction was mid- to high-income housing; some units of public housing were also built, but far fewer than were needed. As a result, the community in the Fillmore was scattered, with the population moving into the suburbs across the bay and into housing throughout the city. More than 4,000 families were moved out of the area, although many were given "Certificates of Preference" to return once the project was complete.[21] Most could not afford to move back, however, given the newly inflated values of property and rents in the neighborhood, and thus the certificates were rendered useless. The widening of Geary Boulevard and the construction of a Japan Center acted as "a moat that separated the city's largely Black Fillmore District from its recently reestablished Japanese community and the wealthy enclave of Pacific Heights."[22]

COMMUNITY RESISTANCE TO REDEVELOPMENT

The population of the Fillmore District required a large mobilization effort to defeat what at the time seemed an insurmountable foe: a city seeking to eject black renters and homeowners from their established neighborhood, to cut social services to their population, and to destroy the social fabric of an African American neighborhood that acted politically and socially as a community. Although federal requirements for redevelopment projects required community input, redevelopment in the Western Addition was planned mainly without the community's involvement. Because many believed that the promises made by the SFRA would lead to better housing and improvements to their community, organized resistance to A-1 was either nonexistent or came too late.

With A-1 still incomplete, a plan was submitted in 1964 for a larger area of the Western Addition, encompassing 73 blocks. The project area, named A-2, was outlined roughly as the blocks between Van Ness and Baker Streets and Bush and Grove Streets. Residents of the Fillmore had begun to organize to stop A-1, but they redoubled their efforts to halt A-2. Despite the protests of the fledgling community-based organization Freedom House and other community activists and leaders, the Board of Supervisors unanimously approved the plan in October of 1964. But due to the resistance and repeated calls for input on the project from the residents of A-1 and Freedom House, the project did not start until 1966, much later than originally planned.[23]

Freedom House was started by the Congress of Racial Equality and white activists in 1963. The organization began publishing a newsletter, *A-2 Stand!* aimed at informing the neighborhood residents of their rights as tenants. Freedom House also provided assistance in the form of legal aid and called people together for picket lines. After Freedom House failed to halt A-2 in October 1964, a group of activist white ministers took up the fight in 1966, calling on supporters of Freedom House and going door to door to form the Western Addition Community Organization (WACO). Created to provide the necessary structure to unite the diverse groups affected by the project, WACO formally announced its existence on 21 April 1967. The principal organizers of WACO were the Reverend Tom Dietrich of the Howard Presbyterian Church, the Reverend Dave Hawbecker of the Christ United Presbyterian Church, and the Reverend Ed Smith of St. Cyprian's. The ministers hired a white activist leader named Tom Ramsey to lead WACO.[24]

Black members of WACO, however, "challenged the authority of the white ministers and working class blacks who had directed WACO's early program" and succeeded in driving out Ramsey by the middle of 1967. The core group of activists in WACO consisted of Hannibal Williams, who became the chief spokesman and, by the end of the year, the temporary chairman,[25] Ken and Eva Brown of the Homeowners' Association, and Tenants Union activist Mary Rogers, who saw in WACO the means to resist and fight for her own rights for self-determination:[26]

> The bottom line was to remove all blacks out of the Western Addition, build high-rise and high income apartments, and bring all

the suburbanites to San Francisco. . . . The plan was to move us out. . . . There wasn't anything you could do about it. My position was, I refused to accept that I couldn't stay where I wanted to stay. I refused to go somewhere else because I was black. I decided I wasn't going to move. I wasn't going anywhere until I got good and ready.[27]

Between 1967 and 1968, the tactics of WACO included picketing the SFRA site office, organizing meetings of up to 300 people, and taking the stage at public meetings and hearings to demand input into the agency's project and an increase in the number of subsidized units in the plan. They also sat in front of bulldozers, stopping demolition to halt displacement of tenants.[28] In 1968, WACO, with the aid of the San Francisco Neighborhood Legal Assistance Foundation, filed for an injunction against relocation, demolition, and federal funding in Western Addition A-2 pending a valid relocation plan.[29] In December 1968 a federal judge issued a restraining order against the SFRA until it had a more feasible relocation program. Additionally, through WACO's persistent and angry confrontations with the SFRA, the Western Addition Project Area Committee (WAPAC) was formed in January 1969, becoming the official citizen's advisory group to the project, responsible for reviewing building proposals. WACO dominated the new committee, electing Hannibal Williams to head the board. One of WAPAC's victories included appointing Wilbur Hamilton, an African American from the Fillmore, as the A-2 Project Director. Later, in 1977, Hamilton became executive director of the SFRA under Mayor George Moscone.

The end of the displacement of African Americans and other groups from the Western Addition was in some part due to the efforts of WACO and WAPAC, but it was also due to a larger shift in urban planning policies away from "slum clearance" to preservation of existing structures.[30] Effectively halting redevelopment, however, was President Richard Nixon's 1973 moratorium on all federal housing and community development assistance, and further legislation by President Gerald Ford in 1974.[31] The 1975 election of Moscone, whose campaign promises included an end to the pro-growth era that had led to the new skyline of San Francisco, also signaled a change in the overall redevelopment of the city. On the whole, the era that closed with Moscone's election has come to be seen as a model of the devastation, rather than improvement, that came out of urban renewal projects in the 1950s and 1960s. The SFRA itself acknowledges its past mistakes publicly on its official website with the following admission: "[S]uffice it to say there were numerous problems with the policies and approaches of this period. Among the most fundamental of these problems was the top-down approach to urban planning which characterized these efforts. This approach inevitably led to widespread community dissatisfaction."[32]

PEOPLES TEMPLE IN THE FILLMORE

As early as 1970, while Peoples Temple was still headquartered in Ukiah in Northern California, Jim Jones began leading weekly services in the Ben Franklin Junior High School auditorium on Geary Boulevard in San Francisco. The church members incorporated both San Francisco and Los Angeles into their weekly bus trips, leaving Ukiah on Friday evenings for San Francisco, traveling on to Los Angeles, and returning to Ukiah late Sunday evening. In 1972 the Temple had purchased its San Francisco facility at 1859 Geary Boulevard in the heart of the Fillmore District. The church was near the corner of Fillmore and Geary, in the center of the mainly completed A-1 project. The decision to locate the Temple in the Fillmore rather than in the other predominantly black neighborhood in San Francisco, the Bayview, may have been due to the neighborhood's historic nature, which gave it more political visibility, its proximity to downtown and the civic center of San Francisco, or the availability of real estate due to the recent redevelopment projects. Regardless, the Temple's presence in the Fillmore was seen as being at the heart of an inner-city neighborhood, despite the new concrete and glass structures that had replaced large portions of the neighborhood. This community provided the perfect setting for the Temple's agenda of outreach to the underserved.

The Temple did not engage itself with the local struggle that continued between the SFRA and WAPAC, but it did have communications with the agency throughout its time in San Francisco, and it considered redevelopment plans of its own. As early as 1972, Peoples Temple, through Temple member and attorney Tim Stoen, had contacted the SFRA with a proposal to develop a site as a senior citizens' home.[33] The Temple also looked into purchasing a new site for the church in 1973.[34] In April 1976, Eugene Chaikin, another Temple member and lawyer, sent an offer letter to the SFRA for Parcel A, Lot 707 (the Temple on Geary was located on the same lot), for construction of a lodge, to be developed by Goodlett and Associates. The offer reserved the right of withdrawal, contingent upon the WAPAC's approval.[35] The church's proposal seems to have been abandoned, but it may have been an attempt to create a "mission" in San Francisco to house all Temple members in one place. The idea of the church buying property in A-2 and building communal housing or a senior home was not generally viewed as inappropriate, at least not by the SFRA. Many churches in the A-2 area sponsored projects with developers, adding their name and support to buildings. This proposal and other early communication with the SFRA indicate that the Temple must have been savvy to the agency's inner workings and the potential for projects.

The Temple also came into contact—and conflict—with the SFRA as a tenant. In August of 1974, the Temple had asked to rent a portion of Lot 707 to use for parking. It again applied to the agency, in February 1976, for permission to convert the lot into a play area.[36] In August, the agency sent a notice requesting the Temple to clean up Block 707, which, according to the agency, had become "unsightly, due to accumulation of debris boxes, trash and old vehicles."[37] The agency wrote a much more forceful letter in May 1978. Following this, a letter signed by Temple secretary Jean Brown was sent to Assemblyman Willie Brown, asking for his assistance. The letter does not directly state for what Brown's assistance is sought, but it starts: "Regarding the controversy surrounding the usage of Block 726 and 707 by Peoples Temple Church." More interesting, however, is the following: "Wesley Johnson, Sr. a representative of our coordinating staff and newly appointed member of the WAPAC Board of Directors obtained . . . a duplicate of our file . . . [from the SFRA]."[38] Having a member on the board of WAPAC gives some indication that the Temple realized the power the organization wielded. (Sadly, the last letter in the Peoples Temple archive from the Temple to the SFRA is a plea from surviving members in San Francisco after the events at Jonestown, dated 21 November. The letter requests 90 days to dispose of the enormous supplies amassed for Jonestown and to clean up the Geary site.)[39]

Despite these interactions with the agency, however, Peoples Temple did not address the larger issue of urban renewal with the same energy it devoted to issues such as education and drug rehabilitation, with the exception of a 1977 article in its newspaper, *Peoples Forum,* which addressed the issue of urban renewal in passing, as a platform for its larger call for church involvement in the community to eliminate blight.[40] This somewhat late concern for blight may have come from the recent appointment of Jim Jones to serve as a commissioner to the Housing Authority in 1976. Another 1977 article in *Peoples Forum,* describing Jones' commitment to his new position, states what most in the Western Addition had known for decades: "There are many more applicants for housing than there are vacancies."[41] The Temple hierarchy, though it could not have been unaware of the housing crisis, may have been too insular to realize the enormity of the struggle for affordable housing in the larger community. As Jones became embroiled in big-city politics, however, they could not avoid addressing the issue.

JIM JONES, PEOPLES TEMPLE, AND THE HOUSING AUTHORITY

Jim Jones and the Temple's assistance to many politicians has been well documented.[42] One of Jones' most valued relationships for his own personal advancement, and the advancement of Peoples Temple into the public's awareness, came from his support of Mayor George Moscone. To reward this support, with some pressure from Temple member Mike Cartmell on the Moscone nominating committee, Jones was appointed to the San Francisco Housing Authority, after initially rejecting an offer to serve on the Human Rights Commission. Jones was elected as the chair of the Housing Authority in March 1977. John R. Hall writes:

> Perhaps this was an appropriate appointment for a man who had devoted considerable efforts toward putting a roof over people's heads, albeit under his own organization's auspices. Perhaps that was the point, for two years earlier Jones had already been scheming with Dr. Carlton Goodlett about obtaining a redevelopment project grant to build communal housing for Temple members in the Western Addition.[43]

As a new appointee, Jones and the members of the Temple quickly became involved in one of the largest tenant actions of the redevelopment era, the struggle against eviction of the tenants of the International Hotel.[44]

The International Hotel, located at Kearny and Jackson, was a 100-room residential hotel largely for elderly Chinese and Filipino Americans. When the owner, Four Seas Development Corporation, attempted to evict the tenants, the tenants formed the International Hotel Tenants Association and refused to be relocated. The tenants petitioned the Housing Authority to purchase the building from the Four Seas Corporation and turn the building into public housing.[45] In the 23 December 1976 meeting, Jones gave an eloquent speech on the need to support such groups and the need of the Housing Authority to act on their behalf. The Reverend Cecil Williams of Glide Memorial United Methodist Church, however, had done much more. Addressing the Housing Authority in the next meeting, he stated that he had mobilized a coalition of 65 community groups and organizations, in what could be termed WACO-style activism. According to the minutes for the meeting, Cecil Williams acknowledged the agony of the housing commissioners and the risks, but he felt "nothing is accomplished unless a risk is taken by self-determination." He urged the commission to allow the tenants "to determine the destiny of their lives, to purchase the Hotel they are living in."[46] The Housing Authority voted to acquire the building by invoking eminent domain, but it was unable to secure funding, a problem that plagued the International Hotel tenants throughout the struggle, which ended with the building's demolition.

In January 1977, the tenants were to be served with eviction notices. Large numbers of protesters formed barricades around the building to prevent the evictions, with most protesters coming from Glide Memorial and Peoples Temple.

> Neighborhood, ethnic and church groups (including massive contingents from Reverend Jim Jones's People's [sic] Temple) rallied to prevent the evictions, with demonstrations as large as 5000 people. The political pressure was so intense that Sheriff Richard Hongisto, elected in 1975 by a liberal-gay coalition, at first refused to carry out a court-ordered eviction, for which he served five days in jail.[47]

After Jones' show of public support, however, the tenants of the International Hotel wrote Jones a scathing letter in May of 1977 expressing their disappointment when Jones supported limiting the Tenants Association to only 30 days to meet their obligation to secure funding. Jones must have taken the rebuke hard, as it called him on what had always been one of his major tenets, that he would never "sell out":

> We have known you to champion the interest of poor people. In this meeting [of the Housing Authority] yesterday, we feel you compromised your moral and political principles because of pressure. We can only assume that it was external and unfortunately we feel you buckled under.[48]

The tenants were evicted later that year.

Amid a flurry of bad press and a pending investigation by the San Francisco District Attorney's office, and coinciding with the final days of migration of Peoples Temple members to the Jonestown agricultural mission, Jones resigned from the Housing Authority in August 1977, phoning in his resignation from Guyana.

ANALYSIS

The entrance of Peoples Temple into the Fillmore in the early 1970s followed on the heels of WACO's successful lawsuit in 1968, one of the largest struggles the black community of San Francisco had faced. The WACO suit had forced the African American community into a position of political action to negotiate the difficult space between individuals and large bureaucracies, with churches and their leaders playing a significant supporting role. In the long view, this successful bridging of the space between individuals and their neighborhoods on the one hand, and the large and seemingly inaccessible workings of municipal and federal policy on the other, emerges as perhaps the most radical change brought about in the Fillmore's political and religious cultures through WACO-style activism. John Mollenkopf defines this bridge as "political space," or the space in which urban politicians and administrators are forced to interact with neighborhood activists and their demand for power and input into their community's fate. Often these contenders for power, though successful on a small scale, ultimately lose in the long run in their attempts to change city development.[49]

Peoples Temple, with its emphasis on political activism and service, worked at the edges of this "political space" opened by WACO, providing in some part the representation that the neighborhood required, especially as social services and opportunities for political participation were often withheld and even actively undermined by existing governmental structures. As Hall states:

> In the conventional modern world, relatively powerless individuals, especially those on welfare, confront bureaucratic demands on their own. With Peoples Temple, they could counter corporations and the state with their *own* bureaucracy that could create and process data for members . . . with more of a personal touch. . . . The Temple short-circuited that alienation by establishing an advocate organization that would negotiate the twists and turns of the bureaucratic world. [emphasis in original][50]

The need to mediate between the individual and the bureaucracies that administer the individual's needs, which had so often resulted in the failure of the bureaucracy to meet its obligations (such as the SFRA's failure to find new housing for those it displaced) was met by the Temple and its own organizational structures.

The battles against the SFRA during redevelopment had reinforced the expectation that black churches would step up their political involvement with city, state, and federal politics, addressing a need beyond the spiritual afterlife with increasing frequency and urgency, something Peoples Temple showed a willingness to undertake. Calls were issued by the radical younger generation for unification of the goals of social justice with action on the part of the black churches. In a 13 March 1965 issue of *Fillmore Stand* (formerly *A-2 Stand!*), Pleasant Carson Jr. called upon "Negro ministers" to take a stand and "come out in voice and action, especially action, for the movement and call for your congregation to support and act with present organizations for justice."[51]

This call coincided with a more general shift in the political emphasis of the Civil Rights movement, from issues of political franchise at the national scale to a more direct engagement with issues of economic justice, municipal policy, and social services at the level of the neighborhood. This shift is often explained in terms of generational differences within the movement, presented (perhaps too simplistically) as the difference between an older, liberal generation and a rising generation of young activists from the radical and progressive left. Peoples Temple was situated at this collision between Civil Rights–era activists that had brought the churches into the national political arena and the revolutionaries at the forefront of Black Power, who were seeking to re-establish themselves in the community at a local level. Such a collision mandated the need to shift from the large issues of national consensus building to the local and particular level of the individual. This meant addressing the basic needs of food, housing, jobs, care for the elderly, and education, issues that Peoples Temple highlighted as fundamental to its mission. As Hall states:

> It was into this strain between the congregations of conservative Black churches and the radical popular movements that Jones inserted his ministry. . . . But he also offered a mainstay of Pentecostal practice, faith healing, in an apostolic socialist dispensation.
>
> He put the Black clergy of urban California on the spot. They could hardly criticize a social action ministry without deepening the gulf between themselves and parts of their own congregations, but few of them were prepared to engage in more militant social activism, and the Temple made steady gains.[52]

With its agenda of antiracism, political activism in the form of protest, and the ideals of apostolic socialism, Peoples Temple exemplified what they themselves termed a "human service ministry" in an article entitled "Social Ministry for Social Justice."[53] This mix of traditional Pentecostal practice with radical activism brought into the Temple not

only the dispossessed, but also the intellectual bourgeois black population, who sought to further the strides made in earlier movements.
The Temple's recruitment efforts and its methodology were incredibly
successful, whether through directly drawing members away from
other congregations or through encouraging dual memberships. Between 1972 and the mass exodus of the members of Peoples Temple
members to Guyana in 1977, the Temple managed to move from a
small congregation of approximately 200 to as many as 3,000, consisting of roughly 90 percent African Americans.[54]

The answering of the community's demands for social action and
the reluctance of most other black ministries to meet this demand (a
notable exception was the Reverend Cecil Williams' Glide Memorial
United Methodist Church) gave the Temple the boost it needed to woo
churchgoers, as demonstrated by the extremely high percentage of
blacks from San Francisco among the Temple's new members. Because
the demands of the constituents were largely dictated by the needs of
the urban black community, such as the need for meaning and the
means of achieving self-determination in a racially and economically
unjust society, Peoples Temple became a black institution despite the
white leadership of Jones and the largely white power structure that
ran the church. This combination of political aggressiveness and apos-
tolicism, attempting to meet the need for direct engagement in the
style of WACO and its constituent churches, put the church in a par-
adoxical position with political structures that legislated the scope of
that involvement.

One index of this paradox is the apparent contradiction between
the Temple's outspoken political stance and its lack of interest in joining with other religious and political organizations to meet greater
goals of self-determination through the transformation of local politics. Oddly enough, given the events that in part gave rise to the community's dislocated state and arguably contributed to the Temple's
recruitment success in the Fillmore, the Temple stayed out of housing
politics to a large extent, rarely addressing what must still have been
big issues in the minds of the congregation. This avoidance of the
wider political arena of city housing and urban renewal may perhaps
be attributed to the successes of the Fillmore community in the 1960s
and early 1970s. Also, this terrain for activism was staked out by
WAPAC, a political movement in which the more powerful members
of the Temple may have been uninterested or excluded from becoming
players. There also may have been a lack of knowledge about the issue
on the part of the church bureaucracy, although it is difficult to imag-

ine that the newly recruited members did not have some affiliation with or knowledge of the efforts of WACO or WAPAC. One of the Temple's most steadfast allies, Carlton B. Goodlett, editor of the *Sun-Reporter*, had devoted much of his newspaper's space to the issue throughout the 1960s, and the Reverend Cecil Williams of Glide Memorial United Methodist Church, who often shared the stage with Jones, had worked with Freedom House. It may in some small part be attributed to the dislike between Jones and the Reverend Hannibal Williams, who had headed up most of the protests against redevelopment, although by the late 1970s he no longer held a position of power in WAPAC. Hall reports that Hannibal Williams and Amos Brown "met with other Black leaders in [Brown's] Third Baptist Church in late 1976 to discuss the threat Jones posed to the Black church." The result of the meeting was to redefine membership in the Black Leadership Forum to require that members be an "adult person of African descent."[55]

Whatever the reasons, Peoples Temple mainly addressed issues of drug rehabilitation, medical care, child care, and feeding the hungry, all of which bolstered its standing as an organization committed to meeting the immediate needs of an impoverished community in what the Temple termed "the ghetto." Although it did concern itself with housing issues for the elderly and often assisted individuals with making their rent, the Temple appeared to circumvent housing politics simply by providing housing for its own members, consolidating them in communal dormitories which it purchased or rented. Housing in the Temple's insular world was more geared toward congregating members into communal spaces and consolidating members' assets to benefit the whole than it was to solving the structural impasses that beset the black community around housing issues. This agenda was perhaps Jones' attempt to follow Father Divine's advice, as Carlton B. Goodlett explains:

> Father Divine gave Rev. Jones some tremendous insight into the building of a financial institution, being able to house the people and fulfill their needs in every respect. He came away from Father Divine convinced that the first prerequisite for establishing a viable mission was to have all the people live on the same premises in dormitories.[56]

Taking into account the Temple's utopian inclination, this move toward communalism represented the group's attempts to become a self-supporting, self-sufficient entity, providing for members' needs. As C. Eric Lincoln and Lawrence Mamiya note,

Jones' followers lived in communal houses, while Father Divine called his hostels "heavens," but both leaders required their disciples to contribute their entire economic holdings to the central organization in return for food, shelter, a variable "need-stipend," and the security of inclusion.[57]

For the Temple, political activism to meet the community's demand for housing meant literally to put a roof over peoples' heads; such politics do not have as their intention ownership of the roof. This denial of self-determination in the larger sense—the right to decide where that roof was—may have been seen as a reasonable alternative to the denial of self-determination practiced by the secular world in the form of eminent domain and removal; with the Temple's "rejection" of self-determination, however, came food, health care, and community. The move to Guyana might have encompassed, on the part of the rank and file, both their aspirations for self-determination and their loss of faith in the secular democratic system, with its legal assurances of their rights and systematic denial of those rights. More cynically, it could also be seen in terms of the Temple hierarchy's stake in the move as an extension of such an authoritarian politics of living space.

Ultimately, the Temple may have shied away from the relinquishing of power that bridging political space required. At a certain point for most activist organizations, the bridging comes to require interaction with large government structures not only through standard bureaucratic channels—something the Temple excelled at—but also through the struggle to change those structures and their norms through direct, and often unpopular, confrontation. That confrontation, exemplified by the activists of WACO, may have seemed too aggressive for a church that was so inwardly focused. It also might have been an implicit admission of the control exerted by the state, a control that Jones refused to acknowledge, since he advocated a "take what you can" approach, pitting the congregation against the state and predicting the ultimate failure of the state. The Temple did publicly advocate on many issues, but often was conservative and "safe" in the causes it championed, such as freedom of the press, provision of food, education, and individual rehabilitation, issues that are, politically, uncontested work for a mission-oriented church. The Temple to some extent failed to fully meet the political needs of San Francisco's black community by shying away from full engagement with the city and federal bureaucracies in a transformative way. At the same time, Jones wielded enormous power in local elections.

As a tax-exempt religious organization, it was prohibited from politicking, but the calls from its own community called for political action.

The demands for equal housing and a halt to redevelopment made by WACO and its member churches should not be seen as a small feat—it meant potentially alienating not only constituents of the community but the wealthiest potential patrons in the city that formed the support for urban renewal. But throughout all of the literature of the 1960s and 1970s addressing the issue of redevelopment, the recurring theme is the call for self-determination. Hannibal Williams said it best when he told Mayor John F. Shelley in 1967 that:

> [O]ne thing I'm sure of, somewhere in federal law there must be something about self-determination. It's our right and we're here to get it. We're not begging or asking for anything. It's our right, and we want it.[58]

Ultimately, this definition of self-determination reflects the community's call for agency in the local government, its demand to have a say in its fate, and to act rather than be acted upon. Williams' statement reflects the resistance of the community to having the terms of its existence dictated by others, and an aspiration to the autonomy that redevelopment in San Francisco undermined. Tragically, given the optimism with which Peoples Temple was received by many in the Fillmore District who had suffered through redevelopment, the narrow focus and self-serving politics of the Temple's forays into housing issues, culminating in the emigration from the United States and murders and suicides at Jonestown, in the end substituted one denial of self-determination only by imposing another far more absolute.

NOTES

1. Peter L. Stein, *The Fillmore*. Videorecording (1999), produced by for KQED-TV. Excerpts from the film, along with background material and an extensive bibliography on redevelopment, can be found online at <http://www.pbs.org/kqed/fillmore/>, accessed 11 July 2003.

2. Stein, *The Fillmore*. Excerpts from Williams' interview, including this quote, are available online at <http://www.pbs.org/kqed/fillmore/learning/people/williams.html>, accessed 11 July 2003.

3. Among many others, John R. Hall in *Gone from the Promised Land: Jonestown in American Cultural History* (New Brunswick and London: Transaction Publishers, 1989) and Tim Reiterman with John Jacobs in *Raven: The*

Untold Story of the Rev. Jim Jones and His People (New York: E. P. Dutton, 1982), write on the history of Peoples Temple and Jim Jones and mainly focus on the time period after the Temple purchased their site at 1859 Geary Boulevard.

4. Brian J. Godfrey, *Neighborhoods in Transition: The Making of San Francisco's Ethnic and Nonconformist Communities* (Berkeley: University of California Press, 1988), 95–102.

5. For a more extensive look at the history of African Americans in San Francisco and California, see Douglas Henry Daniels, *Pioneer Urbanites* (Berkeley: University of California Press, 1990), in particular the "Bibliographical Essay," 213–222; and Albert S. Broussard's writings on the subject, most recently "In Search of the Promised Land: African American Migration to San Francisco, 1900–1945" in *Seeking El Dorado: African Americans in California*, ed. Lawrence B. de Graaf, Kevin Mulroy, and Quintard Taylor (Los Angeles: Autry Museum of Western Heritage, in association with University of Washington Press, 2001), 181–209.

6. Godfrey, *Neighborhoods in Transition*, 95–102.

7. Godfrey, *Neighborhoods in Transition*, 95.

8. Godfrey, *Neighborhoods in Transition*, 95.

9. Godfrey, *Neighborhoods in Transition*, 100.

10. Charles S. Johnson, *The Negro War Worker in San Francisco*. Report available at The Bancroft Library, University of California, Berkeley (1944), 29. Quoted in Daniels, *Pioneer Urbanites*, 169.

11. Venise Wagner, "The Fillmore: A Cultural Bridge Endures," *San Francisco Examiner*, 2 August 1999, <http://www.sfgate.com/cgi-bin/article.cgi?file=/examiner/archive/1999/08/02/STYLE1470.dtl>, accessed 11 July 2003.

12. Daniels, *Pioneer Urbanites*, 169.

13. Godfrey, *Neighborhoods in Transition*, 101.

14. Chester Hartman, *The Transformation of San Francisco* (Totowa, N.J.: Rowman and Allanheld, 1984), 2.

15. This is an oversimplification of a much more complex situation that involved city politicians, corporate interests (represented by groups such as the Bay Area Council and Blythe-Zellerbach Committee, and its association, SPUR, the San Francisco Planning and Urban Renewal Association), and federal policies all promoting a "pro-growth" era that would last for decades. A more complete analysis of the intricacies of this effort is available in Hartman, *The Transformation of San Francisco* and John Mollenkopf, *The Contested City* (Princeton, N.J.: Princeton University Press, 1983).

16. San Francisco Redevelopment Agency, *Official Redevelopment Plan for the Western Addition Approved Redevelopment Project, Area A-2* (October 1964, amended 3 August 1970), 3.

17. Ira Nowinski, *No Vacancy: Urban Renewal and the Elderly* (San Francisco: C. Bean Associates, 1979). Quoted in introduction by Catherine Hoover, vii.

18. Hartman, *The Transformation of San Francisco*, 17.

19. Hartman, *The Transformation of San Francisco*, 18. Quote is from Thomas C. Fleming, "San Francisco's land development program," *Sun-Reporter*, 27 November 1965, Editorial.

20. Quoted in Nowinski, *No Vacancy*, vii. Source not cited.

21. Hartman, *The Transformation of San Francisco*, 24.

22. David Habert, "50 Years of Redevelopment," <http://www.spur.org/documents/habert.pdf>, accessed 11 July 2003.

23. See "The Final Hearing on A-2" and "Anatomy of a Sell-out," *A2 Stand!* 1, no. 10 (Oct. 1964): 1–4.

24. Ann Bastian, "The Politics of Participation: A Case Study in Community Organization" (B. A. Thesis, Radcliffe College, 1970), 32–34.

25. Bastian, "The Politics of Participation," 40–41.

26. Mollenkopf, *The Contested City,* 187.

27. Interview in *The Fillmore.* Excerpts available online at <http://www.pbs.org/kqed/fillmore/learning/people/rogers.html>, accessed 11 July 2003.

28. Mollenkopf, *The Contested City,* 188.

29. Hartman, *The Transformation of San Francisco,* 158.

30. Eric C. Y. Fang, "Urban Renewal Revisited: A Design Critique" Available online at <http://www.spur.org/fang.html>.

31. Habert, "50 Years of Redevelopment."

32. San Francisco Redevelopment Agency web site, <http://www.ci.sf.ca.us/sfra/history.html>, accessed 19 July 2002.

33. Tim Stoen to SFRA, 17 February 1972. Peoples Temple Records, California Historical Society, MS 3800/f 92.

34. Gene Suttle memo to William A. Kellar, Area Director WA A-2, 23 August 1973. Peoples Temple Records, California Historical Society, MS 3800/f 92.

35. Eugene Chaikin to Quinton J. McMahon, 12 April 1976. Peoples Temple Records, California Historical Society, MS 3800/f 92.

36. Peoples Temple of the Disciples of Christ to the Redevelopment Agency, 19 February 1976. Peoples Temple Records, California Historical Society, MS 3800/f 92.

37. SFRA to Peoples Temple of the Disciples of Christ, 23 August 1976. Peoples Temple Records, California Historical Society, MS 3800/f 92.

38. Jean Brown to Assemblyman Willie L. Brown Jr., 6 June 1978. Peoples Temple Records, California Historical Society, MS 3800/f 92.

39. Hue Fortson and June Crym, 21 November 1978. Peoples Temple Records, California Historical Society, MS 3800/f 92.

40. "Is There a Way Out of the Trap?" *Peoples Forum* 2, no. 1 (April 1977).

41. "S.F. Housing Chairman Finds Demands Heavy," *Peoples Forum* 2, no. 3 (July 1977): 4.

42. See Hall, *Gone from the Promised Land,* and Reiterman and Jacobs, *Raven.*

43. Hall, *Gone from the Promised Land,* 169.

44. After Jones' appointment, Peoples Temple members flocked to Housing Authority meetings; approximately 40 percent of the visitors to the 9 December 1976 meeting, Jones' first meeting, were Temple members.

45. The Housing Authority, as the administrator of public housing in the city, often found itself the last resort for tenants slated to be relocated by redevelopment; many tenants applied to the Housing Authority to purchase their building in an attempt to stop demolition.

46. San Francisco Housing Authority, Minutes, 23 December 1976, 14.

47. Hartman, *The Transformation of San Francisco,* 234.

48. International Hotel Tenants Association to Reverend Jim Jones, 25 May 1977. Peoples Temple Records, California Historical Society, MS 3800/f 20.

49. Mollenkopf, *The Contested City,* 190–191.

50. Hall, *Gone from the Promised Land,* 95.

51. Pleasant Carson Jr., "Report from the Cleveland Community People's Conference," *Fillmore Stand*, 13 March 1965.

52. Hall, *Gone from the Promised Land*, 70–71.

53. *Peoples Forum* 1, no. 13 (December 1976).

54. Hall, *Gone from the Promised Land*, 72. In a 1976 *San Francisco Chronicle* article, the Temple was reported as having 8,000 members (Julie Smith, "The Unusual Leader of an Unusually Active Church," *San Francisco Chronicle*, 25 April 1976, 2). This number goes as high as 20,000 in 1977. The 90 percent figure comes from Rebecca Moore and Fielding McGehee, personal conversation.

55. Hall, *Gone from the Promised Land*, 162.

56. Carlton B. Goodlett, "Notes on Peoples Temple," in *The Need For A Second Look At Jonestown*, ed. Rebecca Moore and Fielding M. McGehee III (Lewiston, N.Y.: Edwin Mellen Press, 1989).

57. C. Eric Lincoln and Lawrence H. Mamiya, "Daddy Jones and Father Divine: The Cult as Political Religion," in this volume.

58. *San Francisco Chronicle*, 4 May 1967, 2.

6

To Die for the Peoples Temple

Religion and Revolution after Black Power

DUCHESS HARRIS AND ADAM JOHN WATERMAN

Although citizens of the First World commonly think of the 1960s as the decade of youthful rebellion, Civil Rights struggle, pop cultural explosion, and anti-war agitation, for our purposes it is necessary to reassert the overriding significance of Third World anti-colonial revolutions in giving shape to the many popular rebellions of the era and to the global politics of subsequent generations. As Robin D. G. Kelley has pointed out, a vision of global class revolution led by oppressed people of color was "not an outgrowth of the civil rights movement's failures but existed alongside, sometimes in tension with, the movement's main ideas."[3] The anti-colonial movement that swept through Africa and Asia, and that brought socialist governments to power in different locales throughout Latin America, was part and parcel of the geopolitical restructurings of the post-war era, indicative of the political and economic instability of the European powers and of the new non-viability of overt white supremacist or Eurocentric ideologies in the wake of Nazi Aryanism. As it is all too easy to lapse into uncritical readings of this moment in political history, it is important to engage this context of revolutionary change as one borne by the particular, located, social interactions between people. It is a moment in which people, in their daily lives, labor to bring about new social and political relations, grounded in notions of economic equality and racial justice. It is also a moment in which people struggle to understand their relationships to each other and to the forces that are reshaping the world—a moment in which people imagine themselves in global perspective. Such were the labors of subjects throughout the African diaspora as blacks around the world began to imagine themselves in critical relation to each other. It is in these labors of cognitive mapping that we want to situate the work of Peoples Temple.

In this chapter, we assert that the participation of people in Peoples Temple was predicated upon the Temple's attempts to integrate a new cosmology that responded to both the failures and the successes of the Civil Rights and Black Power movements in the United States and to the emerging post-colonial order throughout Africa, Asia, and Latin America. Peoples Temple, as a religious and political project, helped to give meaning to the world that was quickly emerging, and to position collective agency as a lever for progressive change.

We substantiate this argument by examining the multiple forms of meaning and meaning-making in which the Temple was actively engaged. This takes the form of a general examination of the political discourses of leftist organizations in the late 1960s and 1970s, focusing particularly on the work of the Black Panther Party and the contradictions bred of the party's emphasis on personal and communal empowerment in juxtaposition with its conscious development of a "cult of personality" surrounding Huey P. Newton. We then move into a historical analysis of the transformations in the post-war global racial and economic order that were facilitated by, and conducive to, greater black participation in new political spheres. Particularly, we are concerned with the significance of the early 1970s as the historical moment in which post-colonial projects are giving way to neo-colonial enterprises and progressive attempts to dismantle the colonial state are displaced in favor of the hegemony of First World capital. We also examine Jim Jones' use of Black Power rhetoric in his sermons to the Peoples Temple community. We analyze his words for all their suggestive appeal to black people who are actively engaged in a project of making meaning out of the tense and contradictory nature of the historical present, and who are working to project themselves, psychically and socially, into new global concerns. Finally, it is in this context that we consider the salience of Jonestown, Guyana, as both an African diasporic community and as community in practical international solidarity with other cooperative socialist projects for redressing Third World underdevelopment.

CHARTING A NEW PATH:
AFRICAN AMERICANS IN PEOPLES TEMPLE

The ministry of Jim Jones in the mid-1950s was partially a response to the persistence of economic and racial inequality in the midst of post-war First World prosperity. It was similar to the work of the Black Panther Party, of First World black intellectuals in the early 1970s, and of thousands of other ministers, black and white, throughout the United States during the 1950s. It was also partially a response to the emergence of widespread popular protest throughout the American South and in pockets throughout the underdeveloped Third World. In that sense, Jones' perspective was informed from the start by the need to conceive of one's self and one's personal and communal commitments in the broader context of movement building. His crusades against racism in Indianapolis drew him into circles of activists in both the secular and the religious worlds and attracted parishioners who were equally committed to racial justice. Both white and black congregants were drawn into the orbit of a man who promised to integrate the most segregated hours of the week—Sunday morning—and to do so in a manner that promoted other forms of political work and challenges beyond integration.

We would like to suggest that the use of Black Power rhetoric by many members of Peoples Temple in the 1970s expressed a genuine desire to locate themselves and their community in the midst of an emergent global political and religious project. Participants in Peoples Temple, black and white, used the rhetoric of the Black Power movement because it was an available and appealing syntax of revolutionary social and political change. As members of the Temple used this rhetoric, they expanded upon it, challenged it, and appropriated its meaning for use in creative, provocative, and problematic ways. Ultimately, these rhetorical strategies served the members of the Temple to work in a world in which the racial, political, and economic orders were being rapidly reshaped. This is to say that Peoples Temple, as an ever-emergent religious and political project, was directly engaged in an effort to cognitively map the political contradictions and possibilities of the late 1960s and early 1970s.

Jim Jones promoted practical changes, but he also had a vision to share, one that was shaped by black and white participation in the community. That vision ultimately led to more radical forms of commitment and action. The Temple's move from the Midwest to Northern California in 1965 and its relocation to San Francisco in the 1970s represent both a physical and social movement from the margin to the center of the struggle for racial justice in the U.S., just as in 1965 when the most visible sites of struggle moved from the rural South to the urban North.

From the Watts rebellion to the failure of the Southern Christian Leadership Conference to effect housing desegregation in Chicago, the flash points of African American political activism had changed.

Whether consciously or not, Jones and Peoples Temple followed the wave. Urban California would take on greater significance in the years to come, due largely to the sizeable population of non-white racial minorities in California cities. Beyond simply moving to the center of black political activity in the U.S., the relocation of Peoples Temple across the plains also signaled its entrance into a broader coalition of leftist organizations and a new level of visibility in the image-conscious California political milieu.

The move to California and the relationships Jones developed with political figures, official and unofficial, throughout the state did not necessarily entail easy coalitions between leaders. When Peoples Temple entered the California scene, it was involved in a web of local and federal politics that encompassed senior members of the Democratic Party (San Francisco mayor George Moscone accepted the organization and its work on the recommendations of Walter Mondale and Rosalynn Carter) as well as local Black Panther activists. Jones was frequently at odds with these figures, critiquing them in his messages to the Temple. "I'd out freedom-fight [U.S. Representative Ron] Dellums, I out freedom-fight . . . Huey Newton, I out freedom-fight Bobby Seale."[4] Later, speaking of Richard Hatcher, the black mayor of Gary, Indiana, Jones cried: "If these Uncle Tom lackeys can speak this way, you better take note: Things are not going well in the U.S.A."[5] Still, members of Peoples Temple participated in grassroots political activity with members of other progressive organizations in and around the Bay Area. Focusing largely on programs that the Panthers would have termed "survival programs," Temple members contributed to the well-being of poor and working-class racial and ethnic minorities both by staging direct action protests on their behalf and by ministering directly to their needs. Jones himself was appointed chair of the San Francisco Housing Authority, and Temple members worked to support the organization in its more radical aims.[6]

Although this activity itself may not seem to indicate any level of commitment or consciousness of broader intellectual and political visions and projects, the work of the Temple in the Bay Area cannot be divorced from the political education which the members of the group were going through in their dealings with Jim Jones and his leadership cohort. By then Jones had become an obscure socialist thinker, blending elements of atheism, Christianity, Marxism, Leninism, Maoism, and Third World revolutionary rhetoric into a complicated brew of political sentiments. His revolutionary perspective, as confused as it is often described, at the time mirrored the confusion of the left as a whole, as its many organizations struggled to build a unifying perspective that could navigate the changing currents and political fortunes of movements around the world.

THE CULT OF HUEY: THE BLACK PANTHERS
IN THE GLOBAL POLITICAL SPHERE

Clarence Lusane suggests that the processes and political institutions of the 1960s and 1970s provided new opportunities for blacks to participate in a "global civil society." Surely the Black Panther Party must be credited as one of the most significant institutional precursors to the emergence of such a society.[7] While the notion of a global civil society suggests a sort of international hegemony of liberalism that, in the 1960s at least, was out of step with the Panthers' revolutionary program, the Panthers were by and large responsible for the radical reorganization of perspectives among urban communities of black Americans which was necessary to facilitate the imagination of those communities in a diasporic-global community. Huey Newton and the Black Panther Party helped to produce and invigorate a set of leftist discourses, discourses of Black Power that became powerful ways of understanding and organizing one's relationship to the world. In founding Peoples Temple, Jim Jones attempted to occupy similar territories, providing analogous forms of imaginary mapping and direction as he built his movement. In forwarding their ideology, the Panthers built an organizing strategy around notions of personal transformation and revolutionary action that hinged upon young Panthers' identifications with Supreme Servant Huey P. Newton. In this regard, the Panthers propagated a cult of personality that, while thoroughly involved in terms related to genuine desires and programs for political change, could also serve to undermine those same desires and goals. Thus we see not only the rhetoric and discourses of Black Power that would later be expanded upon by members of Peoples Temple, but also an identification with leadership analogous to that between Temple members and Jim Jones.

The story of the Black Panther Party begins in 1965, but for our purposes it is 1970 that demands attention. It was in August 1970 that Huey P. Newton was released from the California State Prison at San Quentin after a three-year incarceration. His release was met with great excitement from both the cadre of Bay Area black community members who had been drawn into the orbit of the party as well as from members of the party throughout the country. During his time in prison, Newton had become the cause célèbre of the Panthers, serving both as an influential ideologue and as a point of imaginary identification—an image and persona that condensed and displayed, in visceral, intimate, immediate form, all that the Panthers stood for in a local and national political terrain. Crowded by a multiplicity of radical voices, nationalist programs, and cultural warriors, the political terrain in which the Panthers found themselves operating was not conducive to organizational longevity. Everyone had an agenda, a manifesto, or a platform; everyone had a particular hook. In the case of the Panthers, however, it was Huey's image, his media presence, that gave the organization its edge. Newton's arrest, his trial, and his jail sentence reflected the insidious and anxiety-ridden power dynamics between black people and local law enforcement in the urban North. These dynamics themselves reflected international shifts in the economic and racial political orders, with the dismantling of the Jim Crow South and anti-colonial movements serving as pretexts for new forms of police repression in the North. Newton, like so many other black people of that time and since, was caught in the web of power that served to discipline all members of urban black communities. But while victimized by the same forms of power that policed the average "brother on the block," Newton refused to become a victim. In prison he remained defiant, strong, and articulate about the structures of racism and class oppression that engineered his situation, and the disciplinary regulation of urban black communities.

Newton's image, as portrayed and purveyed by the party, was intimately bound up in the organization's practical political activity and its platform for black self-determination, as well as in his experiences as a member of the black lumpen of Oakland. These factors infused Newton's image, his visual presence and public persona, with a measure of charismatic power that was key to his success as a political figure and to the party's success in organizing a broad cross-section of black communities throughout the United States. Sharing the very common experiences of police harassment and incarceration bound Newton to the people as much as it bound the people to Newton. In addition, it mattered that he was educated and articulate about the plight of these communities and his comrades and that he could outline concrete strategies he believed would enable black self-determination and revolutionary social change. Unlike many of the cultural nationalist organizations of the day, Newton's work with the Panthers emphasized institution building as much as direct confrontation with authority, and the institutions they envisioned, as well as the revolutionary future they projected, had more to do with the historical present of the United States as the primary representative of global empire than with an imagined history of an idyllic, pre-colonial African past.

The potent image of Newton that came to represent the politics and platform of the Black Panther Party was not an organic product of happenstance, but a consequence of diligent and insightful construction on the part of Panther leadership, as well as the contributions of Newton's constituency. During the three years of Newton's incarceration, the leadership of the party, headed by Bobby Seale, Eldridge Cleaver, and David Hilliard, used the image of Huey Newton as a means of organizing party memberships from coast to coast. While the Panthers emerged in 1966 as a relatively small group designed to monitor the local police of Oakland, after Newton's arrest the party went national, sponsoring forums and meetings in cities across the country. By and large, these meetings were organized as informational sessions, teach-ins designed to raise consciousness about the situation of "political prisoner" Huey P. Newton. More than a leader, he was the ideological engine of the Black Panthers personified. Newton as a person influenced the development of party strategies and agendas; Newton as a media representation served to weave together a diversity of communities into a broad, well-coordinated political constituency.

On a certain level, the image of Newton produced by the party was a rhetorical device on the order of the revolutionary Maoist rhetoric they utilized: both had a certain flash and function, but were limited in their ultimate utility. An example of this problem emerged at the Revolutionary Peoples Constitutional Convention immediately after Newton left prison. While Newton felt strongly about the need for revolutionary struggle, he was dismayed to find, upon leaving prison, that the membership of the party was largely made up of young people who were attracted to its radical, Red Book poetics— the Maoist language of power and guns, the "pigs" and the people. These youth, Newton felt, did not fully realize the implications of their words, nor did they comprehend the varieties of struggle, the need to think pre-emptively about the defense of black communities, and the impact of such words on non-Panthers in the black community.[8] As Newton found the rhetoric of the party difficult to bear, so did he find his persona equally cumbersome. Still, he found ample opportunity to use both to his advantage, and in seemingly uncritical ways. The famous portrait of Newton sitting on a large, throne-like wicker chair, fully uniformed, with a gun in one hand and a spear in the other, was as bombastic a visual device as the rhetorical hyperbole in Mao's adage that "all power comes from the barrel of a gun." And Newton's self-assumption of the title "Supreme Servant of the People" speaks to the uncomfortable paradox between his desire to register both as a critical leader in the struggle and as a powerfully visible media presence.

These ambivalences aside, the images of Newton that circulated through various realms of media effectively brought together a diverse array of black people from urban communities throughout the country. In the cult of images, Newton functioned as a figure of saint-like devotion, a point of identification for those black people who were working to understand their position in the emergent post-war, post-colonial, post–Jim Crow order. Thus, as a media text, Newton effectively served as a site at which different types of imagination came together to produce a stunningly strong set of allegiances to individuals and to ideological doctrines.

THE CULT OF JIM JONES: BLACK PANTHER RHETORIC WITHIN PEOPLES TEMPLE

Jim Jones tapped some of the same sources of political and cultural identity that Huey Newton did, the same historical references to slavery as well as the more contemporary days of Jim Crow laws, to draw in the more politically active segment of the Bay Area's population, both black and white. He also used a number of vehicles to attract blacks into Peoples Temple, including the cadences and language of the black preacher, faith-healings, and health and community services for California's urban indigent populations. Indeed, a typical Jones sermon during a Temple service—which, true to the black style of preaching, was constrained neither by time nor form—included a little bit of all of these elements, shifting seamlessly between the religious and the political, between his announcements of free medical services and the demonstrations of his healing powers.

Jones borrowed heavily from Black Panther rhetoric. American society was so racist, so capitalistic, so fascistic, and so corrupt, Jones said, that only a socialist revolution would cleanse it.[9] He appropriated Mao's adage that political power can come only through the barrel of a gun,[10] and drilled it into the heads of his followers.[11] At other times, however, Jones insisted that the revolution would be nonviolent, either by following the teachings of Christ or by following Christ as he now stood before the congregation in the flesh of Jim Jones.[12] Taking the thought to its logical conclusion, he eventually equated the people of the church as the saved souls of the revolution, and described the rest of society as fallen. "If you're born in this church, this socialist revolution, you're not born in sin. If you're born in capitalist America, racist America, fascist America, then you're born in sin. But if you're born in socialism, you're not born in sin."[13]

Nevertheless, Jones' profession as a minister, People Temple's status as a legitimate political force, and the members' daily interactions with the general public gave the Temple a place in Bay Area society that the Panthers never had, and Jones was careful to acknowledge that. He periodically cited incidents of police brutality in his indictment of fascist America, but his few references to cops as "pigs" were limited to those who were white, racist, and members of the Ku Klux Klan in faraway cities like Chicago, Philadelphia, and flash points of the South.[14] In Ukiah, San Francisco, and other places where the Temple located its members, Jones spoke of his positive relations with the police, his empathy for the working cop on the beat, and his pride when police officers attended his services.[15] The church donated money to families of policemen killed in the line of duty and gave bulletproof vests to officers in Ukiah.[16] According to some Temple apostates, however, Jones had ulterior motives for forming and maintaining good relationships with local police forces. "Jim always said he had an in with the police," a *New York Times* reporter quoted Deanna Mertle as saying, "so we thought going to the police would be suicide."[17]

Although Jones used Black Panther rhetoric and modeled himself after Panther leaders—and even as he attacked the forces within society who would dare to attack those leaders—he was not above criticizing the same leaders over their tactics, their lifestyle,[18] or his perceptions of their disregard of him: "I was willing to go to Cuba to help Huey Newton, [but] he didn't give a fuck, he certainly didn't show any appreciation."[19]

Newton and other Panther leaders might well have dismissed Jim Jones and seen little purpose in forming any alliances with Peoples Temple. In the crucible of the times, Jones would have been seen first for his whiteness, his social status, and his influence in mainstream political circles; with those handicaps, the Panthers would certainly never have gotten around to seeing Jones as Jones saw himself. In addition, the same new members of the Black Panther Party who troubled Newton—those who quoted Mao and threw their fists in the air and brandished their guns with cries of protest, those who had not endured the consequences of the words and the guns with hard jail time—were similar to the people in the pews and, more importantly, in the pulpit at Temple services. Temple members might have stood in court with their brothers and sisters who got in trouble with the law, but despite his claims of persecution, Jones' arrest record apparently consisted of one morals charge, which was quickly dropped.

There was a more fundamental difference between Huey Newton and Jim Jones, though. Newton tried to eschew his cult-of-personality status. Jones created his, developed his, maintained his, proclaimed his, reveled in his.[20] He would acknowledge this at times, but he would immediately add that the only way he could lead his followers to socialism was to model the example.

This model was flawed with troubling complexities, however. He described himself in various addresses as acting for Christ the Revolutionary, as being the returned Christ to bring Socialism, and as not being a man standing before his people, but as the Principle of Socialism itself.[21] Those descriptions imply perfection, and so he was, at least whenever he spoke about socialism. As a result, when he defined socialism for the people or cited examples of socialist behavior or thinking, he was speaking with the ultimate authority. His humanness, with its evolving frailties and passions and demands and stresses, allowed him to create new definitions of socialism as he went along, and thereby gave that ultimate authority the illusive quality of inconsistency. The true socialist revolutionary did whatever Jim Jones said *he* would do at that moment, facing those circumstances, with his purposes.

There may be no better example of this than in the concept of "revolutionary suicide," which Huey Newton articulated and developed with a consistent theme: the revolutionary struggles with the knowledge that his actions may lead to his death at the hands of the oppressor, but with the hope that those same actions will lead others to take up his banner and go on to victory. As Newton used it, the term emphasizes revolution over death.

For Jim Jones, "revolutionary suicide" meant any one of a number of things: dying while fighting for their cause, i.e., Newton's sense of the term; committing suicide so the Temple's enemies wouldn't get them and torture their babies and return the seniors to live in unspeakable conditions in the United States; committing suicide so they wouldn't have to fight their black brothers on the Guyana Defense Force who might be attacking them; committing suicide rather than bring dishonor to the concept of socialism; committing suicide as an alternative to "go[ing] out and start[ing] a fucking war"; or, as he said in the final minute of the death tape, "protesting the conditions of an inhumane world."[22] In all these uses, Jones emphasized the stark finality of death over fluid definitions of what constituted a revolution.

Indeed, it is only on the subject of death that Jones retained any sense of consistency. Whether he spoke of his own sense of *Weltschmerz*,[23] his own unwavering commitment to defend his followers,[24] his followers' commitment to revolutionary suicide, or the inevitable destruction of the earth after "the ultimate horror of nuclear war,"[25] his personal vision was one of apocalypse. It was only on those occasions when that vision included a political element that he intoned the words—and distorted the meaning—of Newton's "revolutionary suicide."

DISCOURSES ON POST-COLONIALISM: BLACK AMERICAN RESPONSES TO THIRD WORLD LIBERATION

[THE] COLONIAL ENTERPRISE IS TO THE MODERN WORLD WHAT ROMAN IMPERIALISM WAS TO THE ANCIENT WORLD: THE PRELUDE TO DISASTER AND THE FORERUNNER OF CATASTROPHE. COME, NOW! THE INDIANS MASSACRED, THE MOSLEM WORLD DRAINED OF ITSELF, THE CHINESE WORLD DEFILED AND PERVERTED FOR A GOOD CENTURY; THE NEGRO WORLD DISQUALIFIED; MIGHTY VOICES STILLED FOREVER; HOMES SCATTERED TO THE WIND; ALL THIS WRECKAGE, ALL THIS WASTE, HUMANITY REDUCED TO A MONOLOGUE, AND YOU THINK ALL THAT DOES NOT HAVE ITS PRICE? THE TRUTH IS THAT THIS POLICY *CANNOT BUT BRING ABOUT THE RUIN OF EUROPE ITSELF,* AND THAT EUROPE, IF IT IS NOT CAREFUL, WILL PERISH FROM THE VOID IT HAS CREATED AROUND ITSELF [EMPHASIS IN ORIGINAL].

—AIMÉ CÉSAIRE[26]

THE CUBA OF THE AGE OF FIDEL CASTRO IS SO CLOSE TO MISSISSIPPI, GEORGIA, ET AL., THAT IT ALMOST BECAME PART OF THE SLAVE EMPIRE OF THE SOUTH JUST PRIOR TO THE CIVIL WAR. THIS ABORTIVE ATTEMPT ON THE PART OF THE SLAVE-HOLDING ADVENTURERS TO CAPTURE CUBA IS NOT COMMONLY KNOWN IN THE GENERAL TRADITION OF AMERICAN FOLKLORE ABOUT SLAVERY. IF CUBA HAD BEEN ANNEXED WHEN SEVERAL SOUTHERN AMERICAN EXPEDITIONS TRIED TO LAND THERE, IT WOULD HAVE BEEN PART OF THE U.S. AT THE END OF THE CIVIL WAR. IN THAT CASE THE CUBAN AGRARIAN QUESTION WOULD HAVE DEVELOPED ALONG THE SAME LINES AS THE AGRARIAN PROBLEM IN THE SOUTH AND THERE WOULD HAVE BEEN NO AGRARIAN REVOLUTIONARY REFORMS AS HAVE BEEN CARRIED OUT UNDER CASTRO.

—HAROLD CRUSE[27]

Although Third World liberation movements shook the colonial world in the 1960s, the heritage of such movements was in the work of previous generations of black Atlantic intellectuals and activists who had begun to chart the path toward a post-colonial future. Intellectuals like Césaire provided the context for the intellectuals of the anti-colonial movement, many of whom struggled to understand the complexities of the present and its relationship to the past in order to avoid certain pitfalls in the future. Radical internationalists W. E. B. Du Bois and C.L.R. James also provided critical insights based in both intellectual activity and political activism—both had worked to establish analytic and political trends that redescribed the nature of the relationship between Africa, Europe, the Americas, and political economic power. Harold Cruse, watching and reading in the United States during the late 1950s and early 1960s, went on to use the perspectives that emerged from the movements of the Third World—and from intellectuals like Césaire and Frantz Fanon—as a means of positioning the black populations of the U.S. in an international historical and political perspective. In addition to Cruse's writing, 1960s community leaders brought the situation of African Americans into a discussion of global politics, as Malcolm X did with his Organization of Afro-American Unity (OAAU). Immediately prior to his assassination, Malcolm X was working to petition the United Nations to investigate the historical human rights violations of blacks in the United States. Although left largely unrealized after Malcolm X's death, the program of the OAAU was enormously influential in shaping the work of the Panthers in their earliest incarnation.

Cruse's work was influential in shaping early Panther ideology as well. During their time at Merritt College, Huey Newton and Bobby Seale participated in the Revolutionary Action Movement (RAM). RAM used Cruse's essays on international politics as a means of educating a young generation of activists into awareness of domestic issues in relation to international political trends. Crucially, RAM emphasized, and Newton and Seale learned, that black American communities were domestic colonies of the United States government and that, as such, they could not be liberated by civil rights reforms, but only by revolutionary struggles analogous to those occurring throughout the Third World. Following Fanon, Cruse contended that it was the lumpen proletariat of these colonies—the people that Newton and Seale would later call "the brothers on the block"—that would lead the anti-colonial revolution in the United States. As this perspective resonated throughout the anti-colonial struggle and was drawn into Panther thought, it indicated the extent to which Third World liberation was working in and against the politics of First World Marxists who believed the lumpen to be too conservative a group to ever articulate itself as a historical-political force. This difference does not so much indicate a break between Marxism and Third World liberation, but illustrates the way in which anti-colonial politics were built out of contending visions. For Fanon, Cruse, Newton, Seale, and their fellow activists, the lumpen constituted an underdeveloped historical re-source—a population that was bound to nobody and nothing, and that could be directed toward progressive ends given proper organization. In this instance, the Panthers' commitment to organizing the lumpen proletariat provided one of their most salient conceptual connections to Third World liberation struggles.

The Panthers not only borrowed organizational strategies from Third World movements, they also borrowed other forms of vision and direction. As Kathleen Neal Cleaver notes, the demands that the party set forth in the original ten-point platform were not that different from the demands articulated by the Kenya Land and Freedom Army, known as the Mau Mau. "[W]hat did [the Mau Mau] ask for? They wanted self-government. They wanted to get rid of foreigners. They wanted an end to the trial of criminal and murder cases by the Europeans. . . . [The Panthers] insisted on power to determine our destiny, full employment, decent education, and an end to police brutality."[28] Cleaver tells only one side of the story here and neglects to address how significant these demands were in the context of a socialist ideology. These were not components of liberal reform, but elements of a program that questioned the hyper-development of certain communities at the cost of the underdevelopment of others, and a critique of attendant notions of inequality and injustice. In addition to borrowing significant practical points from Third World movements, the Panthers expanded upon ideological perspectives that would enable them and their membership to understand the conditions of their lives in the United States and to imagine *and bring about* a different future. Such intellectual work was carried out in a social context, in one important instance, at the Revolutionary Peoples Constitutional Convention (RPCC) of 1970.

The RPCC had been a long-term Panther project, the meaning and fortunes of which shifted as the political context of the leftist movement in the U.S. changed. Nonetheless, in the early 1970s the RPCC was envisioned as a forum in which many oppressed and activist people from around the United States could meet and begin to articulate an alternative social and political vision in the form of a revolutionary constitution. The conference opened with an address by Huey Newton—recently released from prison—and featured a working group on international relations that positioned the U.S. struggle in the context of other Third World struggles.[29]

In his address, Newton outlined a unique contribution to international revolutionary thought—the theoretical practice of revolutionary intercommunalism. He argued that capitalist expansion over the course of time had eroded the sovereignty of all nation-states. As the foremost capitalist country in the world, the United States and its financial institutions had entered into a new imperial phase in which its funds directly dictated policy in many parts of the world. Through these processes, Newton argued, all the countries of the world were now functionally colonies of the U.S. Countries could no longer be discussed as sovereign entities protected by a patrolled and impermeable border, but only as communities open to all who had an interest in the movement and expansion of capital, with attendant notions of development or underdevelopment. In order to alleviate the conditions of this historical development, Newton argued, it was necessary for the community-colonies of new American imperialism to bind together in a wave of solidarity he described as revolutionary intercommunalism.

Newton's ideas, emerging at a historical juncture immediately following broad decolonization, were a salient cautionary note, an important reminder that decolonization was not the end of struggle, and that it was jeopardized by the machinations of U.S. capital. In many ways, Newton simply reconfirmed a point that Césaire had made 20 years earlier when he argued that the colonies of the world should not look to the U.S. as a liberatory power, because the U.S. was poised to become the superpower of all imperialist superpowers.

PEOPLES TEMPLE AND POST-COLONIAL DISCOURSE

Jim Jones held many of these same beliefs, but his analysis was much less sophisticated, indeed to the point of being one-dimensional. If the United States government supported a regime, he opposed it; conversely, if the U.S. supplied an existing government with weapons to put down an insurgency, then God and Peoples Temple were on the side of the rebels. He castigated the white minority governments in Rhodesia and South Africa,[30] savaged the American role in the assassination of President Salvador Allende of Chile,[31] and catalogued the CIA's coups around the world.[32]

Similarly, according to Jones, communist countries contained perfect societies:

> There [is] no need to operate on anyone in China. . . . Now they've got nuclear reactors. Now they have modern jets. They have a perpetual pump. They have synthetic insulin. . . . The Chinese have the only country in the world that has a synthetic insulin that's not made from [animals] dying. No animal has to die to give the Chinese

people insulin. But more than that, in 20 years, China has stopped all violence. They only had seven murders all last year, and we have more than that in San Francisco on Friday night.[33]

But the communists don't get mentally ill so they don't have any psychiatrists. That's the truth. China, it's an unknown profession. They just don't have any.[34]

The uncritical acceptance of communist societies, coupled with Jones' dependence upon the Soviet Union's official media agency Tass as his primary source for news, especially after the Temple's migration to Guyana, blinded him to Soviet hegemony and use of client states in its war of brinksmanship with the West. Struggles against Soviet-supported regimes and governments—whether those struggles originated from outside forces or grassroots dissident groups within—were undoubtedly financed and armed by the CIA. The only difference of opinion with the USSR he voiced regarded its treatment—the ouster, vilification, and purging—of Josef Stalin, whom Jones considered the great defender of the Soviet state, especially during his courageous stand against the Nazis in Stalingrad. "You're never gonna make me dislike that man, no matter how many tales you tell me."[35]

Much of Jones' political analysis was also transitory, influenced by one day's headlines from the Tass news agency, supplanted by the next day's headlines, renewed when news of a crisis flared a second time. At the same time, he recognized the opportunities to make a political point to the Jonestown community when a story presented a parallel object lesson. In May 1978, after reading an item about the radical black group MOVE, which had been in a house in Philadelphia under police siege for 12 months, he said, "That gives some point of what we could do if anyone was threatening our internal freedom here. We've certainly got a better capacity to resist, and more bodies and more arms, although we are not offensive in our design, we do not believe in violence. . . . But we will protect our freedom. Obviously, we will fight for our freedom."[36]

But if Jones' political message was predictable and repetitious, to the point of being simplistic, it was deliberately so. One recurring theme in address after address was that "two out of three babies are going to bed hungry tonight."[37] While the problem he described was worldwide, his specific solutions were not. Instead, they were local; more specifically, they were the programs initiated and administered by the church to meet the needs of its members. Jones could condemn the world for its inability—or lack of political will—to feed the starving masses, but in Peoples Temple, no one went hungry.

In this way, the political analysis itself was decidedly secondary to greater goals: to attract people to the church, to build the Temple as a strong institution, to maintain loyalty, to establish a community where Jones' followers could live apart from American society. In short, the goal was to create a utopian society that would correct the failings of the country from which they emigrated.

This, then, is the basic difference between the Black Panther Party and Peoples Temple. The Panthers fought the revolution on the streets of Oakland, Watts, Harlem, Detroit, and Chicago, to bring about a better life for black people where they were. Peoples Temple had the opportunity to broaden its base to include black activist groups—even if not the Panthers themselves—as well as students, unions, and community associations, but it didn't. Indeed, as Rebecca Moore points out, "A more ideologically correct, or consistently leftist, position would have been to turn outward beyond the group's boundaries. . . . Under Jones' guidance, however, the group turned inward, and tried to establish the new society from within."[38]

THE POLITICAL SIGNIFICANCE OF JONESTOWN, GUYANA

Jonestown, the Peoples Temple's experiment in cooperative, communal living in the jungles of Guyana, was founded in 1974, less than ten years after the group established itself in California. The decision to develop the Peoples Temple Agricultural Project in Jonestown did not necessarily represent a rejection of the exigencies of politics or engagement with the political milieu of the United States. Instead, it provided a concrete example of the Temple's mission, a place where theory was put into practice in the service of an agenda for broad political change. The decision to participate in the building of Jonestown itself follows a long history of utopian communities in the U.S.—a history that is as marked by the glimmer of potential as by the pall of failure.

Jonestown, Guyana, however, was not an ideologically isolated or unconsidered endeavor. While the distance between Jonestown and urban Guyana is analogous to the distance between nineteenth-century utopias and the urban U.S., Jonestown was planned as a means of participating in the project of cooperative socialism with which elements of the Guyanese government were engaged.

In the late 1960s, Guyana wrote a new constitution that proclaimed itself a cooperative socialist state, one devoted to the cultivation of equitable economic development in the service of racial justice. Cooperative socialism was itself a bold idea, one that emerged as a consequence of the work of diasporan black intellectuals like Walter Rodney, a Caribbean intellectual engaged in politics throughout the black Atlantic world. After Rodney was forced out of Jamaica during his late twenties, he settled in Guyana and moved throughout the African diaspora. Observing anti-colonial movements in Africa, Asia, and the Caribbean, Rodney came to the conclusion that Third World nations could not disarticulate themselves from the political dominance of the First World without first pursuing a course of economic development—along capitalist lines—into national self-sufficiency. In his classic text *How Europe Underdeveloped Africa,* Rodney argued that 500 years of European exploitation had so thoroughly drained African nations of their natural resources that even post-colonial African nations would remain underdeveloped as long as they pursued economic paths that were shaped during colonialism and imperialism.[39] Rodney's solution was a radically Leninist one—to reclaim the means of production from foreign owners and set those means to work producing surplus that could be reinvested into national development.

Throughout his life, Rodney's work remained a sophisticated reinterpretation of the post-colonial period and the policy measures necessary to manage the impact of the new global reordering. In moving to Jonestown, the members of Peoples Temple, black and white, found themselves working in and on Rodney's vision, sharing in its assumptions, even as they challenged some of its prescriptions. Jonestown was, if anything, an experiment in social and political development along cooperative socialist lines—an attempt to develop the land and apparatuses of economy in support of communal development. It was, among other things, the place in which people found themselves engaged, most significantly and concretely, in the processes of both symbolic and material production outside the racial capitalist economy—a place where they constructed a vision and mapped their relationship to the social and political world as they tilled the soil and planted their seeds, as they erected their homes.

Jones' choice of Guyana—even the location of Jonestown within Guyana—reflects his own political shrewdness and sophistication. The Temple leader sought to establish his community—what he called the "Promised Land"[40]—in a country that would embrace his political views. Apart from Cuba, a migration to which would have created problems for the U.S. government, the Cuban government, and Jones himself, the only country in the Western Hemisphere which met his political criteria was Guyana, the self-described cooperative socialist republic.

The former British colony on the north coast of South America had other advantages as well. The people speak English. The country has a large black population. The climate and the physical surroundings of the Northwest District are reminiscent, although exaggeratedly so, of the Southern and border states in which many Temple members had been born and raised.

The arrangement to lease twenty-five thousand acres of jungle to an American religious group also benefited the government of Prime Minister Forbes Burnham and his political party, the Peoples National Congress. The heavily jungled area of the Northwest District had been a subject of a longstanding border dispute with Venezuela to the west. By allowing the Temple to establish its new home there, the Guyanese government was making a firm claim to the area and was backing up that claim by involving American citizens on its side of the dispute. If Venezuela decided to challenge the claim, it would suddenly and unexpectedly find itself fighting the interests of a superpower.

Jones knew who his patron was, and he made sure his followers did too. Government officials who visited the project were always treated well and always gave glowing reports of what they saw. When Jones voiced criticism of a Guyanese political party, it was of the opposition, the Peoples Progressive Party led by Cheddi Jagan. And, since the PPP was more pro-communist than Burnham's PNC, Jones was placing his political fortune with the party with better ties to the U.S. government. For both Jones and Burnham, then, and despite their rhetoric to the contrary, the United States loomed in the background of their negotiations as the ultimate protector for each of them.

RELIGION AND REVOLUTION AFTER BLACK POWER

In this chapter we have tried to address why African Americans would be attracted to Peoples Temple (which was perceived as a white movement) and why they would follow Jim Jones (a white man). As stated earlier, black congregants were enamored of a man who promised from the start to promote racial healing while encouraging political work that a black community suffering from post-traumatic Watts syndrome could appreciate. Any reconsideration of Peoples Temple must take the relation of religion and ideology very seriously because of the Temple's function as both a religious and political vehicle. Even if one is inclined to maintain separate understandings of religion and ideology, one cannot ignore the need to think of these phenomena in tandem where the Temple is concerned. Temple members were encouraged, if not required, to participate in traditions of social and political activism beneficial to their own group and to the broader concerns of the progressive left in and around the San Francisco Bay area in the 1960s and 1970s. Such political participation was crucial to Temple members' sense of belonging in the Temple community. It contributed to a powerful sense of collective destiny. This destiny called for making the ultimate self-sacrifice: dying together to protest the conditions of an inhumane world.

In Peoples Temple, religious commitment was a close associate of political consciousness. It is difficult, if not impossible, to consider the legacy and meaning of the Temple as a religious organization outside of its function as a political body. In their deaths, as well as in their lives, Peoples Temple members saw little distinction between the personal and the political or between religion and revolution.

NOTES

1. Huey Newton, *Revolutionary Suicide* (New York: Writers and Readers Publishing, 1973), 7.
2. U.S. FBI Peoples Temple Recording, Q 042. Transcript available on *Alternative Considerations of Jonestown and Peoples Temple*, <http://jonestown.sdsu.edu>, accessed 11 July 2003. All tapes marked "Q" come from the FBI.
3. Robin D. G. Kelley, *Freedom Dreams: The Black Radical Imagination* (Boston: Beacon Press, 2002), 62
4. Q 1059 Part 3.
5. Q 235.
6. Rebecca Moore, *A Sympathetic History of Jonestown: The Moore Family Involvement in Peoples Temple* (Lewiston, N.Y.: Edwin Mellen Press), 170–172.
7. Clarence Lusane, *Race in the Global Era: African Americans at the Millennium* (Boston: South End Press, 1977), 217.
8. Duchess Harris and Adam J. Waterman, "Babylon Is Burning: Race, Gender, and Sexuality at the Revolutionary People's Constitutional Convention," *The Journal of Intergroup Relations* 27, no. 2 (Summer 2000): 17–33.
9. Q 284, Q 952, and Q 1059 Part 5.
10. See for example Q 235, Q 599, and Q 638.
11. Q 242 and Q 805.
12. See especially Q 612, Q 1057 Part 5, Q 1058 Part 2, Q 1059 Part 1, and Q 1059 Part 4.
13. Q 1053 Part 4.
14. For example, Q 242 and Q 384.
15. For example, Q 162, Q 612, Q 686, and Q 1059 Part 3.
16. See Q 612a and Q 1058 Part 3.
17. Q 1058 Part 3.
18. See Q 1058 Part 3, and Q 1059 Part 3.
19. Q 595.
20. From Q 135: "If I'm the only socialist alive, then I'll die a socialist. I hardly think that's true, that I'm the only one, but I know one thing. I've not found any better one. No, no, not one." And from Q 1059 Part 3: "You got

nothing better than me. You haven't got anything as good as me. You haven't got anything one-tenth as good."

21. David Chidester, *Salvation and Suicide: An Interpretation of Jim Jones, the Peoples Temple, and Jonestown* (Bloomington: Indiana University Press, 1991), 56–59, 73–77.

22. Q 042, Q 599, Q 637, Q 639, and Q 757.

23. For example: "I could die tonight, then I'd be out of my misery. But [that would mean] the death of the movement." Q 757.

24. For example, Q 635, Q 807, and Q 1059 Part 1.

25. See Q 049a, Q 235, Q 284, Q 932, and Q 1059 Part 5.

26. Aimé Césaire, *Discourse on Colonialism* (New York: Monthly Review Press, 1950), 64.

27. Harold Cruse, "A Negro Looks at Cuba," in *The Essential Harold Cruse: A Reader*, ed. William Jelani Cobb (New York: Palgrave, 2002), 8.

28. Kathleen Cleaver, "Women, Power, and Revolution," in *Liberation, Imagination, and the Black Panther Party*, ed. Kathleen Cleaver and George Katsiaficas (New York and London: Routledge, 2002), 127.

29. "Revolutionary People's Constitutional Convention Philadelphia Workshop Reports," reprinted in Cleaver and Katsiaficas, *Liberation, Imagination, and the Black Panther Party*, 289.

30. See Q 162, Q 242, Q 323, and Q 741.

31. See Q 956 and Q 1059 Part 5.

32. For example, Q 320, Q 353, and Q 599.

33. Q 1053, Part 4.

34. Q 639.

35. Q 161.

36. Q 284.

37. For example, Q 134, Q 569, Q 630, Q 678, and Q 743.

38. Rebecca Moore, *In Defense of Peoples Temple and Other Essays* (Lewiston, N.Y.: Edwin Mellen Press, 1988), 164.

39. Walter Rodney, *How Europe Underdeveloped Africa* (Washington, D.C.: Howard University Press, 1970).

40. See Q 612a, Q 953, Q 1058 Part 1, and Q 1059 Part 5.

7

Jim Jones and Black Worship Traditions

MILMON F. HARRISON

Decades after its tragic end, the Peoples Temple movement remains a singular moment in American religious history. But one of the things that still seems to have been overlooked, or forgotten, in our subsequent attempts to make sense of this phenomenon and the events of November 1978 is that its membership was overwhelmingly African American. As Rebecca Moore writes in this volume, 70 percent of the residents of Jonestown were black, while 90 percent of the membership in California may have been African American. These were particularly women, children, and the elderly. While whites, including working-class families who migrated from Indiana to California, and young, middle-class professionals who joined in the Golden State, made up a portion of membership, urban blacks constituted by far the largest group of members.

A commonly asked question when considering the numbers of people who were attracted to Jim Jones, the white charismatic leader—an attraction and subsequent relationship that ultimately led many to their deaths—is "what type of person would follow a madman like Jim Jones?" The suggestion is that only a particular personality type, one that is weak or with low self-esteem for example, or the socially, politically, or economically marginalized—the disinherited—would find succor and compensation in a religious movement like Peoples Temple. This chapter approaches the question of Jim Jones' and the Peoples Temple movement's appeal, particularly for its African American members, from a slightly different perspective. It addresses the issue of how certain elements of the traditional black worship style were drawn upon and used by Jones as part of the services in such a way as to make the experience *resonate* with the large numbers of African Americans who participated in and helped shape them. It also locates the presence and privileged position of those elements of black worship traditions squarely within the context of Jim Jones' leadership role in the worship setting and his defining and reinforcing the range of acceptable expressive norms.[2]

JIM JONES' PERSONAL AND RELIGIOUS BACKGROUND

The specific details of Jim Jones' personal and spiritual history have been well documented elsewhere, so I will not reiterate them here.[3] However, I do think it important to point out how certain aspects of his life before Peoples Temple may have served to shape his worldview and give him access to culturally specific modes of expression that would later lead him to shape a message that would resonate with his African American audience.

First, the early influence of Jim Jones' mother, Lynetta, on the formation of his overall spiritual outlook and the doctrine he would later develop should not be overlooked. Mrs. Jones was not particularly fond of organized religion—in fact, she was outright derisive of what she termed the "Sky God," a term Jim later used frequently in his sermons in an equally derisive manner.[4]

Although she thought many of her devoutly religious Holiness-Pentecostal neighbors took their beliefs far too seriously—after all, she drank and cursed and habitually committed any number of acts they considered sinful—Mrs. Jones did believe that the world was inhabited and enchanted by numerous types of spirits. She also was a great lover of nature and of animals. Like many during the Great Depression, when Jim was born, the Jones family was poor and dependent upon Lynetta's income to make ends meet. His father, James Thurman Jones, or Big Jim, had become disabled during World War I. In addition to her views on religion and the spirit world, Mrs. Jones was always quite sensitive to issues of social class. Her husband's family had looked down on her because of her family's class background. Labor unions and the plight of the exploited proletariat were major concerns for her, reflecting her experience as a woman supporting a family during the Depression.[5]

Despite his mother's views on organized religion, young Jim was still exposed to the Holiness-Pentecostal traditions of belief and practice through the efforts of some of the neighbors who brought him to their churches for services and Sunday school. In fact, according to John R. Hall, were it not for his mother's intervention, young Jim Jones' life might have been similar to that of other well-known child evangelists on the Holiness-Pentecostal revival circuit, such was his interest and talent with preaching even as a child.[6]

Perhaps another formative issue concerning social inequality arising out of Jones' family background was Big Jim's affiliation with the Ku Klux Klan when Jim was a boy. In Peoples Temple sermons, Jones remarked upon his father's virulent antipathy toward blacks and Jews and the hypocrisy he saw in whites. He even said he had researched his family's history and claimed to have found an African American ancestor. He related the story in one of his sermons:

> Jones: . . . or black. I rather suspect it was the latter, because my family tree was suddenly disposed of, because we came back from one of the *kings* in England. They were so proud of that family tree, but I, I smelled, as the old whites used to say nastily, I smelled sweetly, a nigger in the woodpile.
>
> [*Laughter and applause*]
>
> Jones: So I went to look at my family tree, because my father was such an autocrat and he was such an *aristocrat* and such a *blowhard* and such a *mean* soul, that he was trying to *hide* something. He talked too much against blacks and Jews. I knew something was *wrong* with this man. He talked down about the Indians, and I *knew* when people start kicking others, they're hiding something themselves.
>
> [*Laughter and applause*]
>
> Jones: Hmm? So I got that family tree—the *original* one, they'd taken the one out of the courthouse, and they had—oh, it was all prettied up and had a seal on it and it was surrounded with a silver trim or gold trim—it was just beautiful. But I went to the courthouse and I searched and I searched and I went *way* back to South Carolina and I found that Grandma went out to somebody's back cabin.
>
> [*Laughter and applause*]
>
> Jones: And when I came home and told my dad what I found, he didn't talk about family trees anymore. He forbade me to speak, and he kicked me out of the house, because I had found out what's happened to many, many millions in this land, across the land. Some of you're here, you think you're white and you got that, that inner soul spirit and you feel that vibration for freedom and you got that love for oh, justice and—and then there is something to this, an intrinsic appreciation for art and aesthetics and

rhythm, and you feel it in you and you look white, but honey, a nigger slipped in your woodpile somewhere.[7]

Thus, the oppression of the non-white races in America, along with the injustices of class-based inequality, long held a powerful fascination for Jim Jones. The excerpt above provides an example of the ways in which Jones communicated to his followers that he not only *understood* what it was like to be non-white in America, but that he actually *experienced* discrimination personally—even being kicked out of his house by his father as a result of telling him he had found a black ancestor.[8] When he became a student pastor in the local Methodist church, he severed his ties with the congregation when the church rejected his demand that it be integrated. He and his wife Marceline were the first white family in Indianapolis to adopt a black child, and they suffered discrimination as a result. He spoke often about his "rainbow family" and the experiences they faced in trying to live out the dream of a racially integrated society.

Like many of his time, Jim Jones became interested in socialism and communism as philosophies that could be useful in bringing about the types of social change needed in American society and the world at large. During the mid-1950s a prominent leader of an interracial movement, Father Divine, came to Jones' attention. Divine's movement, built around his Peace Mission, was headquartered in Harlem, New York, but boasted centers around the country, included agricultural communities in upstate New York, communal and interracial living in dormitories, and extensive social service agencies and businesses run and owned by the church. The great influence of Father Divine apparently led Jones to model his own church's activities on those he had seen as part of Father Divine's movement. He even appropriated the black tradition of extended and fictive kinship by encouraging followers to address him as "Father" or "Dad," and his wife Marceline as "Mother," just as was done in the Peace Mission movement.

Certain events in Jim Jones' personal and religious background undoubtedly served to shape his worldview and his approach to ministry by the time Peoples Temple began attracting the attention of present and former members of traditional, mainline African American churches. Although his parents were not particularly devout practitioners of religion, his early experiences with Pentecostalism, which has a multicultural history and has traditionally been made up of the poor, the despised, and the dispossessed of American society, gave him a certain sensitivity to issues that might be relevant to blacks. He also severed his formal United Methodist denominational affiliation in protest of its racially discriminatory policies and practices in Indianapolis.

BLACK WORSHIP TRADITIONS

Although they may be expressed or manifested in many ways, there are basic, identifiable themes and strains that many scholars of black religion agree are characteristic of traditional African American religious belief and practice. Together these might be referred to as the "Black Sacred Cosmos," which has been articulated by more than one observer of African American religion.[9] These traditions are not to be taken as fixed, static "retentions" of some monolithic and mythical African cultural heritage transported wholesale to the New World in the context of African enslavement in the Americas. Rather they are a composite of a number of worldviews, common to the African population of the region of West Africa from which the majority of slaves came.[10] The emphasis here is on first identifying the themes at work in the overall worldview before moving on to the more specific practices that give life to those themes and practices.

First, the worldview African Americans adapted from their African cultural heritage gave them what might be referred to as a holistic understanding of the relationship between the sacred and the profane in the lives of human beings. That is, the spiritual realm of experience is not separate but inextricably connected to the material conditions of life. In the language of many traditional African societies there is no word for "religion." This is a reflection of the worldview that, although they may be a different order of being, things that exist in the spirit world do not constitute a separate order of experience from all other aspects of social, economic, and political life, the life in which humans are most directly engaged daily.

Following from the belief that all aspects of the material world are subject to the spirit world, the traditional African worldview includes the belief in an immanent, as well as transcendent, supreme being and creator God, who cares about and actually intervenes in the course of human history. One of the central motifs in African American Christianity in particular has been the Hebrew Bible story of God's chosen people, the children of Israel and their exodus from Egypt, led by the man appointed to the task directly by God. Another way in which spirit beings may intervene in the lives of humans is through spirit possession. To this day, many traditional African-based religions maintain the belief that certain spirits, corresponding to various forces in nature or to departed and venerated ancestors, can and do "ride" worshippers in the course of ritual activity used to invoke and entreat them to work on the behalf of those in attendance. In the context of charismatic Christian traditions, the appearance of the Holy Ghost, as many African Americans refer to the Holy Spirit, is analogous to spirit possession and is a desirable goal of worship and preaching.

Another theme running through African American spirituality is a strong emphasis on social justice, the ultimate judgment of evil, and the rewarding of the oppressed. Although God may extend grace and mercy, God is—first and foremost—on the side of the just rather than the unjust. The righting of an oppressive, unjust social system has always been the expectation expressed through the religion of African Americans in the midst of their experience in the West. The notion that we *all* will eventually have to "reap what we sow" has formed the basis for African Americans' ideas concerning social justice.

Extended family and fictive kinship is another important element found in the worldview that Africans in America expressed in their religion. At its heart, black worship invokes a communal ideal in terms of people's interactions in the social world. That is, the needs of the group are privileged over the individual in most matters. Black spiritual or religious bodies have existed with some sense of relative autonomy from white control even before there was an autonomous black family in America.[11] The institutions constructed upon this ideal have had to fill in the gaps and meet needs in the black community that were not being met through mainstream institutional means. One of the most important of those institutional functions was providing a sense of family to those most in need of it. In particular, single mothers, their children, and the elderly played essential roles in these extended and often fictive kinship networks that were maintained through the church (although not exclusively so).

These core values are expressed in worship through several elements of the traditional style of black worship. First, *freedom* of emotional and ecstatic display in the context of worship are emphasized and encouraged. This includes the use of music and the body in dance, clapping, swaying, stomping of feet, and the playing of individual percussive instruments like tambourines by people in the congregation. The worship service is also a collective construction as expressed in the "call and response" vocal, musical, and preaching patterns. Thus it is highly participatory, requiring or encouraging all in attendance not to remain outside the experience but to join the collectively produced celebratory event, thereby sharing in the blessing to follow.

Finally, based upon the value traditional African societies placed upon oral transmission of cultural meanings and understandings, personal testimony of spiritual experience occupies an important place in the black worship tradition. Bearing witness to the truth of what is being said is yet another important way the group participates in worship. The preacher usually elicits that witness with such phrases as "Can I get a witness?" or "Y'all don't hear me!" to which the people respond, communicating their agreement with what the preacher is saying. Expository preaching style includes storytelling, the use of metaphorical rhetorical style, variation of cadence, "sing-song" vocal style, repetition, physicality—including jumping from the platform, dancing or other ways of performing and dramatizing scripture to make a particular point or highlight a principle for the audience. W. E. B. Du Bois, an astute observer of traditional modes of black worship that were developed and adapted in the context of slavery, summed up the experience as "the Preacher, the Music, and the Frenzy."[12]

BLACK PENTECOSTAL WORSHIP STYLE
IN PEOPLES TEMPLE SERVICES

At their essence, the worship services at Peoples Temple were constructed around the model of the emotionally expressive Pentecostal tradition. The black style of worship has shaped this tradition from its origins even though organizationally white Pentecostal denominations like the Assemblies of God have moved away from identification with the black origins of their movement.[13] Although some attribute the Holiness-Pentecostal style of worship more to Southern folk culture in general rather than to existential blackness, Cheryl J. Sanders finds its origins in traditional African worship traditions.[14] On this matter I would tend to agree with the latter opinion: that the style of worship common to Holiness-Pentecostals has its origins in the traditional black worship styles of the African Americans who played a prominent role in and made up large numbers of these movements from their inception.

In examining the transcripts and listening to tapes of Peoples Temple services, one of the first things that stands out about Jim Jones and his audience is the way in which the "call and response" mode of collectively constructing worship was employed throughout. Jones' speech is punctuated and actually buoyed along by moments of applause, shouts of "amen," "hallelujah," and other forms frequently found in African American worship services, especially in a Christian context. In this way the speaker and the audience participate in a carefully orchestrated conversation, with the speaker making a claim upon the sensibilities of the audience members, who then bear responsibility for validating that claim (or not) and encouraging the speaker to continue in his or her present vein (or not). To the casual observer or outsider—particularly those more attuned to the emotionally controlled atmosphere in many mainstream white congregations—this part of African American worship services may appear to be out of control when, in actuality, it requires that one learn the proper times and places in which to insert these seemingly spontaneous vocal interjections.

Another important element of black worship services that is consistent with the "call and response" modality is the role that music, especially the organ (but also percussion instruments), plays throughout the course of the service. At certain times during the sermon—most notably when the audience, being carried along by the preaching, begins to reach a high point—the organist or pianist will begin to strike musical chords on the instrument as a type of musical voice that accompanies the collective voice of the people in the audience. It is not only the vocal shouts of "Amen!" "Preach!" "That's the truth!" "Tell 'em" or simply shouts, cheering, or the clapping of hands, people standing, etc., that the preacher responds to, but it is also the notes played by the musicians in response to his preaching that help to carry the entire assembly along to the goal: a sense of collective emotional catharsis. It was at these times that the "frenzy" brought on by the people's perception and expression of the Holy Ghost's overtaking them would become part of the corporate worship experience. Usually accompanied and invoked by music, the majority of the congregation would be involved in fast, rhythmic clapping while individual people might run around the church, dance in a very stylized manner referred to as "shouting," oblivious to those around them; they might speak in tongues, or some might simply cry or shout. The following excerpt from a Temple service in which personal testimonies of healings have already taken place shows exactly this kind of emotional display. Apparently some members of the congregation have begun dancing ecstatically and even running around the church building rejoicing.

> Jones: . . . I said again in this ministry, under my ministry, how many have had cancers healed? Good God Almighty. No wonder the people stay, you see, the ones that stay, the ones that get healed of those cancers. Good God. Good God! (Pause) Holy holy holy. (Pause) (Hums).
> [Organ plays]

Jones: Mighty God. (Pause) Yes, my God. (Pause) Just look at her run like that. I never get tired of seeing her dance, because I can remember when her heart was so bad, that she died back there, and had to be brought back. So I can always enjoy her running. It makes me feel good. Somebody says that she dances all the time. Well, that's fine. I'm glad she can dance. I can remember when she couldn't even walk. (Calls out) Hey, God. (Pause) (Normal tone) That's beautiful, to see someone run like that, when they were dead. Died of a heart attack, she died right back there on that aisle. (Pause) Don't talk to me—let'em run, boy, when they can—run when they couldn't walk. I'll say, thank you, God.[15]

As the excitement that accompanied the last emotional climax subsides in preparation for a later one that is likely to occur, it appears that Jones admonishes those whom he perceives as not understanding or even looking down on the people engaged in this type of behavioral display.

Jones: You know, it's—it's something that uh—I look out over some of you, and you look like you're feeling sorry. I looked at one woman down there, who looks like she's feeling sorry for these people who were once cripple, and they have had cancer and they been healed. And you know, you shake your thoughts at them. You put your thoughts out at them. And you shake your head at them. And really, you're the one that's the loser.

[Applause]

Jones: To have something you can rejoice over, some people would live all their life, to find something they can rejoice over. (Pause) Bless you. We—This is our house, you know.

[Stirs]

Jones: We paid for it, every stick of it, not a honky dollar in here. (Pause) You can go down and look at the county clerk, and you'll see it's in the name of the Peoples Temple, and there is not a honky dollar in it.

[Light applause]

Jones: Don't go in here—I'm going to tell you one thing, if you come in here, and you're light-skinned, don't come in here and look at your—don't crane your head at us. 'Cause this [is] our house and there's not many churches in this town that are paid for, and we paid for every nail in it, and we'll shake and rattle and roll, if we want to.

[Cheers]

Jones: (Laughs) (Cries out) Oh, yes, we will.

[Cheers][16]

Jim Jones also made use of the style of preaching that, although perhaps not the exclusive province of black preachers, found its fullest development in the Black Church. The style of preaching that characterizes Holiness-Pentecostal revivalism can also be seen and heard in the services of Peoples Temple. As part of this style of preaching, Jones frequently changed his cadence and the rhythm of his speech as he and the audience together reached varying levels of excitement. He also routinely used the sing-song type of vocal cadence in his sermons characteristic of the black preaching tradition.[17] His sermons also drew upon the oral traditions of expository preaching common among black ministers. That is, they would use scripture, or the day's text—as they often referred to the passage that would be the basis of the day's message—as the point of departure from which they took the audience on a journey that included personal anecdotes, testimony of audience members, bits and pieces of song lyrics—even the actual movement into and out of song, accompanied by the musicians—to illustrate certain points or drive home a particular principle.

Rather than a strict adherence to biblical exegesis as may be the case in the churches of whites, the tradition of black preaching has been one in which the word of God is not merely communicated but is indeed performed. It is acted out in an attempt to make it real in the lives of the listeners. Jones' sermons were filled with stories, some of them personal anecdotes and some testifying to the experiences of people present in the services. Although there were numerous biblical references throughout his sermons, they were often used without a clear thesis or theme. His invocation of the charismatic notion of inspiration and the working of the Holy Spirit through the preacher may have been the basis for this type of spontaneity. There often seemed to be no discernible pre-determined thesis for the sermons; rather they would go wherever the Spirit led, an important value in traditional black preaching.

In terms of the manifestation of the charismatic gifts of the Spirit, Jones also was instrumental in shaping the degree to which the public ministry of glossolalia (speaking in tongues), faith healings, or things like public prophecies would become part of the behavioral norms in the services. Excerpts from sermons show that he invited members to participate in the public ministry of prophesying in tongues and provided the accompanying "interpretations" of such prophetic messages, what he referred to here as "admonition":

> Jones: . . . Continue as you feel, if you—if someone wants to exercise their faith for another, just three or four minutes by saying some admonition, do so.

Voice in crowd: (speaking in monotone tongues for several seconds) God has come. Love has come, in other man. And the light has come in other man. True apostolic (unintelligible word—sounds like "charity") exists.

[*Several people shout*]

Jones: Shh!

Man in crowd: . . . upon this earth. It has come. And it is coming. And God has (unintelligible)

Jones: Shh!

Man in crowd: Jim Jones has come to bring socialism to the United States of America. Hallelujah, hallelujah hallelujah!

[*Many people shout*]

Jones: It's beautiful. It's beautiful. I would add one thing to it. *Christian* socialism. That's where you take them, that stage. You take them stage by stage. Or *apostolic* Christian socialism. Very beautiful.[18]

Later on in the same service Jones asks the congregation whether anyone else wishes to "make an expression" and gives them permission to do so. Several people respond to his invitation:

Man in congregation: Behold, I have said unto thee. Give up thy capitalist ways. I have returned with my power and glory to build a new Jerusalem. Hallelujah.

[*Several echo*]

Jones: Yes. To build a new heaven and new earth would probably be more sound theology.

Woman witnesses in tongues: . . . had all things in common, and distributed to these, as they had these, (unintelligible word) had this, here, true Christian socialism, here now on earth. Ah hallelujah.

[*Several echo*]

Jones: You'll need to preface these things with "The *Lord* hath declared," or "The *Spirit* speaketh," *expressly* to the church, something of this nature, to give an endorsement. But now qualify your thoughts in the days ahead with knowledge. Get some knowledge in there. Go through these scriptural concordances and *find* them, beautiful quotes that you can push it in between a scriptural phrase, and it'll be of *great* help in building the ideal. One voice will reach someone where another one won't. One testimony will open a door, and no one else could succeed. My voice might be associated with its tenor, with a type of voice that has been reflecting negation to the person. Well, they shut you off. Or my prototype, my physique might be of a negative nature to someone. But some voice out of the great anonymity of the collective whole *speaks*, opens the door, when I've not been able to open the door. But we have to get knowledge there. So let's increase it with knowledge. I'm going to expect *more* knowledge at next meeting. Hmm?

[*Crowd reacts*]

Jones: More knowledge. Anyone else? I like uh, sweet love's tongues, and listen to it, sweet love's speak—speak forth.

Woman speaks in tongues: The Lord God is (unintelligible word). Behold, the people his word. Yeah, he is—

Jones: Umm-hmm. Yes. Now, with a message like that, to *lengthen* it a little bit. If someone even picks on her tongue—she has a beautiful tongue—gift, if someone then gives the *prophetic* interpretation, because it's a language, almost, her, it's just as, someplace deep in the very recesses of her consciousness. I wouldn't make a stake on it that it's a language that she's *used* at some, at some stage, in her *unfoldment*, in some prior life. (Pause) But we're not here to theorize about the supernatural meaning of it anyway, we're here to *utilize* it for good.

Several voices: Yeah.

Jones: Beautiful.[19]

In the above excerpts we see some of the ways in which Jones provided space for the exercise of the charismatic gifts of the Spirit, the public ministry of prophesying in tongues, and providing the interpretation to the listening congregation. He actually invited people who felt they had a word for the people to exercise their faith in this manner and come forth with their particular utterance from God through the Holy Spirit. Jones also quieted those who, in their fervor, would have interrupted the utterance, basically instructing them to continue to listen for the interpretation of the tongues. Further, he instructed those giving prophetic utterances, shaping the content of their messages. For example, Jones himself shaped the interpretations offered of the tongues in several ways: according to the doctrine at Peoples Temple when he urged the man to preface socialism with "Christian"; urging the woman to preface her interpretations with "the Lord hath declared" and instructing her to go through scriptural concordances to find beautiful biblical quotes to insert; telling the congregation that some voices and testimonies can reach certain people while others cannot. He also commented on the interpretations with endorsements like "beautiful." He suggests that people "parallel" their interpretations of tongues, saying, "You need to *parallel*. And you have to, you have to make your tongues comparable to—I mean the sounds should be comparable." He instructs the congregation on the proper way to conduct this type of activity. These are all examples of the ways in which Jones allowed the charismatic gifts of the Spirit to become part of the behavioral norms in the services at the same time he shaped the acceptable means by which they would be experienced.

In addition to the free expression of religious devotion and experience of the Holy Spirit, Jim Jones provided the black constituents of his congregation what he assumed they would expect from him: a highly participatory, celebratory, dynamic form of expository preaching, along with a message that sharply criticized the Christian church's hypocrisy and complicity in perpetuating the oppression of the poor, the weak, and the racially and ethnically marginalized segments of society. Even more, he offered concrete programs to actually do something about the problems of those people most in need. Jim Jones seemed to understand the importance of the prophetic role of the black preacher and the prophetic stance assumed by African American religion in general. That is, his messages included a great deal of commentary on contemporary issues in the larger society as well as issues in the more traditional churches out of which many of his followers had come. Some members of his church had actually belonged to other, mainline Black Church denominations in addition to being members of Peoples Temple. His sermons were filled with social commentary and critique of the injustices of the capitalism, racism, sexism, and ageism that structured American society.

CONCLUSION

Whether consciously or not, Jones brought various aspects of his own personal life and background to bear in his attempts to construct a message and worship services that his African American followers could relate to and identify with. This material can be broken into a set of symbols that Jim Jones invoked and combined and recombined into messages and worship services that seemed to "speak to" large numbers of African Americans. In other words, Jones learned to speak the symbolic and religious language of black Americans quite fluently and made that language an integral part of the worship experience. He made it part of the behavioral norms in Peoples Temple.

Timothy Nelson looked at the role played by leaders within some black congregations to define the norms of emotional display.[20] On the basis of what church leaders found to be acceptable or not, certain churches exhibited more or less ecstatic forms of emotional and devotional display. In other words, emotionalism in worship services— while appearing to be an essential part of certain groups' response to the spirit world—is actually the result of the power relations within the setting. We can say that the emotional worship service is produced, rather than just occurring "naturally." What this means is that the forms of worship and the types of emotional display that African Americans had grown accustomed to were privileged in this particular congregation based on the continual endorsement and personal identification with it of its principal leader, Jones. If Jones had not appreciated black worship traditions or had not wanted them included as central parts of the services, he could have rejected them and deemed them inappropriate, unacceptable. Although members of the congregation might have spontaneously sought to express their religious devotion in ways consistent with the traditions found in black worship, if Jones—the leader, the person with the power in that setting to define and enforce those expressive norms, and a white man—had defined their attempts to do so as an inappropriate emotional display, then the services would not have looked and sounded and felt as they did. The result would have been far fewer African American participants. With worship being such an important basis for a sense of community and cultural continuity, to reject (or accept) a group's traditional modes of expressing their devotion and experience of the sacred is, ultimately, to reject (or accept) them. And in the history of African Americans, their churches and other institutions were among the few places their own heritage could be affirmed and celebrated in white-dominated American culture and society.

This principle can be seen at work in Jones' attempts to create and maintain an atmosphere that the African Americans in his church would recognize as genuine, provide validation of their experience, and become the basis for a much more politically active spirituality than the churches from which so many had come. That is, from the variety of forms of religious devotion and its outward expression, Jones chose to use patterns, meanings, and understandings that were consistent with and therefore would resonate with large numbers of African American worshippers. He did this in the content of his sermons (shockingly and provocatively identifying himself and anyone else who was oppressed along with African Americans as "niggers"). He performed public, community works that reaffirmed his commitment to selflessness and the construction of a self-sustaining communal lifestyle rather than being like many of the so-called "jacklegs," ministers whose only interest in the congregation was getting their money for personal gain. Jones drew frequent attention to these in his sermons. He made public space for the continuation of traditions found in the African American religious as well as secular culture: the full range of emotions in worship, giving testimony and bearing personal witness of his power, for example, to heal the body. He gave positive sanction to the African American race and culture and privileged it in the worship services. Thus it was not only the words of his mouth, as indicated in the epigram at the beginning, or by stating how much he had enjoyed watching people dance and run around the building, that communicated that the black worship style would be welcome. It was also his actions that demonstrated the important message that helped shape and prepare the way for future occurrences by defining the black worship style as not only acceptable but desirable.

Of course, the content of Jones' sermons did change over time, with his earlier ones being far more concerned with spiritual things: implementing a social gospel; inaugurating a communal lifestyle based on the principles of "Christian apostolic socialism"; and supporting social justice, faith healing, and so on. His later messages seemed to center on conspiracies against not only the movement in general but against him, its leader, in particular. Ultimately, his ministry changed from being one focused on the needs of the people that he claimed to care for so deeply, to one in which he worked out his own personal paranoia and the siege mentality that arose from that paranoia and from his increasing drug use. The movement that had once affirmed its African American members became the one that led to their demise. That shift in focus was one of the factors that ultimately led to the mass murders and suicides that have come to characterize the names Peoples Temple, Jonestown, and even Guyana to this day.

NOTES

1. U.S. FBI Peoples Temple Recording, Q 612. Transcript available on *Alternative Considerations of Jonestown and Peoples Temple*, <http://jonestown.sdsu.edu>, accessed 11 July 2003. All tapes marked "Q" come from the FBI.

2. Timothy J. Nelson, "Sacrifice of Praise: Emotion and Collective Participation in an African-American Worship Service," *Sociology of Religion* 57, no. 4 (Winter 1996): 379–396.

3. See, for example, John R. Hall, *Gone from the Promised Land: Jonestown in American Cultural History* (New Brunswick, N.J.: Transaction Books, 1987), and Tim Reiterman with John Jacobs, *Raven: The Untold Story of the Rev. Jim Jones and His People* (New York: E. P. Dutton, 1982).

4. Hall, *Gone from the Promised Land*, 6. Also, in his sermons through the years Jones can be heard using the term "Sky God" and contrasting faith in his power with that of depending on the image of God put forth in the more traditional, Judeo-Christian sense.

5. Hall, *Gone from the Promised Land*, 5

6. Hall, *Gone from the Promised Land*, 10.

7. Q 612.

8. This was not actually confirmed and may have been made up for the purposes of the sermons.

9. For example, see Mechal Sobel, *Trabelin' On: The Slave Journey to an Afro-Baptist Faith* (Westport, Conn.: Greenwood Press, 1979); and C. Eric Lincoln and Lawrence H. Mamiya, *The Black Church in the African American Experience* (Durham, N.C.: Duke University Press, 1990).

10. See, for example, Albert J. Raboteau, *Slave Religion: The "Invisible Institution" in the Antebellum South* (New York: Oxford University Press, 1978).

11. W. E. B. Du Bois, *The Souls of Black Folk* (New York: Library of America, 1990 edition).

12. Du Bois, *The Souls of Black Folk*, 138.

13. Iain MacRobert, "The Black Roots of White Pentecostalism," in *Down by the Riverside: Readings in African American Religion*, ed. Larry G. Murphy (New York: New York University Press, 2000), 189–199.

14. Cheryl J. Sanders, *Saints in Exile: The Holiness-Pentecostal Experience in African American Religion and Culture* (New York: Oxford University Press, 1996).

15. Q 956, from a worship service held in Los Angeles in 1973.

16. Q 956.

17. Gerald L. Davis, *I Got the Word in Me and I Can Sing It, You Know* (Philadelphia: University of Philadelphia Press, 1985); Henry L. Mitchell, *Black Preaching* (New York: J. B. Lippincott, 1970).

18. Q 1016, from a worship service held in Los Angeles in 1972.

19. Q 1016.

20. Nelson, "Sacrifice of Praise."

8

Breaking the Silence

Reflections of a Black Pastor

J. ALFRED SMITH

If we are to learn anything about the tragedy of Jonestown, we must begin with an understanding that it is not about a single day sliced out of our history. In my judgment, there was an earlier tragedy—pieces of which I noticed and did nothing about, pieces of which I should have noticed and didn't—prior to the migration of hundreds of Peoples Temple members from San Francisco to Guyana. I believe there were continuing tragedies in Jonestown itself leading up to 18 November 1978, even though I did not witness them. I do know that there is another ongoing tragedy, one that causes me great pain. That is the tragedy which stops my brothers and sisters in the black clergy in the Bay Area from giving a voice to the grief, to the sense of betrayal, and to the internal struggle to understand how we played a role in the success of Jim Jones in our midst. It is the tragedy of profound and unforgivable silence.

It is time to break the silence.

THE BLACK CHURCH IN THE BAY AREA

The 1970s were a dark age for the Black Church in San Francisco. Most churches had become little more than social clubs, where chicken dinners and raffle tickets were the only activities on the agenda. In these houses of worship, the red carpet in the church narthex became a fashion runway for the fur coat and Brooks Brothers suit crowd. After the Sunday morning service was finished, the church fathers would seal the buildings up tighter than Pharaoh Ramses' tomb.

Upward mobility was the hallmark of the African American church establishment. Many of those churches had not yet *arrived*, but still held upper-crust aspirations. For many of San Francisco's children of the African diaspora, Christianity was primarily a middle-class expression. And so it became for the churches as well.

As far as I could see, these churches practiced an other-worldly Christianity that was more concerned about saving the soul than saving the environment. Their pastors preached the sweet by-and-by: "When we get to heaven, we're going to put on our shoes. When we get to heaven, we're going to sing and shout. When we get to heaven, oh, what a great time it will be." They had little outreach to the underclass. They had no ministries to address the needs of the hurting people who made the sidewalks of San Francisco their beds and used yesterday's newspapers as blankets. Their followers did not want to be bothered with the huge numbers of disenfranchised and disaffected people around them.

Coming out of my own sense of inner integrity, I have to say, I don't know anything about the furniture of heaven, I don't know anything about the temperature of hell, but my very location in a community of decay and deterioration means that I know a great deal about the nasty now-and-now. As senior pastor of the Allen Temple Baptist Church in Oakland, I'm going to lend the stubborn ounces of my weight toward trying to bring about social change. I'm not talking about the social welfare that merely gives Christmas baskets and turkey baskets and used clothing and second-hand furniture to poor people. I mean the work I am called to do, to try to bring about some grassroots change.

I know—how deeply I know—that this puts this church in a minority. There are a few others, like Glide Memorial United Methodist Church, where the Reverend Cecil Williams still serves as pastor, and nearby Third Baptist Church, where the Reverend Amos Brown presides, but once you turn the corner past these churches, you might have to look a long time to find another.

These scattered churches—our lonely voices almost drowned out by the evangelistic, revivalistic, sawdust-trail, tent-meeting, salvation-oriented invitations to Christianity—follow the prophetic line of the Bible. Ours are the roots of Black Theology, of Liberation Theology, of the Social Gospel movement of Walter Rauschenbusch out of Rochester Seminary and the Baptist Church, and Washington Gladden out of Williams College and the Congregational Church.

The prophetic line taps an ethical religious motivation to bring about societal change. It tells us to service all the needs of all people of all ages, from the womb to the tomb. I do understand that one role of the church is to deal with life after death, but I'm going to trust Jesus to take care of that. The prophetic line gives us another commandment, to deal with life after birth. And that's what I'm concerned about: life after birth.

It's called the prophetic line because it arises from the social prophets Isaiah, Micah, and Amos, who preached the word of God eight centuries before Christ. I begin with Amos 5:24: "Then let justice surge like water, and goodness like an unfailing stream." And now the more complete articulation of the tradition within Isaiah:

> The Spirit of the Lord God is upon me; because the Lord hath anointed me to preach good tidings to the poor; he hath sent me to bind up the brokenhearted, to proclaim liberty to the captives, and the opening of the prison to them that are bound; To proclaim the acceptable year of the Lord . . . To appoint unto them that mourn in Zion, to give unto them beauty for ashes, the oil of joy for mourning, the garment of praise for the spirit of heaviness; . . . And they shall build the old wastes, they shall raise up the former desolations, and they shall repair the waste cities, the desolations of many generations. (Isaiah 61:1–4)

And of course, the prophetic line came to fruition in the gospel of Jesus, who used this same scripture when he stood up in the Temple to preach his inaugural sermon, and who admonished his disciples to feed the hungry, clothe the naked, and visit the prisoner.

I am an inheritor of that tradition. This is how I define myself. I wanted this church to be an institution that tries to service the needs of the community. And this is what I've been about for 32 years. We've built housing for the elderly, housing for people who are HIV-positive. The J. Alfred Smith Skill Center trains people for jobs. We have a ministry in anger management, where 300 men come each week, men who've been guilty of domestic violence. We have the Malachi Project to help men who have deserted their children, to get them back to care for their children.

I think we have succeeded in ways that other churches in our community have not. We are more than a Sunday go-to-meeting church. If you stop at other churches, you will see locks on their doors. If they have parking lots, you will not see cars there. But not here. We have programs going on here all the time. The place is alive.

We have also grown. When I came, this church was a little building on the corner of 85th Avenue and A Street. Now we take up the whole block. The Family Life Center which houses most of our programs was built on top of what used to be the headquarters of the Black Panther Party. When the Black Panthers needed to sell their place, they decided they wanted us to have it. More than that, some of those former Black Panthers are now part of this ministry. The chairperson of the board of deacons for 2003 is a former Black Panther. Our radio announcer is Bobby Seale's sister. The way we have grown tells me not only how much we respect the community, but also how it respects us in turn.

THE PREACHING OF PEOPLES TEMPLE

There was another minister who claimed the prophetic line in San Francisco during the 1970s. Jim Jones arrived and stretched out his hand to the hurting, the poor, and the broken. He opened the doors of his house of worship, and to those whom Jesus referred to as the least of these, he said "Come." He answered the call to social justice that most mainline churches of the time had abandoned, forgotten, or never even heeded. The letterhead of his church, Peoples Temple, identified him with the Disciples of Christ, but it was the Temple's commitment to Jesus' Parable of the Last Judgment—which also appeared on the letterhead for all to see—that commanded allegiance and admiration.

He spoke persuasively, so I believed—or at least convinced myself to believe—that he spoke sincerely. Most importantly and impressively, he used the same metaphorical, theological language and vocabulary that I used, that Cecil Williams and Amos Brown used, that Martin Luther King Jr. used, speaking with the thunder of the historical prophetic line of the Black Church. The rapport I felt with my black brethren in the faith, I suddenly felt for a white man.

The rapport we all had, the bond we all felt, did not come about by accident. And when I say that Jim Jones spoke our language, I'm not just talking about his enunciation of the prophetic line. I'm talking about his rhetorical style.

I don't know who influenced Jones as a young man back in Indiana, but he must have been around some black preachers, and he must have listened, and he certainly learned. There's a difference between the Anglo style of preaching and the black style, and you can't learn it from a book or a classroom. You have to experience it.

The Anglo style emerges from the seminary. It's more cognitive. It has a goal of imparting information, information, information. And there's a very straightforward manner to it. It has to proceed from

Introduction to Roman numeral I, then A under that, and points under that. It becomes so mechanistic. There's no soul. And it has a clock on it. You go to a white service, and you see what happens if the preacher doesn't finish what he has to say in 20 minutes. People get restless, they look at their watches, they don't hide their yawns.

Black preaching comes out of our oral tradition, because our earliest preachers did not know how to read. Our earliest preachers heard the white clergy read. They remembered the stories, they embellished the story. They worked with the story. They romanced the story. They experienced the story.

African American preaching has a tendency to produce an event, to help people experience an event, or to experience truth. So when the preacher talks about the cross—"Were you there when they crucified my Lord?"—you end up listening to the way he or she paints the picture, the imagery, until everyone in the congregation can say, "Yes, I was there." Because you were there. It's an experience of the truth.

And it's a joint experience, known as "call and response," between preacher and congregation. My congregation reacts to what I say, but they don't just follow me. It becomes a conversation. They encourage me, they push me, and when they talk back to me in a continuous voice, that means I'm doing well. Because it's true, I may *think* I know the general direction I'm heading when I start out, but it's my congregation that lets me know when I'm reaching them and when I'm not.

The black oral tradition as reflected in the black preaching style also doesn't concern itself with time as much as white churches do. It's not that black churches allow the preachers more time. Rather, it's that both the preacher and the congregation have the freedom to suspend time to develop where we want to go.

Great preaching is like playing a musical instrument. When you look at a text, you have to look at it as you would look at a piece of music, and see whether it is in a major mood or a minor mood, whether it's joyful or whether it's ecstatic, or whether it's mournful, whether it's like the blues. The sermon should have a theme. There should be improvisation. There are movements. And when you close out, you bring it home. I have learned more about preaching from listening to music than I have from academia.

Jim Jones knew that. He felt it. He understood it. He captured it. He worked his story and his message, and he worked his congregation. He asked for his followers to respond, and they responded, and he gave them more, just like any black preacher would. In fact, if you closed your eyes and just listened to him preach, you would swear you were listening to a black man.

Let me stay with music to illustrate what I mean. I come out of Kansas City, Missouri. Music is a part of my early experience. I have pictures around my study of John Coltrane and Miles Davis. I used to see the jam sessions with Count Basie. I also used to listen to a great tenor saxophone player named Flip Phillips, who played with Woody Herman. They had that great song, "Woodchopper's Ball," with Flip Phillips taking off on that tenor so low, and if you didn't see him playing, you would say he was black. When people heard him on the radio, they would fight over whether that was a black man playing. But Flip Phillips was white.

Jim Jones was like that too. He had the gift of communicating with black people. He didn't communicate in the sterile way of the seminary. He didn't follow the sterile texts. No, if you listen to Jones' sermons, you can hear him following the rhythms and cadences to match the beating of the human heart.

THE TEACHING OF PEOPLES TEMPLE

Jim Jones first called me in 1976, during a very difficult time in my ministry. I had been serving as the pastor of the Allen Temple Baptist Church for seven years. The church had experienced tremendous growth, but we had suffered growing pains too. The open door between this historic Baptist institution and the community was swinging both ways, and I found myself involved in local problems—and local politics—more than my predecessor had and, in some ways, more that the longtime members of the church thought I should. Still, when people found themselves abused by the police, we stood by their side. When people felt themselves cut apart from the political establishment, we invited the establishment in the form of the mayor to come down to the ghetto to hear them. We were already working with the Black Panthers to create a safer, cleaner neighborhood.

As Allen Temple grew, my name began to appear in the newspapers with frequency. Through some act of providence, I became one of the most recognizable clergypersons in the San Francisco Bay region. I was well known for my position as a thermostat in society, as opposed to being a thermometer. My church and I labored to correct the moral climate in Oakland as it pertained to the poor, rather than to simply mirror it. You could count on us to upset the apple cart.

It seemed as though my efforts were misunderstood. Even people within the church thought I was too militant. They could not understand why I believed that the church should build housing for the elderly and host job fairs for the underemployed, why the church should implement programs to tutor African American and Latino youth in the disciplines of science and mathematics.

I also received criticism from the other African American preachers in Oakland. They wanted to know whether I was a communist. They wanted to know whether I was saved. They wanted to know whether I really preached the gospel. They did not think that a pastor should point out the misdeeds of the land he loved. Because I criticized America's insensitivity to the have-nots, these men wanted to know if I was a good American. They labeled me a "troublemaker" and a "radical."

And, of course, I felt the ire of the power structure which, as I understood it, had been elected to make life better for all the people of the city. At one point in a crowded city council meeting, the mayor became so angry with me, he abruptly turned his chair around so that his back faced my church members and me. I was unmoved, but I was growing weary.

Jim Jones' telephone call, with his sweet words of encouragement, was a balm to me against the smoke and flames of that fiery furnace. He said that he had become aware of the work that I was doing in East Oakland and had a very positive opinion of me. He said he wanted to meet me face to face.

I went to visit him at Peoples Temple in the Fillmore District of San Francisco. It was a huge, converted synagogue situated in a tough neighborhood. The Reverend Jones came across as a very friendly man, a godly man. He dressed and behaved like a normal pastor of a mainline church. Jones talked to me with the wisdom and clarity of theology that one of my seminary professors might have possessed. He could make a point without becoming bombastic.

He asked, "What can I do to help you? Is there anything I could do to help you? I hear good things about you. I read good things about you. I know what the needs are, and here you are, endeavoring to carry on a ministry like Jesus. What can I do?"

I thought to myself that this man was a godsend. Over the years I had accumulated a number of social justice prayers which I very much desired to see in print. I told him that I had tried to get my little book of prayers published, but everywhere I went, doors slammed in my face. All I needed was a little bit of money to get the book published.

Jones said, "I will have them printed for you, Reverend Smith. I won't even charge you for this. Consider it a gift." And he made good on his word. In 1978, Peoples Temple published *In The Name Of Our Elder Brother*.

My joy of that day was diluted, though, by something I noticed on my way to the parking lot after meeting the Reverend Jones. A short little lady walked up and talked to me. That's when I learned that he had people living there at the church. And I remember thinking, this building held more than a church. There was a type of commune there too. This caused me some apprehension. It planted a seed of doubt, but it was a tiny seed, and that was all.

In a way, that encounter was like everything else about Peoples Temple. Whenever I heard of them at their best, I would learn about something else that dulled the luster. But whenever I picked up the rumors of some troubling impropriety or activity, the next thing I heard would turn the spotlight back to what they were doing for their troubled community. Throughout the time Peoples Temple was in San Francisco, the intimations that something wasn't right would surface, and then go back down, then come back up and go back down. I think they surfaced permanently just before everyone left for Guyana, but who knows? If they'd stayed, maybe the ebb and flow would have continued until people figured out what they had to have found out in Jonestown: that Jim Jones wasn't what he seemed.

While I want to reiterate that I am writing from my own perspective, I need to add in total honesty that all of us were taken in, because all of us wanted to do what Jones seemed to be doing. We may all want to remember just the misgivings we had about Jim Jones and to overlook the ways we tried to forge mutual and reciprocal bonds with him, but those bonds were there. Listen to the words of the Reverend Cecil Williams, who concluded a broadcast conversation with Jim Jones in this way:

> Here's a man, I have to tell you, I think he's a genius, I think he's a prophet. He's charismatic. He's one of our great leaders. I'm glad to be associated with you. Brother, we're going to stay together, because I know, if I stay with you, we're going to make it. We'll bring about justice. Walk that walk, and talk that talk. And be that be, and love that love, and struggle that struggle. Look for us. We'll be there.

When Jones and his followers left for Jonestown, they left quietly. I did not even know that he was in Guyana until the terrible reports of mass suicide came interrupting the morning news telecasts. However, he had said something the day I visited him that should have given me a clue as to what was on his mind. He said, "If America ever becomes repressive and follows the path of Nazi Germany and turns against people of color, we will have a place to go." I thought perhaps he was using rhetoric to impress me with the fact that he was leaning to the left theologically. After all, it was something that had been said about me.

As I reflect on Jim Jones today, I am reminded of Matthew 7:15 in the New Testament: "Beware of false prophets, which come to you in sheep's clothing, but inwardly they are ravening wolves." The issue is, was he a wolf all along, or did he change? What happened to change him? When did he become the wolf? At the time I met him, he convinced me that he was authentic. I heard him speak the words of the prophetic tradition. He could say just what I'm saying, and say it convincingly. Maybe I was naive, but I judged him by the way I judged myself. That's one of the mistakes that I made. I allowed myself to be blinded by his works. I didn't check him out. I didn't try to get to know him. But now I really believe that he knew all the time that he was taking us for a ride. I don't think something cataclysmic happened to him that made him detour. I can't prove that. The truth is, I don't know. I don't know. I don't know.

I do know that his message changed. When he began his ministry in Indianapolis, he preached with passion and fervor, urging, imploring, daring the members of his church to accept the invitation to pick up the cross of Jesus. Even when he was in San Francisco, he would draw people in with the Christian message. After the deaths in Guyana, though, we began to hear stories about what really happened during some of the services. More than once, Reverend Jones threw the Bible to the floor and said, "Too many people are looking at this instead of me." He told Archie Ijames, a black assistant minister of Peoples Temple, "You go out and preach about me, and I'll back it up with miracles." But even when he changed his message, he didn't change his style. That was his delivery wagon. He was able to bring people along with him across the country from Indiana, down from Ukiah to San Francisco and Los Angeles, and eventually to Guyana, because he kept the same style. The problem was that eventually, people responded only to the style of preaching instead of what he had to say. The delivery wagon had become more important than the groceries.

His fatal flaw was his own proclamation that he was God. But more than that, he said, everyone was God. When he did that, he forgot who he was working for. He lost his humility. In its place, he put forward the ego that corrupted him. And when I say "ego," I mean he Edged God Out.

That's what saves most of my brothers and sisters in the church from becoming like Jim Jones. It's true, there is an occupational hazard that makes us want to play God, that makes us forget that we're not God. We can become so mechanistic in doing our job as preachers that we lose the sense of the sacred and we start to think of ourselves as the sacred. But most of us are able to remain in touch with our fragility. We know that saints have to take baths, and saints have to use the toilet, and saints have to use deodorant.

THE PEOPLE OF PEOPLES TEMPLE

I do think it is important to separate the people of Peoples Temple from Jim Jones, and to talk about the similarities and differences between the congregation at Peoples Temple and those of black churches in San Francisco and Oakland.

Peoples Temple had a unique presence in San Francisco, but it would have been unique anywhere. By that I mean that most churches—including Allen Temple Baptist Church—draw their congregations from their surrounding neighborhoods. The congregation may change over the years as the neighborhood flourishes and decays and revitalizes, or as the church offers different ministries and services to respond to local problems or address national concerns, or as different preachers bring their own style of worship to the pulpit. But Allen Temple Baptist Church was born as an African church. My congregation is mainly African American. The church is located in an African American neighborhood. And I am located in the heart of this community, both physically and spiritually.

Peoples Temple was different. It had changed locations more than once. It had remnants of its Indianapolis roots as a Holiness church tempered in the fires of the Civil Rights movement, and there were several families, black and white, from its intentionally integrated congregation from those early days. There were people, mainly white, who were attracted to Jones' message of peace, equality, and brotherhood when the church made its home near the small northern California town of Ukiah. Then there were the people whom Peoples Temple ministered to in San Francisco, families in need, mainly poor, mainly African American, many of them elderly, many of them migrants themselves to San Francisco from rural areas of southern and border states. It was an interracial congregation then, in part because of the people Jones had attracted along the way, in part because of the places that the church made its several homes.

We can make other contrasts, though, and I would certainly offer

Allen Temple Baptist Church as an example of that contrast, in part because of the many other ways we mirrored what was going on within Peoples Temple.

Our church was rapidly growing at the same time that Peoples Temple was growing. Our growth was coming from everywhere, but principally from three sources. We were able to attract the youth. We were able to bring back people who had been disenchanted with the church and who decided to return and try it one more time. And we were able to attract people who had previously been unchurched but who were drawn to the social activism of our ministry. I remember more than once, when I would be asked to give the invocation at the Urban League dinner, that people would come to me afterwards and say, "Where is your church? Do you preach like you pray?" I would invite them to come see for themselves, and they would come. And then they would come again and again.

We also lost a number of people who did not respond to my social gospel ministry. Folks have said, well, he doesn't preach the gospel. I want to go where they're going to preach the Bible. By that, they mean that all they wanted to hear was scripture, and what it meant when it was written, but with no application as to what it means now. If I were to bring up the president during a sermon—which I do—and castigate his policies when they need castigation—which I do—they would say, you're not a preacher, you're a politician, you shouldn't talk like that. These are the people who attend church if the preacher gives them religion as an emotional catharsis. For these brothers and sisters, Karl Marx was profoundly correct when he wrote that religion was the "opiate of the masses." But if they were looking for a narcotic with which to anesthetize themselves, they realized they wouldn't find it with me.

There were some other old-timers who were frightened by our rapid growth. They heard about the way Peoples Temple was growing too, and they knew about my earlier interactions with Jim Jones. They began to wonder if I was that kind of person. After all, Jim Jones preached the same social ministry that I did. Jim Jones preached all of the biblical truths upon which I had staked my very soul. I was young and charismatic—and if I'm no longer young, I do hope I still have charisma—but the combination and the example across the Bay in the form of Jim Jones made people question if I was a cult leader. But there were also enough people around who could sense that I was not like him, that I was not building a church around me, that my style of leadership was more democratic, that my call was to bring people to their God *and* their community, not to renounce them.

Still, I knew that telling some of these old-timers that I wasn't a cult leader was not sufficient. I had to show them. What I had to do was to stretch myself, to hold on to them, while trying to honor others. And it worked. We were able to do that because we had some of what the old crowd wanted in worship, and we had some of what the new crowd wanted in worship.

THE MINISTRY OF PEOPLES TEMPLE

If the history of Peoples Temple gave it a unique congregation when it came to town, there's no denying that it continued to build, and to reach out, and to continue its growth and transformation where it found itself newly planted. In that way, Peoples Temple wasn't separate or different from black churches as much as it was separate and different from *all* churches.

The Temple had members with good jobs, well-paying jobs, professional jobs, because Jim Jones brought them in. He was smart. He was no fool. When it was necessary, he would play the anti-intellectual card. He would say in his sermons, "We don't need any of those college professors in here." But when he needed to prove the intellectual integrity of his message and his ministry, he was quick to call out the names of the professors and teachers who stood by him. Jim Jones would rail against the government in his sermons, but there were members of the Temple in city government, county government, state government, people he could turn to in a single heartbeat and ask to get things done on behalf of his people. Jim Jones would blast the legal system that locked up minorities and the economic system that condemned them to poverty, but he had lawyers and accountants who could manage the Temple's affairs from within the church. Jim Jones would sprinkle his sermons with references to innumerable faith healings and resurrections from the dead, but his congregation included nurses and care home administrators who tended to the elderly and sick and made sure they had decent housing, adequate health care, and companionship. And he intended these professional resources to grow, with students attending college with the benefit of Temple financing.

But the majority of his members were the people who came to the Temple in need. And I'll be blunt about this. If you're hungry, you need food. And Jones provided it. So they came, and they stayed.

Let me also say this about his followers: they were sincere. They weren't what the missionaries to China used to call "rice Christians," the people who would stick around for a sermon because they knew they would get something to eat when it was over. They weren't like people in the Bowery or the Mission, who knew they would get a meal if they sat through a bad sermon. No, these people were really genuine. They were coming because their needs—first their basic human needs, and then, through the church, their need for a caring community—were being met.

The Gospel of Luke tells us that John the Baptist asked Jesus through his disciples, "Are you the one? Are you for real? Or should we look for somebody else?" And Jesus replied, "Go and tell John what you have seen and heard: the blind regain their sight, the lame walk, lepers are cleansed, the deaf hear, the dead are raised, the poor have the good news proclaimed to them." That's what Jim Jones said he would do for his followers, and he did enough that they believed the rest.

It hurts me to say that, because this is where we as the San Francisco Bay Area Christian community must shoulder a portion of the blame for Jim Jones' success. If more African American churches had built holistic ministries rooted in justice, Jones would have not been able to find a toehold in San Francisco. If my African American pastor peers had met the needs of the people, instead of just preaching about them, Jim Jones would not have flourished in San Francisco. The people of our community wanted their needs met, and they needed them met right then. They were not waiting for some eschatological heaven. There was a vacuum of services, and Jim Jones filled it. He acted much like the Black Panther Party in this town, which filled a vacuum.

The Bay Area Christian community did not offer services along with the sermons. In that way, they—we—helped to create Jim Jones.

The black pastors know this truth, but we can't talk about it, even to each other. Even a quarter-century after Jim Jones took all those people to Guyana—why, oh why, my Lord, did he take them to Guyana?—we *still* can't talk about it. And the reason we can't is we'd have to begin the conversation with an acknowledgment of our responsibility. More than that, we'd have to acknowledge the conversations that we *did* have back then, when we complained about Jones' ability to draw black folk from our own pews. Here was this man, coming and taking our people, but we didn't talk about the theology of Peoples Temple that might have disturbed us, and we didn't talk about the ways we could duplicate the social services that Peoples Temple offered. No, instead we talked about our own growing congregations and the terrible competition that Peoples Temple represented to that growth. After the deaths in Guyana we were stunned—shamed—into silence. Even now, it pains me to speak of our failings, our missed opportunities, our culpability in this tragedy.

THE WHITENESS OF JIM JONES

Without minimizing anything I've said before, I do need to add one aspect of the Peoples Temple minister which we could not control, which we could not change, which we could do nothing about: Jim Jones was a white man. Especially for his elderly followers, there was an authority that a white leader has that the most educated black man can't have. It is a thriving vestige of racism that damages the black community and—to my way of thinking—damages the white community too.

In this case, though, there was an even more powerful combination at work. Jim Jones had both the authority of being white and the rhythm and the cadence of the preaching style of black. The combination drew black people to the church, and it kept them in the church. They not only had a man who could speak their language, they also had a white leader who could speak the language of the dominant society. And they knew it. They knew they could move forward with that church more than they could with any other. They suddenly had the strength, power, and influence of being white.

There's a similar phenomenon in America right now as it relates to charismatic churches. They are all led by white ministers. And they have blacks, although not necessarily poor blacks, as Peoples Temple did. They're not a part so much of the administration, but they are a part of the music, the choirs, the celebration, the liturgy. They have a prominent role there, even if that role is to set the stage for this dynamic white preacher. Jim Jones understood this dynamic and knew that even as his leadership gave his black congregants power, their presence—their sheer numbers—gave him power.

A BLACK CHURCH?

Even though Jim Jones had a large black following—reflected most tragically in the percentage of blacks among the dead in Jonestown—I am reluctant to characterize Peoples Temple as a black church. A black church is rooted in the community, its strength percolating up from the foundation of that community. Its members may travel around the country on behalf of the church, and it may even have a national presence, but it will remain part of its home community. It certainly would be impossible for a black church to accept the defeat that a move to a foreign country would represent.

The leader of a black church must also have the power. It's a power that eludes definition, a power that can only be demonstrated—perhaps "illuminated" is a better word—through the example of Martin Luther King. When Dr. King came to town, the pastors showed up. And even today, when Jesse Jackson comes on the scene, the pastors show up. Pastors that I never see otherwise show up. Fellows drop what they're doing. Jesse's popularity may not be as great as Dr. King's, but when he comes, we show up. When we show up, some of our people show up also. And it is through us that Jesse has a platform or a base. But Jim Jones did not have that kind of a base. His base did not go beyond Peoples Temple.

In some ways, I am also hesitant to describe Peoples Temple as a church at all. It certainly had the trappings of a church, the offices and rituals and robes and music of a church. But it fell away from any kind of religious message. And because everything in the Temple was invested in one man, it could not—and it did not—survive his death.

Let me return to Allen Temple Baptist Church as an illustration of what I mean. Allen Temple was a church when I arrived 32 years ago, and it will be a church after I leave. It has grown in part because of the message that I preach. The people have responded to the message that I preach. Part of that response is in their taking leadership roles within the church. And that's one thing that separates us from Peoples Temple.

I mentioned earlier that I have a more democratic leadership style than Jim Jones. My style is to try to empower people, empower people, empower people. We have a prison ministry; I don't run it. We have an AIDS ministry; I don't run it. We have a job training center; I don't run it. We have a skills center; I don't run it. We have tutorial programs, we have a children's minister, we have a youth minister, we have a senior citizens ministry, and I don't run any of them. We have a Latino pastor on the church staff, we have a minister's training program, and I don't supervise them. But I launched all of them. It was my leadership that got them started, and I keep them encouraged and keep them inspired.

I don't have anything to do with the money. When they bring a check to me in the service and say we want to present a certain amount to the pastor from some community association, for a tutorial or for a scholarship, I say, "Wait while I call a trustee," because I never even touch the checks.

After I retire, other people will be able to provide the leadership and the inspiration and the encouragement, because we have a long-range planning committee that's studying the future needs of the church. It will be a seamless transition from me to my successor and to where the church will go. I won't have to worry about the program dying, because it's not built around me. They're studying how to build on the foundation that the church has right now, the foundation that would be there if I left tomorrow. Peoples Temple did not build a foundation, and it left nothing after it died.

WHEN RELIGION BECOMES SIN

There's a hillside at Evergreen Cemetery in Oakland, beneath which rest the remains of hundreds of people—mainly children—who died in Guyana and who were never identified or whose bodies were never claimed. I was summoned as one of the pastors to deliver a eulogy, to offer words of comfort, solace, hope. Over the years, I have spoken at more funerals than I can remember. But I remember this one. Sometimes, the family can turn the graveside ceremony into a cauldron of human emotion. That did not happen on this inclement day. The mourners seemed numb. They stared at me in disbelief as if to ask, "Who are you, and what are we all doing here?" I saw emptiness in the sockets of their eyes. They were a people beyond sorrow. I shudder to recall it even this many years later.

I preached a sermon on that occasion entitled "When Religion Becomes Sin." I spoke about the justice of God. I believe we need to do everything in our power to struggle for justice in this life, but I told the mourners that we are not always successful, that justice does not always arrive in this life. Oftentimes, God rewards his children in the world to come. I do believe in eternal life. I told the mourners that, too.

I have had plenty of opportunities to reflect back on that time, and I feel I have learned a few things.

I have learned that true prophetic religion must always create a space for critical analysis and reflection prior to the enactment of social justice. The failure to do so will always result in the exchange of one oppressive pharaoh for another.

I have learned that the potential for evil is latent in the best of us. There's so much bad in the best of us, and so much good in the worst of us. And that defines the human predicament. When we think that we have flowered into a culture where there is a garden of Eden, we find out that Eden is not a perfect environment. Because there's a serpent there. Germany, the home of great culture and music and literature and philosophy and education, produced a Hitler. We may think that we have taken an upward step, but I view it more like Sisyphus trying to get the stone up the mountain, and he stumbles, and he and the rock fall again to the bottom of the slope. I have learned that the struggle to become human will always remain a perpetual struggle, and we have to always pray, "Lead us not into temptation, but deliver us from evil."

I have learned that the growing anti-intellectualism of the African American church is inexcusable. Black people who desire that their medical professionals have knowledge of the latest technological advancements in the field of medicine, and who desire that their financial planners have impeccable educational credentials, should always look into the training and background of the man or woman in the pulpit. But they don't, so that anti-intellectualism is still there. It is still there. If we would visit an African American ministerial association, you would discover that 80 percent of the men call themselves "Doctor." But the inconsistency is that they are anti-intellectual. But yet you've insulted them if you don't call them "Doctor."

On the other side of the coin, the fellows in the church with no training are suspicious of those of us who paid our dues, who made the sacrifices. Our church has been stigmatized as the bourgeois church. "Allen Temple is bourgeoisie," they say, "you don't want to go there." They say, "Pastor Smith pastors out of a book," and they don't mean the Bible. They're talking about my library.

I have associates who are college and seminary graduates. They write. But they have no pulpit. But a fellow with a little money can go right down to a storefront in East Oakland and rent it, call himself "Doctor," get him some drums, some tambourines, some musicians, and he's in business. He'll take advantage of the people who are looking for the wrong thing in a preacher. They want a preacher that will make them feel good. Not to think. That troubles me. That troubles me. That troubles me. I feel it as sharply now as I felt it 32 years ago.

There is, of course, another trend that arises from this anti-intellectualism, and that is the trend toward prosperity Christianity, the packages that merely market religion to strive for the unholy dollar rather than deal with *any* ethical concern whatsoever.

I am deeply concerned about younger pastors and seminarians who are impressed with the mega-church movement, which says that if a church is very large, it is good, and so all of the ministers' efforts go into building a big church. I am concerned about some of the younger pastors and seminarians who are not only sexist and homophobic and materialistic, but who instead of preaching the gospel of prophetic Christianity, preach a prosperity gospel from Sunday to Sunday. Unless they change, they leave the door wide open for another Jim Jones to appear with false messianic hopes.

Unfortunately, the seminaries are contributing to the problem rather than solving it. In my opinion, the staff of a seminary has a responsibility to make sure it trains preachers who could lead a child in today's world. But there's a gap between the town and the gown. And many of the fellows who do the teaching don't want to have anything to do with the preaching, and by that I mean the parish church. They look down on the parish church, they make fun of the parish church, they make fun of parish preachers. They even have the audacity to say to seminary students who are not so bright, "You would make a good pastor."

So the anti-intellectualism comes from both directions. And the result is that many of our churches still do not have a theology. They cling only to a shallow moralism. They have shut the door that hinges between reason and faith.

We have lost many of those whom W. E. B. Du Bois called "the talented tenth." The educated lost now wander down the corridors of sophistication and materialism and narcissism, or they embrace the hip-hop rap gangsta mentality that preaches a different gospel. They no longer accept the invitation to pick up the cross of Jesus, because they don't hear it, because no one in the churches—and definitely no one outside the church—wants to talk about the sweat and blood and sacrifice and loss we must endure before we reach the reward. We just want the reward.

GRIEF AND RESPONSIBILITY

But what's more important than what we've learned is what we have not learned. I wrote before of the conversation that we in the black clergy have not had. We are afraid of acknowledging our responsibility, yes, but we are also afraid of expressing our grief. And so we have bottled it up inside. It's ironic that we are so encouraging, so insistent, that the families in our congregations do their grief work after a loss, and yet here we are, a quarter-century later, trained in counseling and experienced with death, and we have not yet learned how to do our own grief work over the deaths in Jonestown. Even now. Because if we had, we would have some paradigms to make sure that it would not happen again. You hear the Jews saying in response to the Holocaust, "Never again!" But because we have not done our grief work, because we have not looked at the Jim Jones phenomenon critically, and because we have not examined our own implication in the whole process, we have not come forth with a synthesis to determine what preventive steps we need to take to ensure that this never happens again. And we thereby leave the door open for it to happen again, and again, and again, and again.

So this would be my challenge to the new generation of black ministers coming onto the scene in the Bay Area. The older generation—my generation—has demonstrated that we are incapable of processing, much less understanding, Jim Jones. It's my challenge to the ones who follow to pick up the pieces that we didn't.

The new generation does not have to shoulder our burdens of responsibility for the success of Jim Jones, for the emigration of the members of Peoples Temple to Guyana, for the deaths in Jonestown. The new generation does not have to explain or justify or defend or weep or examine their own failings on these issues. They do not have to linger behind the wall of silence.

This, then, is my call to action. This is my pained plea to the new generation of African American men and women. We need to go deep within ourselves to bring forth evidence of the intellectual respectability of the whole religious experience. Within the context of that dimension, we need to question what it was within the Black Church that Jim Jones addressed and that we didn't.

And when we come to terms with that, when we reach an understanding, when we can name the poison that drew our people away as surely and insidiously as the poison in Jonestown that took so many of our brothers and sisters, we will finally confront the power that Jim Jones had, and we will know how to defeat it.

And we will have broken the silence.

Amen.

9

America Was Not Hard to Find

MUHAMMED ISAIAH KENYATTA

In these, our troubling times, I find no clearer signal of God's call to repentance than the phenomenon called Jonestown. Whether American Christians comprehended Jonestown may well determine their answer to an important question: Did those nine hundred shed the fertile blood of martyrs, or did they do nothing more than add another pointless footnote to the annals of bizarre decadence which chronicle these last days of the American empire?

As Christians, our only authenticity is in living and telling the greatest Good News. We should therefore know better than any others that transcendent significance is not simply in events. It is also in the stories that illuminate the meaning of events. So whether Jonestown is merely superfluous evidence of the banality of evil or becomes a precious lesson which renews our faith depends largely upon our articulate understanding of these nine hundred lives and deaths. But beyond that, our understanding of Jonestown hangs on the cross of our understanding of ourselves and on our call to continual witness in America.

First, we need to look squarely at the bare facts, unadorned by the meanings ascribed to them in pop journalism.

Peoples Temple embraced two congregations affiliated with the Christian Church (Disciples of Christ) communion or "denomination." These two, one in California and one in Guyana, are reported to have been among the five largest congregations of the Disciples. Pastor

This article first appeared in *The Other Side* 93 (June 1979), and is reprinted by permission. The ellipses which appear are in the original.

James Jones, by all indications, was a minister in good standing within his denomination. The Disciples have long been recognized as a *bona fide* ecclesiastical body, according to secular law and to the maxims of various local, national, and international Protestant ecumenical groupings.

Peoples Temple was no more or less legitimately Christian than many other local churches, be they Episcopalian or Southern Baptist or United Methodist or Lutheran or African Methodist Episcopal or what-have-you. Disclaimers after the fact that Peoples Temple was a renegade cult are both self-serving sophistry and conspicuously hypocritical exercises in self-denial when propounded by less-than-Christian American Christians.

Furthermore, Christians ought to be very wary of attempts to minimize the significance of Jonestown. Some do this by scapegoating James Jones as a mind-manipulating, charismatic leader. (I'm using the term *charismatic* in the sociological sense.)

American Protestant Christianity, especially as expressed by the poor and marginalized classes, is notoriously inclined toward the elevation of charismatic personalities. But we cannot, with integrity, nail James Jones to the cross of the cult of personality. For if we do, we must also raise the hammer to such cherished figures as Billy Graham and Martin Luther King Jr. (not to mention such lesser lights as Chuck Colson, James Cone, William Sloane Coffin, or our favorite local preacher).

What we do know is that Jones and Peoples Temple undertook a ministry largely focused on the poor, on oppressed minorities, and on others alienated from mainstream U.S.A. We know that ministry flourished (if the numbers of adherents and the dollar value of contributions are indices of successful ministry). And numbers and money *are* appropriate measures of evangelical success and commitment, if we are to believe the wide range of effective media campaigns with which we are regularly bombarded. (I think of the efforts of such diverse ministries as those of Robert Schuller, Tom Skinner Associates, the Christian Broadcasting Network, the Presbyterian Major Mission Fund, and many others.)

Of course, numbers and money are not the only signs of effective ministry. All of the aforementioned (and the vast majority of Christians) also affirm our responsibility to heed the charge of our risen Lord, who said, "Feed my sheep." Contemporary missions, from the Voice of Calvary in Mississippi to the World Council of Churches' Program to Combat Racism, recommend themselves to us. And they recommend themselves to us as creative models of sheep-feeding in the context of current social realities. So, too, do efforts like Bread for the World or the American Friends Service Committee or the American Committee on Africa, all of which owe their inception to impulses of Christian service.

Additionally, there are more traditional approaches to Christian service. I think of Catholic Charities, Oral Roberts University, church-affiliated schools and hospitals, settlement houses of varying denominational genesis, and the plethora of hunger programs. Whether innovative or traditional, ameliorative or reformist, these approaches share a common understanding. They all affirm that our faith lives in our works for and among those in need.

On this score, none can deny that Peoples Temple compiled a commendable record of socially good works and progressive social advocacy. If the needy themselves are in any way appropriate judges, then Peoples Temple stood in quite favorable judgment.

Further, we know that Peoples Temple became, in part, a pilgrim church. Following a tradition at least as time-hallowed as the colonial settlements symbolized by Plymouth Rock, a large contingent of Peoples Temple uprooted itself from its native land. It set out to a frontier place in the hopes of better perfecting the practice of its faith. Just as the pilgrims of U.S. folklore migrated to the New World, so these Peoples Temple settlers migrated toward the attraction of virgin territory and away from perceived persecution.

To the credit of Peoples Temple, its leaders did not do as the European colonists did in their New World; that is, unlike the European Christians who brought genocide and race slavery, Peoples Temple secured permission from legitimate authority before colonizing Guyana's jungle. And once there it manifested a multiracial familyhood in sharp variance to the racist society from which Peoples Temple had fled.

It may be helpful to note something about the settlement policy of the Guyanese government. I was privileged to hear this policy delineated by Prime Minister Forbes Burnham when he met with a group of U.S. blacks in Guyana in 1970.

Guyana is a multiracial nation. It includes descendants of African slaves, descendants of indentured servants from the Indian subcontinent of Asia, descendants of European colonizers, remnants of various native American populations, and assorted other descendants from various subject peoples of the old British empire.

Slavery and imperialist domination has strongly characterized Guyana's history. So has conflict between subject peoples—notably African Guyanese and Hindu Guyanese. In 1970, when Guyana declared itself a "cooperative republic," it set for itself twin goals. One was ending foreign economic domination. And the other was ending internal ethnic conflict.

The Burnham government has been influenced largely by the Christianized cultural inclinations of the politically dominant African population. It has also sought an alternative path to socialism, divergent from the doctrinaire Marxism espoused by Guyana's major opposition party.

In this political and cultural context, and confronted with the demographic reality of huge expanses of underpopulated jungle areas, the Burnham government evolved a policy of welcoming settlers. These settlers would contract to undertake development of wilderness areas on a cooperative economic basis. (This policy blends characteristics of homesteading with cooperative economic schemes such as those used by John Perkins in rural Mississippi today.)

Thus, there is nothing surprising or sinister about the terms under which Guyana welcomed Peoples Temple. Peoples Temple had all the right things going for it. It had an anti-capitalist bias, commitment to cooperative ownership, multiracial composition, and a profession of Christian communalism reminiscent of the early church described in Acts.

Moreover, the Peoples Temple settlement was approximately 70 percent black. That very significant fact surely could not have been lost to Guyanese observers, keenly aware of the vicious racism which still oppresses U.S. blacks.

Had the Peoples Temple story continued along these visible lines, it would have stood as a challenge to the majority of North American Christians. It would have called us to take seriously the holistic message of our faith.

Think about it:

A band of Christian pilgrims and social visionaries leaves the ghettos and spiritual catacombs of a decadent empire. A called-out people is reborn in a contemporary Antioch of Christian communalism. The third world, in a telling irony, offers a refuge to the oppressed and marginalized of this Yankee Babylon.

Wow, one can easily imagine Jonestown being "discovered" by its counterpart communities in the U.S. I can see it being celebrated by publications like *The Other Side*, the Episcopal *Witness*, and *Sojourners*.

But the story did not unfold so felicitously. Rather the story spilled, like the shocking red blood of Jesus, across the headlines of the chronicles of our era—the *Los Angeles Times*, the *Washington Post*, *Newsweek*, and the *National Enquirer*. The grisly mix of mass murder and suicide left over nine hundred dead. Count them—one by scarlet one—children, women, men, infants, elders, perhaps rich and surely, surely poor. Wretched dead, stinking rotten sacks of flesh that had been the abodes of living souls . . .

In one day, in the twinkling of an eye, they died and died. Outstripping the body count of that day's casualties in the Namibian and Zimbabwean liberation wars. A number equaling one out of every thousand residents of Cleveland, Ohio. More than ten times the number of Black Panthers murdered in the FBI's conspiratorial war on black militance. Nearly half the population of Plains, Georgia. Forty times the victims of Lt. Calley at My Lai. Sixty-odd tons of human meat fetid in the tropical sun . . .

How can we begin to really comprehend the carnage? Before so monstrous a testimony to human sinfulness, dare we begin to shed even a single tear for fear we could never stop crying? Can we test the limits of our sanity by trying to take it all in?

But dare we tempt the living of our spirit by not trying? Can we risk not remembering forever that these nine hundred were flesh of our flesh and blood of our blood?

And what, oh Lord, is the meaning of this sacrifice?

To hear the answers and to understand why Jonestown calls us to repentance and to renewal, I believe we must recall the message that was the immediate trigger of the event. We must, for a moment, arrest our despair and soberly complete our chronicle.

Newspaper evidence indicates that one trigger of the Jonestown dying was a message the leaders gave the settlers. The message was that if the settlement closed down, all the people would have *to return to the United States*. Distraught over this possibility, one settler sent Jones a note, imploring him to save them "from having to go back to fascist Babylon."

What triggered this carnage? Not just the Ryan murder. Not just the threat of a deeper probe or individual indictments. Not even a sudden recognition that the cultic, charismatic James Jones was, despite all of his visibly good works, a man overcome by a demonic psychosis. No, not just these. For under all of these lingered a haunting fear. And according to several newspaper investigators, it was the haunting fear of the masses. It was the fear—whether true or false, chance or calculation—that if the settlement closed, they would have to go back home.

Home. To the United States. To us!

Here is the question that we, the body of Christ in the United States, must wrestle with. It is not simply a question of cults or demonicized charisma or ecclesiastical authority or political conspiracy or financial skullduggery. It is not a racist fantasy of civilization succumbing to Conradian forces of jungle darkness. Above all, Jonestown is not a question of the validity of Christian communalism and radically holistic witness against the structures of injustice. And we must not let it be so construed.

Rather, the question of Jonestown is that of return to America. To understand Jonestown, we must see our country, our church, ourselves as the nine hundred saw us.

One of the Fathers Berrigan once wrote a poem, the title and refrain of which was "America is hard to find." I do not think America was hard to find for the nine hundred. They had found it and found it hopelessly hard.

The blacks in Jonestown had found America in Oakland and Harlem. They, and thousands of other blacks who, but for God's grace, might have been among them, found America blazing from the muzzles of police guns. They had found it as naked as the racism beneath the fig leaf of Proposition 13. They saw America sitting at breakfast in the White House with Richard Nixon and Billy Graham.

They watched America loading the moving vans when thousands of white Christian families fled Cleveland, Ohio, to avoid school desegregation or returned to re-gentrify Georgetown in Washington, D.C. They felt America's hand thrusting the flagpole like a red-white-and-blue bayonet as a "southie" attacked a black bystander at a Boston anti-busing rally. They heard America when the mayor of this country's fourth largest city bellowed the call to "Vote white!" They heard America even more clearly when half of Philadelphia's white voters rallied to that call.

They, and others locked in the inner-city underclass, found America daily. They found it riding like a white ape on the backs of black and Hispanic teenage dope fiends in Newark and the South Bronx, where heroin is more plentiful than jobs. Daily, they felt the warmth of America in fire-trap tenements going up in smoke and roasting their babies like made-in-U.S.A. marshmallows.

White and black, the adolescents and young adults found America packaged in green plastic bags bearing brothers home from Vietnam. They heard America when born-again Jimmy Carter sanctified and idolatrized Nelson Rockefeller and muttered not a mumbling word for the 43 guards and inmates butchered by Rockefeller's bullets at Attica.

Those idealistic Christian visionaries, bold in the flawed hope of Jonestown but ignored on the back pews of our own worship places, found America turning the key that slammed the lock that sealed the cage where Ben Chavis is jailed in Wilmington, North Carolina. They caught America looking over the gun-sight at the balcony of a Memphis hotel on April the fourth, the year of our Lord 1968.

The elderly at Jonestown and down the street from our own homes in Ourtown, U.S.A., found America, too. They found America in lonely convalescent homes and other age-ghettos where America casts them away like yesterday's fashions. Some of them heard America in the clanking of their spoons inside the dog-food tin-cans that hold the best meals their pensions could buy. They saw America in our eyes averted from their sagging flesh and knobby-jointed unsightliness.

The women, too, found America as she jiggled in a braless-look bra and looked like she was wearing nothing at all under her oh-so-tight clothes. And indeed she wore nothing at all between the pages of *Hustler* magazine because, even if Larry Flynt is reborn and half-dead, business must go on.

And the women heard America explain that business is teeny-bopper prostitutes on Times Square street corners dreaming of promotions into massage parlors where Mr. America damn sure expects more than a rubdown for his 20 dollars. And they heard America teaching our daughters that love is sex is women for sale in their places on America's bargain basement shelves like Farrah Fawcett posters all in row.

And we who are of the same body and blood of Jesus Christ, who was crucified anew nine hundred times on one afternoon in the jungle, must confess that we, too, have found America. And we are it. We are its sustainers and sufferers, its victims and executioners.

We must repent of what America has become. And we must repent that our church has become so indistinguishable from America. When the message reached Jonestown, that it was time to return, the nine hundred could not find us. They could not find us waiting here, in America but not of America. We must repent of having become so much like America that the nine hundred could not see us standing here with arms outstretched, saying, "Welcome home."

We must take upon ourselves the responsibility of America. We must and we can, by God's grace, be transformed and transforming even in this desolate land.

We must and we can give meaning to the sacrifice of Jonestown. From the flawed vision of Peoples Temple, we must and can resurrect that which is good and authentic in the Way of Jesus.

We must. We *must* because that is our peculiar, historic calling as

God's church in this land of no-return. We must because we owe it to the nine hundred and ourselves.

And we can. We can because that is the universal, eternal promise of God's Son who is resurrected and returned to us for this and all times, from Golgotha to Guyana to tomorrow.

Shalom.

10

The Church in Peoples Temple

MARY R. SAWYER

In the mid-1970s, some one thousand members of the movement known as Peoples Temple relocated from California to the South American country of Guyana to build a settlement that they intended would exemplify the principles of communalism and racial harmony. Within days and even hours of receiving word of the tragic ending of this settlement, most of America had become persuaded that those who perished there were either politically or psychologically demented or both. Consequently, their dignity as human beings was utterly denied.

At the time, in our shock and in the face of public reactions, those of us living in northern California who had worked with the people of Peoples Temple in various capacities and who had developed a positive regard for their social and political activities could do little else but offer feeble defenses of the members: "But they were individuals just like you and me." For the most part, our voices were silenced. While some have integrated this experience into their life journeys, many still are reluctant to speak of the personal ties they had to the group and its members, in large part because of the sense of shame generated by the demonizing and caricaturing of the movement and its leader, Jim Jones, by those who did not know the people personally.

The dehumanizing of the victims of Jonestown by the journalistic community was tantamount to the withholding of permission to grieve. And America's religious community—that vast potential reservoir of pastoral care—was unable to facilitate a proper grieving, either on the part of the families immediately affected or on the part of the nation, because they, too, did not know the people, and what we do not know in a personal way, we cannot mourn. Indeed, because of not knowing the people, the church and its national congregation could not begin to fathom how very much there was to mourn.

Martin Amos was a beautiful, precocious, biracial 10-year-old who loved books and plants. Annie Moore was the artistic daughter of a United Methodist minister who, together with his wife, had routinely included all three of their children in peace and civil rights demonstrations; Annie followed her older sister Carolyn Layton into the movement. Richard Tropp was a Jew who had been in the South during the Civil Rights movement. Fred Lewis was never a member, but 27 of his relatives, including his wife and children, died in Guyana. Marcie Jones had the most gentle spirit of any woman I have ever met. She was the abused spouse of Jim; she was dearly loved by the Peoples Temple family.

People joined the Temple for one of two reasons: in order to give help, or in order to receive it. Caring individuals were drawn to the movement's emphatic commitment to racial equality and economic sufficiency. They were deeply impressed that the Temple helped drug addicts recover, found new vocations for prostitutes, served food to the hungry, provided shelter for the homeless and homes for senior citizens. The people who joined had grand ideals and big hearts. Or they had trouble. They *were* the drug addicts or the prostitutes or the hungry or the financially insecure.

In practical terms, Peoples Temple was a movement that offered sanctuary from racial discrimination, opportunity for education and employment, and the promise of lifelong economic security. In spiritual terms, it offered the experience of community and the occasion to be a part of something larger than oneself. It did what religion does: it met people's needs. It provided meaning and purpose. It addressed ultimate concerns.

Throughout its entire history, Peoples Temple was commonly understood to be a Christian organization. Certainly in San Francisco, it was regarded as a church. When its Christian credentials were brought into question, however, the problem arose as to how to categorize the movement.

A voice I hear with clarity across the chasm of time is that of Mervyn Dymally, who from 1974 to 1978 served as lieutenant governor of the State of California. A native Trinidadian and naturalized citizen, Lieutenant Governor (later Congressman) Dymally brought to his public service a keen sensitivity to the social inequities of race and class. Throughout his tenure as a state senator in the 1960s and early 1970s, he was a leading author of progressive civil rights and social services legislation. As such, he earned from the Peoples Temple movement the same enthusiastic endorsement and support that was enjoyed by other justice-minded public officials in California.

Thus it was that Dymally exclaimed to me, following one of his visits to Peoples Temple, "This is what church *ought* to be about: community and a concern for social justice. Peoples Temple," he exclaimed, "is a *real* church."

I met him in 1975 while I was conducting research on the emerging problem of harassment of black elected officials, a pattern that was becoming all too evident a decade after the passage of the 1965 Voting Rights Act. Dymally referred me to Peoples Temple as a group that would likely help support my research. They did, immediately grasping my thesis that our country was threatening to repeat that historic event known as post-Reconstruction when blacks, having been momentarily enfranchised, were once again excluded from the democratic process.

Late in 1977, I joined the lieutenant governor's staff as his speechwriter and liaison with social change movements, which at the time ranged from the United Farm Workers movement to the Native American Walk for Peace to Peoples Temple. When rumors and allegations about the practices of Jim Jones and the Temple surfaced in the communications media, staff members of Peoples Temple asked our advice on how to respond. We replied, "If you have nothing to hide, the best policy is an open door." In the meantime, Dymally charged me with finding out "whether this group was in fact a real church."

My personal observations inclined me to answer, "No." While visiting the Temple one Sunday morning, I was invited to speak extemporaneously to the congregation—an experience I commonly had when visiting black churches. Immediately upon concluding my remarks I was publicly chastised by the Temple's attorney, Charles Garry, for invoking the word "God." "We don't use that word here," he declared. "Well," Marcie Jones hastened to amend, "we use a lot of different words to refer to what some call 'God.'" Her reassurance was short-lived. The service concluded with the congregation of hundreds of people joining the service leaders in a raised fist salute and a shout of "long live socialism."

It has taken lo these many years to begin to formulate a "Yes" response to Lieutenant Governor Dymally's question. "Yes, but . . ." Yes, but not as he meant it.

A MULTILAYERED MOVEMENT

Peoples Temple began as an independent Christian congregation and ended as a congregation in good standing with the Disciples of Christ (Christian) Church.[1] In the aftermath of Jonestown, some ceased regarding Peoples Temple as a religious movement at all. Others were quick to label the movement a cult, with attendant allegations of brainwashing. In subsequent years, some sociologists were more inclined to characterize it as a sect; a few argued that it had evolved from a sectarian movement to a cult, while others opted for the lexicon of New Religious Movement. John R. Hall characterized the organization variously as an "unconventional church" and as a "public relations façade" to promote socialism.[2]

Mary Maaga suggests that the appropriateness of different categories depends on which segments of the movement's membership one is considering: the white and black working-class families who were its original members when the movement began in Indiana in the 1950s; the young, white, college-educated Californians who found novelty and meaning in the movement in the 1960s; or the urban African American youth and elderly who were drawn to Peoples Temple in the 1970s.[3] Her analysis points to the complexity of the movement, which of itself may account for the struggles of social scientists to classify it. It also points to the reality that typologies of sects and cults often obscure more than they clarify. Not the least of what is obscured are the stories and experiences of the participants themselves.

Most accounts of Peoples Temple acknowledge that at least 80 percent of the movement's members during the years it was based in San Francisco were African American; more recently, Rebecca Moore has suggested the number was closer to 90 percent. Reports of membership have ranged from 2,000 to 8,000 to as many as 20,000. Actual membership figures are elusive, since the Temple itself counted as members those people who came to visit without their going through a formal process of "joining."[4] Two to three thousand is perhaps a reasonable estimate of individuals who regularly attended services or participated in outreach activities.

More precise data is available for members who lived in Jonestown. Moore has identified more than 1,000 Peoples Temple members who were living in Guyana in November 1978—giving names to 900 of the 918 who perished and 122 who survived.[5] More than two-thirds of Jonestown residents were African American, she reports. Black females outnumbered black males by almost two to one. Twenty percent of the members were over 60 years of age—with three-fourths of these being black women. Over a third of the population—36 percent—were infants, children, and teenagers.[6]

African Americans who were drawn to Peoples Temple represented a cross-section of the black community, from low-income to professionals. The religious backgrounds and affiliations of adult African Americans who regarded themselves as members of Peoples Temple—either in San Francisco or in Guyana—are not precisely known. But it is known that many of them—whole families as well as individuals—came to the Temple from black churches. In fact, while still in San Francisco, some continued to attend their traditional church while also attending services at Peoples Temple, a practice not uncommon in black churches. Archie Smith Jr. writes of one such instance:

> One black pastor reported that a beloved member of long-standing and deep involvement in her own church was a Jonestown victim. In a conversation with her pastor, she reported that she was attracted to Peoples Temple because "they did things together, ate and took trips together." They were able to provide a family-like atmosphere, a sense of belonging on a daily basis in ways that she could not find in her own church. For her, the church still functioned as the central community institution which strengthened her participation in a larger social and political process. It was not that her home church failed her, but that she found in the Peoples Temple *more* opportunities for involvement.
>
> This particular woman never gave up membership in her home church, even though she claimed membership in the Peoples Temple. She was not alone in her desire to see the church more involved in issues of social protest and reform. Participation in her home church may well have been a motivating factor for involvement in the more socially active orientation of the Peoples Temple.[7]

Even those who were not previously affiliated with another church in any formal way had quite likely been influenced to some degree by the ethos of African American Christianity. (Many, if not most, African Americans who joined the Nation of Islam or the Black Panther Party, for example, had been brought up in black churches.) Just as Peoples Temple presented itself as a church, so most of its recruits perceived Peoples Temple that way. Maaga points out that in all its developmental stages, the Temple "behaved like a traditional mainstream religious organization in its recruitment strategies."

> Individuals would be attracted to the Pentecostal-style healing services, or interracial congregation and social activism, or social services and supportive community. Individuals would then invite

family members and close friends to participate in this wonderful church they had found. Even the most negative accounts of Peoples Temple generally start with an account of the excitement at having discovered such a lively, committed and caring congregation.[8]

But what became of these religious orientations once these individuals were fully engaged in Peoples Temple? What happened when the realities of internal conflict and abusive control became apparent? What was the response when Jones rejected Christianity and disparaged those who upheld it?

As Anthony Pinn points out in the first chapter of this book, the religious experience of African Americans is not limited to Christianity. While some 80 percent of all African Americans are estimated to have a church affiliation,[9] a large number are Muslim, a few are Jewish, some practice Buddhism, a significant number are practicing quasi-African religions, and an unknown number identify as humanists. It is entirely reasonable to suppose that the religious orientations of those involved in Peoples Temple—both prior to joining and while they were members—were not restricted to a Christian worldview. They may well have adapted or developed new religious understandings. But if the religious experiences of members in this movement were not limited to Christianity, neither were Christian formulations necessarily precluded.

That a critical mass of African Americans might have preserved a black spiritual cosmos in the midst of white-orchestrated chaos and deception seems plausible enough in light of the fact that black religion was formulated and sustained precisely in the midst of the white-orchestrated chaos and deception of slavery and Jim Crow segregation. And a people astute enough to know that Paul's admonition for slaves to obey their masters did not exhaust the parameters of the gospel, surely also were able—if they so chose—to assign Christian meaning to their participation in this movement, even if Jim Jones' dismissal of Christian scriptures rendered his organization not-church.

One is compelled to consider at least the possibility that nestled within the church façade of the larger movement was a *real* church, that is, a body of believers who, in their values and activities and goals—and in their private, internal reflections—understood themselves to be keeping the faith of the African American Christian tradition. Definitive, empirical documentation of this notion would require an analysis of the members' own testimony—testimony that, for obvious reasons, is now largely unobtainable. But anecdotal data and conceptual inferences give a degree of credence to this scenario.

While consideration of the religious understandings of African

American members, Christian and otherwise, does not provide a complete account of the Peoples Temple movement, surely no account can be definitive absent such consideration.

AFRICAN AMERICAN CHRISTIANITY

African American Christianity developed as a confluence of three religious systems—the traditional cosmologies that Africans brought with them from their homelands in Africa, their meaning systems as they were modified during two hundred years of enslavement, and the Christianity they encountered in the evangelical revivals and mission activity of Euro-American Protestants. Peter J. Paris is among the scholars of black religion who argue that the cosmology developed by African Americans preserved key elements of an African worldview—namely, the emphases on spirituality, family or kinship, and community. "Centuries of slavery, racial segregation, and disenfranchisement," Paris writes, "greatly enabled African Americans in retaining the most prominent elements of an African worldview that constituted their only reliable frame of meaning. Hence, all encounters with the world of their Western captors were interpreted through that frame of reference."[10]

As they encountered Christianity in the "New World," African Americans rejected the distorted uses to which whites put the faith in justifying racism and slavery. But many embraced the religion itself, finding its central tenets—the kinship of all people, just relationships, and community—to be consonant with their existing worldview. In these and other respects, Christianity spoke to their own experiences of oppression. Accordingly, they embraced both the promise of freedom in the life to come and the prophetic tradition of Christianity as it related to social justice and the imperative of freedom in this world.

No biblical text was more significant for African slaves than the story of Exodus. While white Christians understood themselves to be a "chosen people" who had been led to the "Promised Land" of America to fulfill a divine mission, African Americans interpreted the story as it corresponded to their own life circumstances. America, for them, was a land of bondage, and they were the enslaved people to whom God had promised freedom. Given a worldview that made no distinction between the sacred and the secular, enslaved Africans readily perceived the active pursuit of freedom to be a central requirement of Christianity. Accordingly, these values were incorporated into their cosmology. "Freedom" was understood as a communal matter, not just an individual concern. As C. Eric Lincoln puts it,

> In Africa the destiny of the individual was linked to that of the tribe or the community in an intensely interconnected security system. In America, black people have seldom been perceived or treated as individuals; they have usually been dealt with as "representatives" of their "race," an external projection. Hence, the communal sense of freedom has an internal African rootage curiously reinforced by hostile social convention imposed from outside on all African Americans as a caste. In song, word, and deed, freedom has always been the superlative value of the black sacred cosmos.[11]

This "black sacred cosmos," with its emphasis on community, justice, and freedom, has found expression in forms ranging from the United Negro Improvement Association to the Nation of Islam to the Southern Christian Leadership Conference. In less dramatic form, it is evident in the roles that black churches and their leaders have played since they first came into being. In the antebellum period, it was working for the abolition of slavery; following emancipation and throughout one hundred years of segregation, it was building schools, starting businesses, and serving as political liaisons with the white power structure; in the mid-1900s it was dismantling the very system of segregation and supporting black political development; since the 1980s, it has been fostering community outreach, building housing complexes and credit unions and providing health care and Afrocentric educational programs.

Not that all black churches and ministers have participated in all these activities. Black churches reflect a continuum of positions, from conservative and otherworldly to radically liberationist. This diversity was represented in the San Francisco Bay Area in the years that Peoples Temple was growing so rapidly. Many of its recruits came from churches that were spiritually oriented but lacked social outreach or political programs. The complaint that these black churches were not meeting the community's needs is not without merit. The larger reality, however, is that these churches did not *create* the needs. Rather, the alienation that brought people to the Temple was a function of the racism and economic exploitation of the larger society. Churches that were deemed sufficient before the Civil Rights and black consciousness movements—that had come into being in a different time and different circumstances—afterwards were not.

In important respects, Peoples Temple was more consonant with the newly generated expectations and aspirations of the day. At least some of the members joined not so much out of a sense of despair as out of a sense of hope and possibility. They were attracted to what, in its external features at least, was both a caring family and a Civil

Rights movement in miniature. In quest of genuine, inclusive community, they joined a movement that posed a challenge to the features of the larger society that were so destructive of community.

THE TEMPLE'S SELF-PRESENTATION: BLACK AND CHURCH

The socio-religious history of African Americans provides a partial, but not total, answer to the question of why African Americans were drawn to this movement—that is, to this particular movement that was led by a white man. Key characteristics of Peoples Temple, and especially of Jim Jones, make their actions more explicable.

First, Jones was profoundly influenced in his youth and young adult years by the reality of racial discrimination in the state of Indiana where he grew up; he was influenced, too, by the anti-Communist hysteria of the 1950s. Putting these together, he became a passionate, persuasive, and ultimately obsessive proponent of racial integration and economic equity. Identifying the church structure as the most viable vehicle for advancing these values—much as was occurring in the Civil Rights movement of the South—he preached a "gospel" that emphasized the communal model of the early church, the democratic value of equality of all people, the Christian imperative of "doing unto the least of these," and the Marxist tenet of "from each according to (their) ability, to each according to (their) need." That he failed utterly to achieve these ideals was all too evident in the fact that the inner circle of the Temple's leadership was predominantly white—but also predominantly consisting of socialistically inclined individuals who, if not religious, were committed to a communal lifestyle.

So invested in the principle of racial equality was he that Jones personally took on the ontological identity of blackness. Here are Jones' own words, spoken during a Peoples Temple service in 1973:

> I know that I'm black, and I've got a little bit of this and I've got a little bit of that, I got a little Indian, I got a little Jewish, and I've a little Scotch, and I've got some Welsh, but I recognize that I couldn't begin to identify what I am.
>
> So black is a consciousness. Black is a disposition. To act against evil. To do good. So I'm not going to label people and typecast. One of the blonde-headed women here was the first one to join me against the racist mob. She got out there and fought with her bare hands. She proved she was black.[12]

Ultimately, Jones even began to claim to have African ancestry. He spoke the inclusive language of "we blacks" and after moving to Guyana sometimes spoke of their intended utopian settlement as "Black Town."[13] In an intentional inversion of color symbolism, he referred to their suicide rehearsals as "White Nights." While in Redwood Valley, both black and white members who adopted the popular dress and hairstyles of the black consciousness movement were affirmed. Jim Jones appropriated the theological vocabulary, the autocratic leadership style, and the messianic themes of many black ministers. The services conducted at Peoples Temple had the ambience of black worship services, with strong emphasis on gospel music, testimonies, and healing.[14]

But their idealism notwithstanding, those who held the power also engaged in masterful deception as a means of furthering their cause. For Jones, the ends justified the means. He and his closest aides succeeded to a large extent in deceiving not only many of the members but most of the public at large.

Survivors recall that while still in Redwood Valley, the membership became divided into two primary groups: a smaller and predominantly, though not exclusively, white group which was committed to social justice but that was essentially secular in orientation, and a larger and predominantly, though not exclusively, black group that was religiously oriented. And Jim Jones gave to each according to their need. To the secular group he spoke the language of Marxist ideology and declared that religion was indeed "the opiate of the masses." To the religious group he spoke the gospel language of community, neighborliness, inclusivity, and justice, invoking the names of God and Jesus and eventually claiming that he, himself, was Christ returned.[15]

The economic and political objectives and the religious rhetoric came together in Jones' program of "apostolic socialism,"[16] a central component of which involved drawing black religious members—"the least" in the eyes of larger society and so the most exploited—away from an escapist, otherworldly version of Christianity to a set of social principles that mandated activism in order to create more just conditions in this world. Always the political program was given religious status and was framed by claims of special powers of perception and healing on Jones' part.

To this day, both survivors and non-members who on one occasion or another had the experience of being in his presence attest that Jones was indeed possessed of extraordinary charisma. More than human charm, he had unusual, if not supernatural, spiritual power. Some among these survivors speak of his powers for good that over time were transformed into powers for evil.[17] Some witnesses continue to believe that healings he performed in the earlier years of the movement were authentic, although no one questions that in the later years the healings were fake.

As the character of Jones' power changed and as his behavior became increasingly suspect, whatever tolerance for critique he had once displayed disappeared altogether. The discipline administered to those who were perceived to be obstructing pursuit of Jones' social principles was severe both psychologically and physically. An elaborate system of spying and reporting on one another was instituted; false rumors were started, causing friend to turn upon friend, all in the interest of maintaining control. Eventually, Jones declared the Bible itself to be a worthless document and dashed it to the ground in the presence of the members. But he continued to use the language of messianism to characterize himself, and he even continued to allow elderly members, especially, to talk among themselves about their traditional religious convictions—so long as they continued to be the committed workers for which he prized them.[18] So long as they gave according to their ability.

In the very last years of the movement, insofar as Jones himself was concerned, the speaking of conventional Christianity occurred only during the Temple's public worship services when "outsiders" might be present, some of whom he presumed would be Christians. Whatever the ulterior motive, Christian language was spoken and was heard by religious members in attendance at the public services. Even when scriptural language was forbidden in private Temple meetings, those terms that were so much a part of the liberative black religious tradition and had been so prevalent in the years of the Civil Rights movement—words of freedom, equality, integration, and community— continued to be primary.

Christianity was spoken of when Jones and his followers exchanged visits with black churches. Indeed, Christian language was used by Jones and the Peoples Temple staff whenever they interacted with prominent personalities in the black community, the ecumenical religious community, and government entities. Even at the very end, the letterhead of the movement's stationery read, "Peoples Temple of the Disciples of Christ, Jim Jones, Pastor," along with the text of Matthew 25:35–40: "For I was an hungered and ye gave me meat; I was thirsty and ye gave me drink; I was a stranger and ye took me in; naked, and ye clothed me. . . . Inasmuch as ye have done it unto one of the least of these. . . . Ye have done it unto me."

KEEPING THE FAITH

In the confusion that Jones intentionally generated, some who were not intimately acquainted with the scriptures apparently came to be persuaded of his claims. Some who did not accept him as the Second Coming did come to see him as a prophet, after the manner of biblical prophets, who was promising them lifelong economic security and deliverance from a racist, hateful, capitalistic society. Others among them retained a capacity for questioning what was presented to them.

Hyacinth Thrash, who slept in her cabin while the Jonestown community was dying around her, reports in her memoirs, "Already in San Francisco Jim started talking about being God, saying he was the Father and God. Well, I knew he wasn't God, 'cause God is a spirit, but you couldn't tell him that. You could say that only to a few." She goes on to chide those who she felt too completely accepted Jones' "theology," but she also writes, "In San Francisco . . . he had me sell our big family Bible. Said it cost too much to ship to Guyana. The old people, some of them, kept their Bibles but didn't take them [out in public] once they got to Jonestown, for fear Jim'd take them away."[19]

When asked if she had any recollections of the elderly members retaining their Christian convictions, Deborah Touchette, a survivor who was at the Temple headquarters in Guyana's capital of Georgetown, replied that she had not been sufficiently close to them to make that discernment. Then, in an afterthought, she reflected out loud that her grandmother-in-law, who also survived Jonestown, had often remarked that "through it all, I held on to Jesus."[20]

The Reverend John Moore, a white United Methodist minister, and his wife, Barbara, who lost two daughters and a grandson in Jonestown, had several times visited Peoples Temple in San Francisco and stayed for a week at the settlement in Guyana. Both of them remember elderly members saying, "Thank you, Jesus." It is their sense that these members never abandoned their traditional religious understandings. Rev. Moore recalls a production of *A Raisin in the Sun* he attended at Peoples Temple in which the line "In this house there is God!" was changed to "In this house there is no God!" He remarks, "I suspect that many of the older members were saying silently, 'In my life there is God!' "[21]

After joining the movement in 1972, Rev. Moore's daughter, Annie, wrote to her family, "[t]here is the largest group of people I have ever seen who are concerned about the world and are fighting for truth and justice for the world. And all the people have come from such

different backgrounds, every color, every age, every income group. . . .
So anyway it's the only place I have seen real true Christianity being
practiced."[22]

Jim Randolph, a surviving member of the Temple's leadership
Planning Commission, recalls that Jones often expressed frustration
that the people he was seeking to free from the "opiate of religion"
too often stayed too religious and too tied to old forms of religion.[23]

Dr. Margaret Singer, a psychologist who, following the tragedy,
interviewed more than 200 San Francisco members of Peoples Temple
who had not gone to Jonestown, acknowledges that she did not in-
quire about their religious or spiritual worldview. Nevertheless, she
does recall the older people she interviewed—who angrily described
Jones as a "false prophet"—indicating that they still had faith in God
and that they prayed to God.[24]

A survivor wrote to the Moore family that Jim Jones "made Jesus
Christ real for us. Before that, everything I read and tried to grasp
was just a myth. But only then did I understand the followers of Jesus.
When I became angry with Jim and decided to leave the Temple, I
would immediately have a vision of Christ on the cross and everyone
deserting him, so I would trudge on."[25]

It seems noteworthy that following the dissolution of Peoples Temple in California, a number of survivors once again became members
of conventional Protestant churches.

What the religious journey of all the black Christians who joined
Peoples Temple was will never be known for certain; if their voices
were not silenced in Jonestown, most of them, especially those of the
elderly members, have been in the 25 years since. But there is a remnant that still has a voice, and that voice is a witness to an enduring
faith. Some black members kept the faith of orthodoxy—the faith that
Jesus was Lord and Savior, the faith that God had sent a servant to
lead the people out of bondage in biblical times and would do so
again, the faith that all people were the children of God and ought to
be accorded equal privileges and opportunities.

It was the resonance of Jim Jones' words with these core tenets of
the faith that brought many of them to the movement in the first place;
it may in part have been these tenets—these extensions of the historic
African values of community and kinship so deeply embedded in the
souls and the psyche of the people—that kept them there even as the
movement engaged internally in rank exploitation and dehumaniza-
tion of its members.

Every belief, every "knowing," is susceptible to abject distortion.
While some members retained the capacity for criticism, others did

not. In Peoples Temple, loyalty to the community was ultimate. In this, Peoples Temple was no different from many other historical and contemporary religious and secular movements. What was different was the cosmological commitment to community that African American members brought in the first place. The vast majority of their fellow members were, after all, also African American—their "brothers and sisters." If they felt despised by the outside world as the movement came under attack, it would have been a familiar feeling, having long been despised by the larger white society.[26] Solidarity in the face of adversity was the mother's milk of their life experiences.

Writes Hans Mol: "Commitment to the leader was not more important than commitment to the community. They very much belonged together. Instinctively, the members recognized that solidarity was the key to survival. Nothing less than total commitment would leave it intact. Individual freedom was a threat."[27] And so entered the distortion—the loss of balance of individual and community, and the attendant tolerance for extreme controls.[28]

> The choice to them was simple: alienation without, solidarity within. And they were prepared to accept the consequences of their choice for the "within." Communal feeling makes up for personal diffidence. Acceptance by one's group heals the wounds of personal disorder and fragmentation. And so the group becomes precious. In extreme cases members feel that it should be preserved at all costs. Team spirit consoles. To cry one's heart out for one's side cures inner discord. To go all out for a cause relieves anxiety.

And hadn't black Christians, of necessity, been doing this for two hundred years?

SOCIAL MINISTRY

The "cause" of Peoples Temple was pursued through far-flung political activities, all conducted under the rubric of church ministry. Tanya Hollis provides a thorough account of Temple engagement with housing and urban development activities in their own neighborhood.[29] The Temple constituency campaigned for ballot initiatives and supported the tenants' association when residents of the International Hotel were threatened with eviction so the building could be demolished. Mervyn Dymally and Harvey Milk, San Francisco mayor George Moscone and California assemblyman Willie Brown—even presidential and vice presidential candidates Jimmy Carter and Walter

Mondale—were among the many politicians who benefited from the Temple's highly effective get-out-the-vote drives.[30]

In addition to mainstream electoral politics, the Temple was a player in the protest politics of the 1970s. They built coalitions with the Black Panther Party, supported gay rights, protested the California Supreme Court decision on affirmative action in the *Bakke* case, and joined the movement to abolish apartheid in South Africa.[31] They were connected to a network of well-known social activists, including Dennis Banks, one of the leaders of the American Indian Movement; Dick Gregory; Daniel Ellsberg, of Pentagon Papers fame; and defense attorney William Kunstler. Locally, Peoples Temple took over the NAACP chapter. Toward the end of their tenure, they became increasingly public about their support of socialist organizations and movements.[32] In short, as John R. Hall puts it, "Peoples Temple became a firm fixture in the pantheon of organizations mobilizing for social change in the United States."[33]

The Temple far outpaced ordinary churches in its charitable giving, as it regularly mailed checks to worthy causes. But some of the giving itself had political overtones, its donation to the American Civil Liberties Union being a case in point. The letter that accompanied the donation, dated 3 May 1973, began as follows: "At the request of its beloved and principled pastor, James W. Jones, the board of trustees of our church has voted to send you the enclosed check in the sum of $1000 in appreciation of the tremendous witness for justice the ACLU has made over the years." It goes on to say, "Our church is committed to the principle that the highest worship of God is service to our fellow man. The criterion for membership is simply willingness to work for others, not doctrine; our church, for example, has many Jewish members."[34] Peoples Temple championed First Amendment rights, including freedom of the press, as they turned out at rallies in support of newspaper reporters from the *Fresno Bee* who faced charges for refusing to disclose their sources.

Yet, as Maaga argues, the "ministry in which Peoples Temple [leadership] were most skilled was navigating the social welfare system in which many of its urban members found themselves entangled. This was especially appealing," she notes, "to those elderly members and single women with children who were dependent upon the government for financial assistance, housing, and health care."[35] Peoples Temple developed a strong relationship with the mental health and social service network in the area of San Francisco where their headquarters were located. "This network and the Peoples Temple," notes

Archie Smith Jr., "developed a kind of ideal working relationship that many activists and socially concerned church people desired and were drawn to."[36] The Temple itself held clinics for testing sickle cell anemia and hypertension and annually provided free flu shots. The Temple even took in homeless animals, had them neutered, and then placed them in homes.[37]

Some of those homes no doubt included several residential care facilities which Peoples Temple owned in the Redwood Valley area. At one point, according to Hall, they were operating as many as nine homes for the elderly, six for foster children, and a 40-acre ranch for mentally retarded persons. In addition, Hall speculates that "other Temple family-care homes and individual families took in smaller numbers of clients under less restrictive licensing arrangements and guardianships."[38]

Peoples Temple began developing a model of communal living for its members while still in Redwood Valley and then expanded these arrangements in San Francisco to as many as 70 households. The "life-care" agreements that many of the elderly members entered into with Peoples Temple were similar to those of other retirement communities or nursing homes.[39] Their shared living arrangements, at least for some, may well have been associated with the early socialistic communities of New Testament times.

At any rate, it was their extraordinary demonstration of commitment to social service and social justice, together with their public presentation as a Christian church, that garnered so much support for the Temple from progressive elected officials, local church representatives, and the local black press.

PUBLIC PERCEPTIONS OF PEOPLES TEMPLE AS CHURCH

Within the black community, Peoples Temple enjoyed no more ardent support than that extended by Carlton Goodlett and Thomas Fleming, the publisher and editor respectively of *The Sun Reporter,* the largest black newspaper in the Bay Area. Except for the years that the Temple produced its own newspaper (*Peoples Forum*), *The Sun Reporter* was the primary news outlet for Peoples Temple activities. Not only did the paper run supportive stories, but also it repeatedly printed laudatory editorials on behalf of the Temple's good works. Goodlett, who was also a medical doctor, worked with the Temple's health clinics and nursing staff and attended to members of Jones' personal family. Goodlett counted Jones as a personal friend and Jones in turn treated Goodlett as his personal confidant although, in Goodlett's words, "[w]hile he sought my advice on many subjects, I was not unaware that he took my advice very seldom."[40]

Some years after Jonestown, Goodlett recalled that "[o]nce when the Rev. Jones asked my advice I told him I was opposed to his politicizing everything he did, because of the fact that the church was accused of being more a political institution than a religious one. I believed that his enemies would destroy him, at least by minimizing his influence, or that of the church."[41] When the Temple did in fact come under fire, Goodlett issued this public statement of support:

> Jim Jones and the Peoples Temple represent [one] of the most invigorating and challenging religious organizations to appear in California in recent years. . . . In attempting to use the moral force of Christianity in dealing with man-made problems that bedevil and dehumanize the social order, Jones has created a cyclone where formerly the political leaders, economic scoundrels, and even impotent religious leaders have failed the very foundations of their ethics. . . . Their leadership mantles have been torn asunder, leaving these pompous pseudo-leaders naked and to be viewed as the hypocrites that they have been for decades.[42]

Goodlett was not one to mince words, and the power he exercised in the black community was not something that many cared to challenge. His support of Jones assuredly had the effect of discouraging others from speaking their concerns about the Temple leadership. But he was not alone in playing this role. And no one played the role with malice.

In April of 1976, Michael Prokes, who identified himself as an "Associate Minister" of the Temple, wrote the San Francisco Council of Churches requesting that "Peoples Temple Christian Church (of the Disciples of Christ) be considered for membership."[43] The request was approved, and Temple members became enthusiastic participants in council activities. In January 1977, the city-wide observance of the Martin Luther King Jr. holiday, sponsored by the Council of Churches, was held in the sanctuary of Peoples Temple.

The executive director of the council, and the only African American staff member, was Donneter Lane. Lane was herself dissatisfied with the operations of black churches in San Francisco, though her husband, John, was a pastor of a local black church. Donneter Lane's spiritual quest had taken her to the Ecumenical Institute in Chicago, where for two months she had studied faith-based community organizing. To her, Peoples Temple was "the embodiment" of what she had learned at the Institute.[44]

Lane makes the point that in the mid-1970s there were no black leaders in the San Francisco establishment, save for one county supervisor and the head of the Housing Authority. Black ministers generally stayed within their own neighborhoods and did not seek to function as intermediaries with the political system. What the people needed, she believed, was a leader "who was willing to take risks, who knew how to negotiate the system, and who could move a social agenda." Jim Jones fulfilled those requirements. Lane supported Jones because "he was already doing what the San Francisco Council of Churches planned to do."[45] In her presence, she recalled, people from the Temple "always used Christian language—very religious language." It was she who suggested that Jones use the scriptural passage from the book of Matthew; later she realized the Temple was using it as a camouflage. She began questioning, she says, "When she heard Jim was trying to get rid of the Bible."[46]

Lane's support of Jones earned her the ire of a number of black ministers, including two of the more progressive-minded who were critical of Jones; they remained angry with her "for years after 1978." When the bodies of those who had died in Jonestown were finally returned to San Francisco, Lane recalls that the black churches distanced themselves. Out of "anger, resentment at Jim, embarrassment and guilt," they remained silent. Regarding the guilt, she adds, "Many of us had that." But Lane, on behalf of the Council of Churches, assumed responsibility for making arrangements for the burial of some 400 bodies that were unclaimed by family members. In return, her life was threatened—and the IRS asked her for a list of "real churches" in San Francisco.[47]

Peoples Temple was accepted not only in ecumenical circles, but in interfaith circles. More than a few people in San Francisco were astounded when Jones succeeded in establishing relations with the local mosque of the Nation of Islam. The two groups exchanged pulpits and, according to the account of Temple member Harriet Tropp, Jones was responsible for getting the Muslims to "stop their preaching of hatred and racial exclusivity" and become involved in the political process. "Members of the Nation of Islam," she wrote, "are now voting, participating in the community, instead of seeking separate territory. They have dropped their bizarre theological references that engender race hatred." Muslims, Harriet claimed, "admire no other leader outside their own ranks as much as this man."[48] In fact, Peoples Temple files contain a letter dated 2 February 1976, which reads: "Dear Reverend Jones, Our warmest appreciation for the great work you and your community are doing. May Allah increase His favors on you."

It is signed, "W. D. Muhammad, Chief Minister" and is printed on stationery of the Nation of Islam.[49] Jones reportedly was responsible for bringing members of the Nation of Islam to meetings of the Northern California Ecumenical Council.[50]

Jones developed relations with the Jewish community as well as the Muslim. In 1976, Temple staff met with the Jewish Community Relations Council and corresponded with rabbis and other Jewish organizations in the Bay Area concerning the rise of Nazi propaganda in the Bay Area.[51]

In their initial contacts with Jones, black ministers in San Francisco embraced him as a gospel-preaching "brother," disregarding his genetic whiteness in the face of his public ministry to "the least of these." They quickly became hostile, however, as members of their churches left for Peoples Temple. Of the few progressive black ministers in the Bay Area, some, as noted, were skeptical of Jones, but others were laudatory of his ministry and the work of the Temple. Cecil Williams, pastor of Glide Memorial, a social activist United Methodist congregation, frequently joined with Jones in making public statements on political matters and worked with Peoples Temple in organizing protest rallies. J. Alfred Smith, Sr., senior minister at Allen Temple Baptist Church and a member of the Alamo Black Clergy—an ecumenical organization of activist black clergy in the Bay Area—was among those who saw Jones and his congregation functioning in accord with the prophetic biblical tradition.[52]

Untold numbers of individuals perceived Peoples Temple to be church not only on the basis of its social gospel–type programs, but on the basis of the spiritual nurture they personally derived from the Temple's public services and from their fellowship with Temple members. Among the progressive politicians, black and white, who left mass meetings at the Temple inspired and rejuvenated was San Francisco gay rights leader and board of supervisors member Harvey Milk, who, along with Mayor Moscone, would himself fall to an assassin's bullet a scant ten days after the Jonestown holocaust. Wrote Milk, following one such visit: "Rev. Jim, it may take me many a day to come back down from the high that I reached today. I found something dear today. I found a sense of being that makes up for all the hours and energy placed in a fight. I found what you wanted me to find. I shall be back. For I can never leave."[53]

Harvey Milk, J. Alfred Smith, Cecil Williams, Donneter Lane, Carlton Goodlett—these individuals were not alone in lauding the Christian virtues of Peoples Temple. Great was their disbelief when word began to spread throughout the city of what had transpired in a land far away to people with whom they had felt so close. The national Black Church leadership was scarcely less shocked.

POST-APOCALYPSE: REACTIONS OF THE BLACK CHURCH COMMUNITY

The Reverend Muhammed Kenyatta, who was active nationally in black ecumenical organizations that were instrumental in developing black liberation theology, vociferously protested the negative characterization of Peoples Temple by the communications media and by church leaders alike. Rather, he proclaimed, the events in Jonestown should be understood as an indictment of America and America's churches for creating and condoning a society in which marginalized people found it unbearable to live.[54] But Kenyatta was the proverbial voice crying in the wilderness. Mainstream black church leaders had quite another take on what had transpired.

Very soon after the events of Jonestown became known, the Reverend Joseph Lowery, then the president of the Southern Christian Leadership Conference (SCLC), initiated a conference call with Congressman Walter Fauntroy, head of the Washington, D.C. office of SCLC; the Reverend William A. Jones, president of the Progressive National Baptist Convention; and the Reverend Dr. Kelly Miller Smith, assistant dean of the Vanderbilt Divinity School and president of the National Conference of Black Churchmen (NCBC). Out of their conversation came a proposal for a national meeting of Black Church representatives to attempt to "understand and begin to address the issues raised by the Jonestown tragedy." They further agreed that Dr. Smith would go to San Francisco to consult with local black religious leaders regarding such a meeting, while the Reverend Lowery and two other individuals would go to Guyana on a fact-finding mission.[55]

On 27 December 1978, Smith, Lowery, and Jones, along with nine other ministers, including several from San Francisco, met in New York City to discuss what they had learned and to develop the agenda for a Black Church Consultation. Notes from that meeting are revealing. One of the persons who had gone to Guyana reported that the Guyanese information minister, Shirley Field-Ridley, had told them that their visit was the "first expression of concern from the black community." The delegation also reported that the surviving young people in Georgetown told them "they felt accepted into a loving, caring community."[56]

Questions were raised as to how "such a cult could take root and grow. What is there about San Francisco?" A San Francisco minister replied that it wasn't just San Francisco, but the government as a whole—that because the members were black, "the government turned their back." He then remarked on the fact that "memorial services were last week and not one white state official came." Jim Jones, however, was the primary target of criticism. Remarked one participant, "If he's Hitlerarian let's say so." The belief was expressed that blacks were still drawn to white leaders as the locus of power. At the same time, white evangelical leaders came under fire for their message that the church is not to be involved in the world and for the influence this had had on many black churches. Some asked whether black churches were doing enough for their constituents; others lamented the failure of the Black Church to pool its resources to address the needs of the larger black community. In addition, concern was expressed that members of the public would equate Peoples Temple with the Black Church, and that if black churches were seen as cults they might lose their tax-exempt status.[57]

These, then, became the themes of the "Consultation on the Implications of Jonestown for the Black Church and the Nation," sponsored by SCLC and NCBC and held at Third Baptist Church in San Francisco on the first two days of February 1979. But the entire meeting, which was attended by some 200 individuals, was framed on the one hand by the assumption that Peoples Temple was a cult and should be examined in that light[58] and on the other by the organizers' sense of rage that—once again—hundreds of black men, women, and children had been led to their deaths by the chicanery of a white man.

The stated purpose of the consultation was "to explore the meaning which Peoples Temple, Jim Jones, and the catastrophic deaths of hundreds of Black people in Guyana may have on the mission, history, and self-understanding of the Black Church." The planning committee indicated it wanted it understood at the outset, however, that "[i]n no way is Peoples Temple being thought of as a 'Black Church.' "[59] As part of the process of seeking to understand what had transpired and what the implications might be, several scholars of religion—among them Dr. C. Eric Lincoln and Dr. Archie Smith Jr.—were invited to present papers.[60]

Lincoln's published article, which was co-authored with Lawrence Mamiya, excluded the contention he made at the consultation that, notwithstanding that the majority of members were black, Jonestown had nothing to do with black religion. The article also excluded the parallel he drew between Jonestown and the "plantation of the Old South," between Jim Jones and the slave master.[61] But in the published version, he remained emphatic that this movement was of a kind with other white cults of the day. So intent was he on characterizing the movement as a non-black cult that he wrote,

> In spite of the doctrine of the separation of church and state and the differentiation of spheres in modern industrial societies, modern cults like Jones' have consciously attempted to incorporate politics into religion. It is this reintegration of previously differentiated spheres into one total world view that is unique about the present-day cults, and perhaps their most alarming aspect.[62]

This, coming from the scholar of black religion who had written voluminously about the "black sacred cosmos," a prime characteristic of which, he asserted, was the pursuit of freedom in this world. He would never have said of black religion that its historic integration of the sacred and the secular, of spirituality and politics, was "alarming." Like the rest of the country, Lincoln's attention was fixed on Jim Jones—though for different reasons than most others: Jones, for him, was the symbol of white racism. So angry was he at Jones, it seemed, and at white racism in general, that he failed to recognize it was the people's kindred anger at America's white racism that led them to Jonestown in the first place.

Archie Smith Jr., in contrast, asserted that "Black people's involvement in the Peoples Temple movement [could] be seen as an attempt to make Black religion relevant to their social, political and economic condition. . . . Many thought they had found in the Peoples Temple a form of church involvement that spoke more directly to the issues of spiritual uplift, justice, social change and communal empowerment."[63]

A professor from San Francisco State University, Raye Richardson, who had lost a sister in Jonestown, was more direct in her criticism of the Black Church than was Smith, pointing especially to its failure to affirm black women. In contrast to her church experience, she said, her sister felt affirmed in Jonestown and celebrated the movement's use of "black symbols to affirm black values," which most black churches failed to do.[64]

Kelly Miller Smith offered this honest assessment of the Black Church:

> Let us confess that in our history there have been peaks and valleys. Let us confess we have fallen far short of our potential. We have often been a lone voice crying in the wilderness of abuse and oppression, but too often even that voice has been weak and fragmented. Too many have been the times when our community has needed a prophetic voice and we have provided but a pathetic echo!

Like our White counterparts, we, too, have often become so involved in the oiling of our machinery that we have neglected to fight for our people. It is far too difficult to get the leaders of Black churches to recognize a crisis before it becomes full blown. Even then, there are some who identify with the wrong side of the issue.[65]

"Jonestown," he said, "challenges us to rise up to the fullness of our potential."[66]

"MY LORD, WHAT A MOURNING"

As the decade of the 1970s was coming to a close, Vincent Harding wrote an essay in which he reflected about the state of the black religious community generally. In a portion of this reflection, which he entitled, "My Lord, What a Mourning, Jonestown is America," he wrote,

> The horrible tragedy of Jonestown and the degradation and destruction of so many of our people should not allow us to forget the essential message that still remains: Nothing in the arid materialism and individualism of the 1970s has eliminated the fundamental hungers in the human spirit for a deep sense of a caring, responsible, disciplined community and a great human cause to which a person may give himself or herself at the risk of "life, possessions, security, and status." Indeed, perhaps we have learned again that people become truly human only as such hungers are fed.[67]

The people of Peoples Temple had a great cause. They knew, for all their leader's deceit, that Jim Jones spoke a truth, and that truth was that America's "self-evident" principles were not evident in practice. In despair that it would ever be otherwise, they sought to build a community in another land, and then, having been led to believe that their community was threatened by the same forces that violated the principles they held dear, they chose to die—as a community.

The further tragedy is that today we are no closer than in 1978 to the reconstitution of a religio-political coalition that might move our society beyond the structural inequities that concerned the members of Peoples Temple. On the contrary, regression has been the dominant modality of the past quarter-century. Today we seem scarcely any closer to the kind of societal transformation that would obviate the need for a Peoples Temple. People are still hungering. And they are still unfed. Those who hunger—those who seek nourishment in the midst of the arid materialism and militarism of the new century—are the descendants of all those who died trying to fill their hunger for a better world. Now, as then, some are struggling merely to survive. Now, as then, some are being led into death instead of life. Now, as then, prophetic voices of integrity are all too few, and all too faint. In a moment of contemporary despair, some among us might be hard put to suppress the haunting question of whether the people were justified in the choice they made.

Contrary to the dehumanizing image of the people that was etched in the minds of the American citizenry, there was in the Peoples Temple movement a community of creative, caring individuals—individuals who were passionately committed to a cause that they came to believe could never be achieved in their homeland. We may surmise that at least some of those who once saw themselves doing the Lord's work understood their last act to be one that would finally bring them release.

> O freedom! O freedom!
> O freedom over me!
> And before I'd be a slave,
> I'll be buried in my grave,
> And go home to my Lord and be free.

POSTSCRIPT

Ten days after Jonestown, a friend and longtime social activist, Mack Warner, accompanied me to the Peoples Temple headquarters in San Francisco. There we were met by two white staff members who escorted us through the floodlights and police line that surrounded the facility. Inside, we sat in what was a cavernous room dominated by long rows of dining tables where hundreds of people had at one time taken their daily meals.

It was quiet. It was, it later came to me, uncannily *peaceful*. As we prepared to leave, I was approached by a young black girl who thanked me for coming. I remember wondering why she was thanking me and whether she fully comprehended what had transpired. I paused momentarily to greet an elderly black woman who was sitting quietly in a rocking chair, off by herself. As I turned to go, her barely audible words followed me: "God bless you," she said. "God bless you."

There is a refrain commonly sung during black worship services: "Surely the presence of the Lord is in this place." I never hear this refrain but what I remember the feeling of being in a holy place.

NOTES

1. In a statement issued shortly after the Jonestown tragedy, Dr. Kenneth L. Teegarden, general minister and president of the Christian Church (Disciples of Christ), made it known that a review of Jones' ministerial standing had been underway but had not been completed because they were unable to confront Jones due to his being out of the country. The statement also noted that "[w]hen James W. Jones affiliated with the Disciples and during his ministry in Indianapolis there was no forewarning of what was to come. His early ministry was considered something of a model for inner city work, with strong interracial aspects and community service to the poor." This statement was printed in the November-December 1978 newsletter, "Church at Work," of the Northern California Ecumenical Council.

2. John R. Hall, *Gone from the Promised Land: Jonestown in American Cultural History* (New Brunswick, N.J.: Transaction Books, 1989), 94, 144.

3. Mary McCormick Maaga, *Hearing the Voices of Jonestown* (Syracuse, N.Y.: Syracuse University Press, 1998). See note 6 in the Introduction.

4. While interviewing surviving members, I was asked more than once if I was a member myself. I answered that I was not, but that I had attended services at Peoples Temple. "Well, then," an interviewee told me, "You were a member. We considered anyone who attended to be a member."

5. These figures represent Moore's best efforts to identify as many people as she could; they differ from the official figure of 918 deaths, which included five at the Port Kaituma airstrip and four in the Georgetown headquarters. Problems in identifying children who died complicate the calculations.

6. See Chapter 4.

7. Archie Smith Jr., *The Relational Self: Ethics and Therapy from a Black Church Perspective* (Nashville, Tenn.: Abingdon, 1982), 196–197.

8. Maaga, *Hearing the Voices of Jonestown*, 85.

9. This figure represents a compilation of the membership figures reported in Eileen W. Lindner, ed., *Yearbook of American and Canadian Churches, 2000* (Nashville, Tenn.: Abingdon, 2002). The figures are self-reported by denominations and in some instances may be inflated. The best estimates are that of the 35 million African Americans in the United States, 24 million belong to the eight largest black denominations, two million belong to predominantly white Protestant denominations, two million are Catholic, half a million belong to smaller black denominations and sects, and at least half a million are in independent, non-denominational churches. An estimated 200,000 are Jehovah's Witnesses.

10. Peter J. Paris, *The Spirituality of African Peoples: The Search for a Common Moral Discourse* (Minneapolis: Fortress Press, 1995), 72, 77, and 162.

11. C. Eric Lincoln and Lawrence H. Mamiya, *The Black Church in the African American Experience* (Durham, N.C.: Duke University Press, 1990), 3.

12. U.S. FBI Peoples Temple Recording, Q 974. Transcript available on *Alternative Considerations of Jonestown and Peoples Temple*, <http://jonestown.sdsu.edu>, accessed 11 July 2003.

13. Catherine (Hyacinth) Thrash, as told to Marian K. Towne, *The Onliest One Alive: Surviving Jonestown, Guyana* (Indianapolis: Marian K. Towne, 1995), 94.

14. See chapter 7.

15. Deborah Touchette, interviews by the author, 7 and 14 January 1998; Grace (Stoen) Jones, interview by the author, 28 January 1998.

16. For a discussion of apostolic socialism as Jones conceived it, see Hall, *Gone From the Promised Land*, 23–24, 146.

17. Deborah Touchette, interviews by the author, 7 and 14 January 1998.

18. Grace (Stoen) Jones, interview by the author, 28 January 1998.

19. Thrash, *The Onliest One Alive*, 100, 104.

20. Deborah Touchette, interviews by the author, 7 and 14 January 1998.

21. John and Barbara Moore, conversation with the author, 18 November 1997; Rev. Moore to author, 13 February 1998.

22. Cited in Rebecca Moore, *In Defense of Peoples Temple and Other Essays* (Lewiston, N.Y.: Edwin Mellen Press, 1988), 123.

23. Jim Randolph, interview by the author, 4 March 1998.

24. Dr. Margaret Singer, interview by the author, 20 January 1998. Dr. Singer is a well-known anti-cult activist and proponent of brainwashing theories. Most sociologists of religion take issue with her perspectives on these matters. In light of her particular orientation, her recall of survivors' conventional religious commitments seems all the more compelling.

25. Moore, *In Defense of Peoples Temple*, 161.

26. Moore points out in Chapter 4 that more than 30 percent of the members in Guyana were African Americans who were from the South. In all likelihood, the proportion in San Francisco was even higher.

27. Hans Mol, *Meaning and Place: An Introduction to the Social Scientific Study of Religion* (New York: Pilgrim Press, 1983), 37. Mol perhaps overstates the case in saying that "Jones' vision of the collective ego replacing a destroyed personal one was in accord with the wishes of the membership." He is more on target in saying that "[t]hey were all refugees from a cold, alien world in which lack of direction, purpose, was obvious."

28. See Anthony Pinn's discussion of just this phenomenon in Chapter 1.

29. See Chapter 5.

30. See Hall, *Gone from the Promised Land*, 165–171.

31. Hall, *Gone from the Promised Land*, 161–165.

32. Hall, *Gone from the Promised Land*. In my working with Lieutenant Governor Dymally, I observed the presence of these individuals with Marcie Jones and staff members of the Temple and on occasion was myself briefly engaged in conversation with them.

33. Hall, *Gone from the Promised Land*, 162.

34. Examples of letters that accompanied these checks may be found in the Peoples Temple Records, California Historical Society, MS 3800, B1/f15 for the ACLU letter.

35. Maaga, *Hearing the Voices of Jonestown*, 86.

36. Archie Smith Jr., *The Relational Self*, 218.

37. Open letter from the Reverend John Moore, District Superintendent, Bay View District, California-Nevada Annual Conference of the United Methodist Church, n.d. Peoples Temple Records, California Historical Society, MS 3800, B1/f14.

38. Hall, *Gone from the Promised Land*, 82.

39. Hall, *Gone from the Promised Land*, 91–92.

40. Carlton B. Goodlett, "Notes on Peoples Temple," in Rebecca Moore and Fielding M. McGehee III, *The Need for a Second Look at Jonestown* (Lewiston, N.Y.: Edwin Mellen Press, 1989), 51. Also available online at <http://jonestown.sdsu.edu>, accessed 11 July 2003.

41. Goodlett, "Notes on Peoples Temple."

42. Carlton B. Goodlett, Ph.D., M.D., unpublished, typewritten compen-

dium which is prefaced thusly: "The following are a selection of excerpts from statements made in recent days by a wide variety of civic, community, and religious leaders in response to a sensationalistic smear campaign directed at Peoples Temple and its minister, Rev. Jim Jones." There is no date, but it would have been compiled following the publication of an extremely critical article in *New West* magazine in July 1977.

43. Michael Prokes to Mr. Marvin Chandler, San Francisco Council of Churches, 21 April 1976, Peoples Temple Records, California Historical Society, MS 3800, B1/f15.

44. Donneter Lane, interview by the author, 3 June 1996, San Francisco, California.

45. Donneter Lane, interview by the author.

46. Donneter Lane, interview by the author.

47. Donneter Lane, interview by the author. Only one cemetery in the Bay Area—Evergreen Cemetery—was willing to accept the unclaimed bodies, most of which were never identified, including 234 children. For a detailed account of the handling (or more aptly, the mishandling) of the bodies, see Moore, *In Defense of Peoples Temple*, 91–111.

48. Harriet Tropp, undated manuscript printed on the letterhead of the University of California Hastings College of the Law Library in San Francisco, personal files of the author. Tropp was herself Jewish and had written this 14-page statement in defense of Peoples Temple when it came under attack by area communications media. See also Hall, *Gone from the Promised Land*, 164.

49. Peoples Temple Records, California State Historical Society, MS 3800, B1/f14. Shortly after this letter was written, Warith Deen Muhammad changed the name of the organization to the American Muslim Movement and began moving toward orthodoxy. The Nation of Islam was then resurrected as a splinter group under the leadership of Minister Louis Farrakhan.

50. Harriet Tropp manuscript, personal files of the author.

51. Hall, *Gone from the Promised Land*, 164.

52. See Chapter 8.

53. "Operations Correspondence," Peoples Temple Records, California Historical Society, MS 3800, B1/f15.

54. See Chapter 9.

55. Kelly Miller Smith, "The Implications of Jonestown for the Black Church," Opening Statement made at the "Consultation on the Implications of Jonestown for the Black Church and the Nation," San Francisco, California, 1 February 1979.

56. "Synopsis," typed notes, 27 December 1978. Kelly Miller Smith Papers, Box 134, File 23, Special Collections University Archives, The Jean and Alexander Heard Library, Vanderbilt University, Nashville, Tennessee.

57. Kelly Miller Smith Papers, Box 134, File 23.

58. The joint statement made by Joseph Lowery and Kelly Miller Smith at a press conference prior to the consultation reads in part: "When we adjourn, we hope to have learned some important lessons, about such areas as: What attracted people to the Temple, and what can the church and community do to lessen the vulnerability to cultism? What are the methodologies or approaches used in recruiting cult members? How can we enrich the life and fellowship of the church as a family of God, as well as expand the church's resources to deal with the poor and helpless? What is the nation's official posture towards the poor, and how does it relate to individuals' self-concept or sense of hope?" Kelly Miller Smith Papers, Box 134, File 23, Special Col-

lections University Archives, The Jean and Alexander Heard Library, Vanderbilt University, Nashville, Tennessee.

59. Kelly Miller Smith, "Implications," 4.

60. Revised versions of these particular presentations were subsequently published and are reprinted as Chapters 2 and 3 of this book.

61. John Jacobs, "Jim Jones: An Old South Slave Master?" *San Francisco Examiner*, 3 February 1979.

62. See Chapter 2.

63. See Chapter 3.

64. Henry Soles Jr., "Churchmen Hunt Clues on Cult's Lure for Blacks," *Christianity Today*, 23 March 1979, 55.

65. Kelly Miller Smith, "Implications," 7.

66. Kelly Miller Smith, "Implications," 7.

67. Vincent Harding, *The Other American Revolution* (Los Angeles and Atlanta: Center for Afro-American Studies, University of California Los Angeles and Institute of the Black World, 1980), 222–224.

CONTRIBUTORS

Duchess Harris, Ph.D., is an Assistant Professor of African American Studies and Political Science at Macalester College in St. Paul, Minnesota. Her publications can be found in *Women and Politics; The Journal of Intergroup Relations;* and *American Quarterly.* Her first book (with John A. Powell) is *Race and Poverty: Wrongs and Policies.*

Milmon F. Harrison, Ph.D., is an Assistant Professor in African American and African Studies at the University of California, Davis. He is author of *Name It and Claim It: The Word of Faith Movement and African American Religion.*

Tanya Hollis, M.L.S., formerly the Associate Librarian of the North Baker Research Library at the California Historical Society in San Francisco, is now Archivist for Environmental Collections at the Bancroft Library at UC Berkeley. She received her Master's in Library Science at SUNY Buffalo, and her B.A. in religion at the New College of the University of South Florida, with the undergraduate thesis "Acting Womanish: Black Slave Women's Contributions to Their Religious Communities."

The Reverend Muhammed Isaiah Kenyatta was a Baptist pastor, law professor, and social activist from Philadelphia who in the mid-1970s served as a regional vice-president of the National Conference of Black Churchmen and as executive director of the Black Theology Project. He died 3 January 1992, at age 47.

C. Eric Lincoln, Ph.D., at the time of his death in 2000 was the William Randolph Keenan Professor of Religion and Culture Emeritus at Duke University. Widely regarded as the "Dean of Black Religious Studies," he was the author or editor of some 20 books, including the now-classic *Black Muslims in America.*

Lawrence H. Mamiya, Ph.D., is Professor of Sociology and Africana Studies at Vassar College. He is the co-author with C. Eric Lincoln of

The Black Church in the African American Experience and the author of numerous articles on African American religious movements.

Rebecca Moore, Ph.D., is Associate Professor of Religious Studies at San Diego State University. She has published numerous books and articles on Peoples Temple and Jonestown. She maintains a website on Peoples Temple at http://jonestown.sdsu.edu.

Anthony B. Pinn, Ph.D., is Professor of Religious Studies at Macalester College in St. Paul, Minnesota. He is the author of numerous books and articles, including *Varieties of African American Religious Experience* and *Terror and Triumph: The Nature of Black Religion*.

Mary R. Sawyer, Ph.D., is Professor of Religious Studies at Iowa State University where she also teaches African American Studies. She is the author of *Black Ecumenism: Implementing the Demands of Justice* and *The Church on the Margins: Living Christian Community*. Her numerous articles on black religion and black politics draw on her years of practical involvement in human relations work and black electoral politics.

The Reverend Dr. J. Alfred Smith Sr. is the Senior Pastor of Allen Temple Baptist Church in Oakland, California. He is currently Professor of Christian Ministry at the American Baptist Seminary of the West and the Graduate Theological Union of Berkeley and has served as Visiting Professor at numerous seminaries across the country. The author of 16 books, Dr. Smith's work focuses on pastoral ministry and homiletics.

Archie Smith Jr., Ph.D., is the James and Clarice Foster Professor of Pastoral Psychology and Counseling at the Pacific School of Religion and Graduate Theological Union in Berkeley, California. He is the author of numerous articles and books, including *The Relational Self: Ethics and Therapy from a Black Church Perspective* and *Navigating the Deep River: Spirituality in African American Families*.

Adam John Waterman is a doctoral candidate in the American Studies Program at New York University. He is currently researching Black Hawk's War and primitive accumulation on the U.S. frontier. His previous articles, also co-authored with Duchess Harris, have appeared in the *Journal of Intergroup Relations* and *Revista de Estudios Norteamericanos: A Spanish Journal of American Studies*.

INDEX

Milton Keynes UK
Ingram Content Group UK Ltd.
UKHW020946110724
445408UK00005B/216